PRAISE FOR
An Anti-Zionist Path to Embodied Jewish Healing

"Israel-Palestine has been described by many as the 'open wound' of the modern world: never healed, never even bandaged. Somerson brings a healer's perspective to this ongoing injury, focusing on its deep, underlying sources. They explain clearly how the Israeli government manipulates Jewish collective trauma to forward its far-right agenda. Most crucially, they lay out an accessible pathway for healing from historical trauma, releasing it from our bodies and preventing it from being passed onto future generations."

—NAOMI KLEIN, author of *Doppelganger: A Trip into the Mirror World*

"Zionism is not solely supported by Jews, nor does it exist to make Jews safer, but it does manipulate Jews through misuse of Jewish trauma, and this book can help us understand and resist that, so we might build safety for Jews and all people based on anticolonial, anti-Zionist solidarity politics."

—DEAN SPADE, author of *Love in a F*cked Up World*

"In this heartbreakingly timely book, Somerson bravely offers clarity and insight into the unfathomable. Most importantly, this book offers guidance on how we might heal without pretending the work of healing will be easy. But it might be possible, and this book is an invaluable guide to that possibility."

—ABIGAIL ROSE CLARKE, author of *Returning Home to Our Bodies*

"Much that Somerson shares occurs across communities—weaponizing historical trauma, resistance to body-based work . . ., and the broader political meaning of the collective fact of healing—but their words deepen our understanding by being held within the intimacy of Jewish experience and histories. A wonderfully pragmatic as well as visionary book, this is an example of the integrity of collective healing held in a good and truthful way."

—SUSAN RAFFO, author of *Liberated to the Bone*

"This vital exploration of individual and collective trauma and healing in Jews and Jewish communities expertly weaves the personal and political; the body and the collective; past, present, and future; ritual, healing, and organizing. Bringing together trauma and healing studies, history and ritual, and stories from decades of practice as a somatic therapist and organizer, Somerson writes complex concepts in ways that are nuanced, yet accessible. This is a landmark book in the field of Jewish trauma and healing studies."

—RABBI JESSICA ROSENBERG, author of *For Times Such as These*

"Right on time, this book is a true gift for our resistance movements and our healing work, which as this book so beautifully reminds us, are one and the same. I'm so grateful for all the wisdom Wendy Elisheva Somerson shares about embodied rituals for trouble-making toward holy interdependence, a Judaism beyond Zionism, and a free and thriving Palestine."

—DORI MIDNIGHT, community-care practitioner, ritual leader, and writer

The client examples in this book are composites drawn from thousands of somatic sessions. Names and identifying details have been changed to protect the privacy and confidentiality of individuals.

AN ANTI-ZIONIST PATH TO EMBODIED JEWISH HEALING

SOMATIC PRACTICES TO HEAL HISTORICAL WOUNDS, UNLEARN OPPRESSION, AND CREATE A LIBERATED WORLD TO COME

WENDY ELISHEVA SOMERSON

North Atlantic Books
Huichin, unceded Ohlone land
Berkeley, California

North Atlantic Books
Huichin, unceded Ohlone land
2526 Martin Luther King Jr Way
Berkeley, CA 94704 USA
www.northatlanticbooks.com

Cover and interior art by Wendy Elisheva Somerson
Cover design by Jasmine Hromjak
Book design by Happenstance Type-O-Rama

Printed in the United States of America

An Anti-Zionist Path to Embodied Jewish Healing: Somatic Practices to Heal Historical Wounds, Unlearn Oppression, and Create A Liberated World to Come is sponsored and published by North Atlantic Books, an educational nonprofit based in the unceded Ohlone land Huichin (Berkeley, CA) that collaborates with partners to develop cross-cultural perspectives; nurture holistic views of art, science, the humanities, and healing; and seed personal and global transformation by publishing work on the relationship of body, spirit, and nature.

The original work, *Nishmat Kol Chai* (נשמת כל חי), translated by Rabbi Zalman Schachter-Shalomi, was shared under the Creative Commons Attribution-ShareAlike (CC BY-SA) 4.0 International copyleft license. (To redistribute or remix this work in any format, modified or unmodified, you must refer to the terms of the license under which the work is shared.)

North Atlantic Books publications are distributed to the US trade and internationally by Penguin Random House Publisher Services. For further information, visit our website at www.northatlanticbooks.com.

Library of Congress Cataloging-in-Publication Data

Names: Somerson, Wendy Elisheva, author.
Title: An anti-Zionist path to embodied Jewish healing : somatic practices
   to heal historical wounds, unlearn oppression, and create a liberated
   world to come / Wendy Elisheva Somerson.
Description: Berkeley : North Atlantic Books, [2025] | Includes
   bibliographical references and index.
Identifiers: LCCN 2024047899 (print) | LCCN 2024047900 (ebook) | ISBN
   9798889841876 (trade paperback) | ISBN 9798889841883 (ebook)
Subjects: LCSH: Healing—Religious aspects—Judaism. | Mind and
   body—Religious aspects—Judaism. | Mind and body therapies. | Psychic
   trauma—Treatment. | Collective trauma—Physiological aspects. |
   Jews—Psychology. | Anti-Zionism—Psychological aspects. | Israel-Hamas
   War, 2023—Psychological aspects.
Classification: LCC BM538.H43 S596 2025 (print) | LCC BM538.H43 (ebook) |
   DDC 296.3/76—dc23/eng/20250128
LC record available at https://lccn.loc.gov/2024047899
LC ebook record available at https://lccn.loc.gov/2024047900

The authorized representative in the EU for product safety and compliance is Eucomply OÜ, Pärnu mnt 139b-14, 11317 Tallinn, Estonia, hello@eucompliancepartner.com, +33757690241.

1 2 3 4 5 6 7 8 9 KPC 30 29 28 27 26 25

This book includes recycled material and material from well-managed forests. North Atlantic Books is committed to the protection of our environment. We print on recycled paper whenever possible and partner with printers who strive to use environmentally responsible practices.

I dedicate this book to the whales,
whose songs are calling us home.
May we get quiet enough
to hear their call.

CONTENTS

STAY HUMAN

I met Hedy Epstein, of blessed memory, *zikhronah livrakha,* (זכרונה לברכה),
a fiery and fearless organizer when she was in her eighties. She was a
Holocaust survivor who escaped Nazi Germany aboard a *kindertransport*
to England, while her parents and most of her family were murdered at
Auschwitz. She funneled the trauma of her childhood into a lifetime of
committed and passionate activism for justice. At ninety, she was arrested
for protesting in defense of Black lives in Ferguson after the police murder
of Michael Brown. At the protest in Ferguson, she was wearing one of her
favorite shirts—a black tee emblazoned with the words *stay human.* She got
the shirt three years earlier, in 2011, aboard a boat in the Mediterranean Sea
aiming to break the then–seven-year-old devastating siege on Palestinians
in Gaza. Hedy's life embodied how to stay human by fighting to end the
systems that dehumanize people—whether her Jewish family, Palestinian
families, or African American families. Like so many of the elders I work
with in the movement for Palestinian liberation, Hedy was a testament to
the ways that trauma and oppression can create in us an unshakeable commitment to justice for all.

I think of that phrase a lot these days—*stay human.* The phrase comes
from Italian journalist Vittorio Arrigoni, who sent dispatches from the Gaza
Strip during yet another horrifying assault by Israel on Palestinians in
2008–2009. His missives all ended with that simple admonition: *stay human.*
I remember reading it during Israel's 2009 month-long assault on Gaza, in

which Israeli forces killed over 1,400 Palestinians, including more than 300 children. At the time, I could not have imagined a worse horror. But now, I think of his refrain as we struggle daily to resist and end the campaign of extermination and terror that Israel has been carrying out for a full year. It's worsening by the day. The Israeli regime is bombing schools, bread lines, and displaced people's camps. Water is down by 94 percent. Polio is spreading. Israeli soldiers are raping and torturing thousands of Palestinians in mass camps.

The trauma Palestinians are struggling to survive is unthinkable. How can we possibly make sense of such a catastrophe? How did the world end up here—watching a livestream of genocide? Under these dire circumstances, how does one stay human?

In so many ways, this book is a deep exploration of these questions about maintaining our humanity in the wake of enormous trauma. Staying human, it turns out, is not an individual task. We are born into an existing web of relationships and layered histories that make us who we are, but trauma severs these connections. This book helps us chart those breakages along multiple scales: the individual, communal, societal, and geopolitical. And it also helps us start to articulate what might stitch us back into our own humanity: What we need from each other, what our bodies teach us, what our histories and ancestors require of us.

It is essential that we, as Jewish anti-Zionist organizers, understand the way Jewish communal pain, history, and trauma not only inform Jewish life today, but are also used to justify the ongoing communal pain, history, and trauma of Palestinians. This book contextualizes the many layers of catastrophe before us. The Israeli ethno-state, supposedly a guarantee of Jewish safety, provides no true safety for anyone. Decades of colonization and oppression of Palestinians terrorize Palestinians and turn Jewish Israelis into occupiers, while using the very real trauma born of genocidal European antisemitism as a cover for war crimes.

For too long, anti-Zionists have allowed Jewish trauma to be defined by Zionist organizations who would rather freeze and replay it than foster healing in our communities. This book shows us how, as anti-Zionists, we have an obligation to address the trauma within ourselves and our communities or we risk never escaping its misuse by our opposition.

This book restores to us our obligation to do the work of healing. By wrestling back our own agency, Wes also creates a path not just to think and talk about trauma, but to take action in transforming it. Jewish Anti-Zionism in this book, and our movements, is not simply an ideology opposing a Jewish ethnostate that privileges Jews with more rights than indigenous Palestinians on their land. But rather, anti-Zionism is a path that can heal our collective historic trauma through a rejection of the inhumanity of Zionism, and a reclamation of a Jewishness that sees all lives as precious. Here, anti-Zionism is an essential framework for tending trauma, in which Jewish healing and liberation are inextricably bound up with fighting for Palestinian healing and liberation.

This embodied path of healing in an explicitly anti-Zionist framework is also a way to deepen and sharpen our organizing by moving the locus of our solidarity work from a place of shame and guilt to one of accountability and repair. Too often our activism veers into narcissism and self-interest, driven by our immense shame about the horrors being committed in our names. Wes offers an alternative orientation whereby our organizing is driven by a shared stake in Palestinian freedom and a commitment to making repair from a place of accountability.

As someone who has been organizing for decades in this movement, every day I see that fighting for a future of freedom, justice, and equality can help redeem our grief, rage, shame, and despair. Yet I also see firsthand how those feelings—the very emotions that make us human—threaten to overcome us. These overwhelming feelings often lead us to become brittle and unkind with each other, threatening to fracture our coalitions and leading us to abandon our strategies. Wes's book offers practical ways to work with our feelings, so that we don't lose our relationships, focus, or determination. Or worse, give up before we see the results of our work. They help us name the full range of what it means to stay human through the horror. They help us not only understand but feel; not only feel but move through; not only move through but make use of these feelings to fuel our solidarity activism.

More than anything, I think this book teaches us that whereas trauma severs people from our connections, it is through our embodied relationships that we will repair ourselves and the world. That's the lesson I, as an organizer, am most eager for our movements to learn. Political consciousness is incredibly high. But we are not organized. That's an entirely different thing. Organizing is nothing if not the work of human beings trying to stay in relationship to each other, struggling toward a common goal. Organizing is channeling our energies in one direction in order to actually shift power. This requires not only having the right idea for what to do, but actually being able to do that work *with* each other.

Wes's book reminds us that we all have an obligation to our own healing in order to show up to the collective task of organizing. If we bring healing to our organizing for justice, we can help transform our political culture. We can move away from the mindset that the perfect political analysis will free Palestine and truly build a community where we feel safe enough to be wrong, to take risks, and commit to the long-haul struggle that lies ahead.

This book demonstrates how organizing is a healing modality and how healing is essential to being a good organizer. By situating embodied healing within and as part of our ongoing protests, marches, sit-ins and shutdowns, this book helps us stay human. And by that, I mean that it brings us closer to ourselves, each other, and the world we are fighting for: of justice, equality, and freedom for Palestinians, and for all people. May it be so.

— *Stefanie Fox, Executive Director of Jewish Voice for Peace*

CHAPTER 1

IN THE MIDST OF GENOCIDE

The history of the creation of the Israeli nation is in part the history of one displacement after another, in which, time and time again, the enemies of the Jews turn into the shades of past persecution, each one at once real and unreal, infinitely dangerous and a ghost.[1]

Israel, as it comes into being, gives us an exceptional, magnified vision, of how a wound turns into the cut of a sword, how historically inflicted damage arms itself.[2]

—JACQUELINE ROSE, *THE QUESTION OF ZION*

At five AM on November 3, 2023, I am trying to stretch my black "Not in My Name" T-shirt to fit over my puffy jacket, so that I can convey our message but stay warm during our lockdown in front of the federal building in downtown Seattle. Each week since the October 7 Hamas attack on Israel and Israel's assault on Gaza, our chapter of Jewish Voice for Peace (JVP) has been protesting to demand that our Washington state Senator Patty Murray call for a ceasefire in Gaza. As I wait for my friends to pick me up, I hear an NPR reporter describe how the Israeli government has rounded up and detained Palestinians who had been working in Israel on October 7.[3] Weeks later, they are returning them to the war zone of Gaza. Dropped off miles from the border, the Palestinian workers have to walk into Gaza wearing numbered tags on their ankles.*

Numbered tags on their ankles? Did I hear that right? Dizzy and nauseous, I grip the back of the chair near the doorway where I am still struggling to put on my protest outfit. Tears stream down my cheeks. I see the image of a family friend who had numbers tattooed on his arm. We often visited him where he worked at a local discount clothing store, Schottenstein's, in Columbus, Ohio, when I was a kid. My mom would catch me staring at his arm and later reprimand me, making sure that I never said anything about this eerie reminder that he survived a Nazi concentration camp.

When my friends Jen and Zoe arrive, I ask them the same question I have been asking myself since Israel's assault on Gaza began after the October 7 Hamas attack: "How could our people condone this?" By which I mean, "How could Jews enact this form of dehumanizing violence after we ourselves had survived dehumanizing violence?"

In spite of my disorientation at that moment, I already knew at least part of the answer. As a healer who works with trauma, I know that if we don't consciously break cycles of violence, we are in danger of allowing them to be reenacted. Trauma causes us to get stuck in the past, often reliving the feelings from traumatic events that we have not been able to digest. The Israeli state perpetually manufactures consent for its violent apartheid regime by activating Jewish historical trauma from the Nazi Holocaust and centuries of antisemitic persecution. The Israeli government manipulates Jewish historical terror to pit Jewish safety against Palestinian freedom. We are currently witnessing the staggering consequences of unhealed Jewish embodied trauma and grief, which are being weaponized to support the genocide in Gaza.

Jewish folks need healing, so that we can remove ourselves from this zero-sum game that leverages the traumatic history of antisemitism to justify the oppression of Palestinians. Now more than ever, we need to learn

---

* In fact, the Israeli government not only rounded them up, but held the workers incommunicado in inhumane conditions, including torture, for weeks before sending many of them back to Gaza. See "Israel: Gaza Workers Held Incommunicado for Week," Human Rights Watch, January 3, 2024, www.hrw.org/news/2024/01/03/israel-gaza-workers-held-incommunicado-weeks.

the tools of embodied healing to break these traumatic cycles of violence and oppression. And that is why I wrote this book (although I started it long before October 7).

Comprehending the Scale of the Genocide

From the moment Hamas attacked Israel in what has been widely called "the deadliest day for Jews since the Nazi Holocaust"—a phrase that notably suggests that Hamas killed Israelis because they are Jewish, not because they are occupying Palestinian land—so many of us have been reeling. I barely had a moment to experience my grief about the nearly 1,200 Israelis, including foreign nationals, who were killed, and the 247 Israelis kidnapped by Hamas, before I began anticipating Israel's response.[4] My initial grief and fear upon hearing about the attack were quickly subsumed by an overwhelming sense of dread. My shoulders stiffened, and my diaphragm tightened as I braced myself for the brutal attack on Palestinians in Gaza by Israeli armed forces under the guise of "self-defense."

While I have been actively protesting the many deadly attacks on Gaza by the Israeli government since 2005, I could not have foreseen the devastating scale of this current assault. As I write this, we are in the seventh month of Israel's genocidal war on Gaza. The death toll is astronomical: 35,000 Palestinians are dead, over 1.4% of Gaza's entire population.[5] The Israeli military is currently killing an average of 250 Palestinians per day.[6]

How do we comprehend this vast scale of death? In the face of these numbers, I often feel panicked, helpless, and numb. I don't want to understand people's irreplaceable lives as statistics. Shaharzad, a Gaza resident, wrote about this phenomenon: "What scares me the most is the thought of my death as a number among the numbers that increase every minute. I am not a number. It took me 23 years to become the person you see now. I have a home and friends, memory and pain."[7]

Whenever I hear about the rapidly rising death toll, I pause and take a breath. I notice the breath of life moving through me as I bear witness to the precious lives we have lost. As the Jewish concept of *b'tselem elohim* (אלהים בצלם) reminds us, all of us are holy because we are all made in the image of the divine. The Talmud teaches us, "Whoever destroys a soul, it is as if they destroyed an entire world. And whoever saves a life, it is as if they saved an entire world."[8] So many worlds are being destroyed instead of protected.

From the start of this genocide in October 2023, I have attempted to witness some of these worlds by learning more about individual people who lost their lives. I recently read Ruwaida Amer's story about Rawaa Abu Mohsen memorializing her sister Baraa Abu Mohsen, an artist and mother who founded her own business designing and making tiny models to decorate cakes.[9] I read Abubaker Abed's description of his friend, Al-Hassan Mattar, a twenty-one-year-old studying English literature, who was killed along with his father, twelve-year-old sister Tala, grandmother, and several relatives seeking shelter with them.[10] His friend remembered how they used to talk about football and watch *SpongeBob SquarePants* while eating popcorn in between studying for university exams. I was moved by Arafat Abu Massi describing his two sons, Mazen and Ahmed. In high school, Mazen was already determined to become a dentist, while Ahmed sold toys and school supplies in a small booth near their house.[11] I mourn and bear witness for all these individuals and the many others whose lives were taken. May their memories bless the freedom of future generations.

I can't begin to imagine what it would be like to live in Gaza surrounded by death, destruction, and disease. Since 2007 the people in Gaza have been living under a blockade in one of the most densely populated areas in the world with high rates of poverty, food insecurity, lack of access to clean water, and rolling blackouts. They have also suffered Israeli assaults every few years that killed thousands of Palestinians, injured countless others, and decimated Gaza's infrastructure. Once the attack began in October 2023, conditions quickly deteriorated. At the time of writing this in March 2024, 75,400 Palestinians have been injured, and thousands of bodies are buried under the rubble from Israeli air strikes.[12] Half of all buildings in Gaza—people's homes and schools, hospitals and mosques—have been destroyed, and people are sick, starving, and living in makeshift shelters or tents with no privacy, access to sanitation, or medical care.

Since the assault began in October 2023, the most many people can wish for is to die next to their family members. As Gaza resident Aunt May wrote,

"My wish is that they drop the bombs on us while we are sleeping and that we all die together. This is why we are here together. So that nobody is left alive to mourn those who were killed."[13] A new medical acronym emerged in October 2023 in the hospitals of Gaza—"WCNSF"—Wounded Child, No Surviving Family.[14] Gravely injured children who lost their entire families flooded the few overcrowded hospitals that were barely functioning. Most of the population is starving, and diseases are spreading, especially among children and the elderly. Most hospitals have been turned into makeshift refugee camps that double as morgues.

While it is hard to imagine living under these conditions from my comfortable home in Seattle, I feel my ancestors stirring uncomfortably because many of them lived (and died) under similar conditions. My great-grandfather Max, a shoemaker whose house was burned down three times in a Jewish ghetto in Warsaw, was the only one of his siblings who escaped Poland for the United States. The rest of his siblings, their children, and their grandchildren—three generations of this family—died in the Auschwitz concentration camp, with only one of his grand-nieces (from a family of eight) making it out alive.

Many Jews whose ancestors experienced persecution, oppression, and attempted genocide are hearing the echoes of our ancestors' suffering as we witness the ongoing Israeli state–backed genocide being enacted in our names. As Russian-Jewish writer Masha Gessen noted in their *New Yorker* article, "In the Shadow of the Holocaust," the living conditions of Palestinians in Gaza are reminiscent of "a Jewish ghetto in an Eastern European country occupied by Nazi Germany."[15] For the last seventeen years, Palestinians have been crowded into an open-air prison that is now being liquidated, just as the Nazi forces liquidated the Jewish ghettos. In both cases, the occupying forces claimed to be enacting this violence in the name of protecting their own people.

Defining Anti-Zionism

In the face of this genocide, an increasing number of Jews are beginning to question the ideology of Zionism, which drove the establishment of the state of Israel. I will go into more details about Zionism in chapter 5, but for now it is important to note that many of us who grew up in Jewish families and communities were indoctrinated into Zionism, a form of nationalism that insists Jews need our own state to be protected from antisemitism. As many of us discovered as adults, Zionism was and is a colonial project that relies on the dispossession of the Palestinian people. Zionism holds that Jews can only be safe by oppressing Palestinians, but more and more Jews are beginning to recognize that Israel doesn't make Jews in Israel or around the world safer. It actually makes us less safe by enacting violence in our names through its apartheid system that imposes "a system of oppression and domination against Palestinians across all areas of its control."[16]

Some Jews, including myself, identify as anti-Zionists, which means we oppose the idea that Jews need our own ethno-religious state. We work to end the ongoing occupation of Palestinian land, the denial of Palestinian self-determination, and the discrimination against Palestinian citizens of Israel. Many of us support the establishment of a democratic, secular state in a land where both Palestinians and Jews have equal rights.

Increasing numbers of Jews refuse to be bystanders while Israel enacts this genocidal assault on Gaza. For us, "Never Again" means "Never Again" for *anyone*. However, the Israeli government and its supporters also use the phrase "Never Again" as a war cry to justify using the same dehumanizing violent tactics against Palestinians that were historically wielded against Jews. For the state of Israel, "Never Again" means "forever again," repeating the cycle of violence with Israelis in the role of aggressors who must perpetually stave off victimhood.

Weaponizing Historical Trauma

This isn't the first time the Israeli government has evoked the historical trauma of the Nazi Holocaust to justify its unjustifiable attacks on Palestine, but it is one of the most blatant. Wearing a yellow Jewish star on his lapel with the words *Never Again* emblazoned on it, Israeli ambassador to the United Nations Gilad Erdan spoke at the October 2023 UN Security Council meeting to oppose calls for a ceasefire. He declared that Israel would continue its attacks "until we eliminate the Nazi Hamas."[17] On a conservative television station, Israeli Finance Minister Bezalel Smotrich described all Palestinians as Nazis when he said Israel must reestablish a Jewish presence in Gaza, because otherwise "There will be 2 million Nazis who want to annihilate us every morning when they wake up . . . we won't exist, period."[18]

When Israeli Prime Minister Benjamin Netanyahu announced the imminent ground invasion of Gaza, he called the invasion a "holy mission" and referred to the biblical story of Amalek, the archenemy of the ancient Israelites.[19] After the Amalekites repeatedly attacked the Israelites, G-d commanded their extermination as divine justice. Speaking to Israelis, Netanyahu proclaimed, "You must remember what Amalek has done to you."[20] In this formulation, Palestinians not only represent Nazis, but also an enemy of G-d who needs to be wiped out. His insistence on remembering Amalek is meant to prompt a common Jewish narrative that positions Jews as eternal victims who must be perpetually vigilant against the forces of evil—whether Amalek, the Nazis, or Palestinians.

If Palestinians represent the enemy of Jews, whether Nazis or Amalekites, they are no longer humans with their own aspirations and dreams who resist Israeli dispossession and aggression because they want freedom. Instead, the Israeli government flattens their lives by forcing them to bear the weight of symbolic evil. They become yet another faceless adversary of the Jews, another ghostly apparition in the parade of antisemitic history.

By evoking Jewish fear and anger about the Nazi Holocaust and historical Jewish trauma, Israeli officials deflect attention from current power dynamics. In a conversation sponsored by *Jewish Currents* and Diaspora Alliance, "Hijacking Memory: The Holocaust and the Siege of Gaza," Professor of Holocaust and Genocide Studies Raz Segal explains the power differentials:

> The fact is that Jews during World War II were stateless, powerless people who faced one of the strongest armies and states at the time, Nazi Germany. But Israel today is a very powerful state with an advanced army that enjoys the support of all the Western powers,

while Palestinians are stateless, powerless people suffering under decades of Israeli settler colonialism, military occupation, siege, and various other forms of mass violence.[21]

Body-Based Healing

To understand why reactivating the fear from past trauma is often successful, we need to understand how trauma is held in our bodies. And that is what this book is about. The first five chapters set up the historical and current context of trauma, oppression, and privilege for Jewish people over the past 150 years; and the need for Jewish body-based healing. The next five chapters delve into Jewish healing from historical and current trauma, including Zionism, through a political lens. Throughout the book, I use a mix of historical research, sociopolitical analysis, my personal experiences, and client examples to engage with the theory and practice of somatic healing in an anti-Zionist framework.

This is not a how-to book; there are no simple steps to healing from traumatizing systems. Rather, it's a collection of ideas, stories, and frameworks to help us grapple with the impact of these systems and foster healing within ourselves and our Jewish communities. You are welcome to try out the practices, such as centering, for yourself when you are feeling well resourced. However, please do not attempt to teach these practices to others if you are just learning them. Because we live inside such traumatizing systems, we each need our own in-depth learning and practice with skilled mentors to develop the embodied capacity to model the practices and hold what they might open in ourselves and others. If you are excited and moved by the work, I hope you continue to explore a path toward politicized embodied healing.

The premise of body-based healing work (somatics) is that past trauma—including intergenerational trauma—lives on in our muscles, connective tissue, and bones. When we undergo trauma—which can include not being able to escape or protect ourselves and others from harm—our automatic and innate survival reactions of flight, fight, freeze, appease, and dissociate are mobilized. While I will explain these responses in more detail in chapter 4, for now it is important to understand that our survival reactions are meant to be engaged when we are in danger to help us escape or fight off the danger. Then they are meant to be released. When we undergo a traumatic experience during which we are powerless to stop harm from occurring, these automatic responses don't release, but instead become trapped in our bodies.

These reactions can easily be reactivated in the present moment, prompting us to relive the original trauma itself. When that happens, we tend to feel disempowered because we are experiencing the feelings and sensations of the original trauma. Regardless of our current circumstances or actual power, we may feel like a victim. In *Power-Under: Trauma and Nonviolent Social Change,* mental health worker and activist Steven Wineman argues that trauma often leaves us feeling rageful about our perceived powerlessness.

Because so many of our ancestors were unable to protect themselves or their loved ones from harm during the Nazi Holocaust and other periods of violent antisemitic persecution, many of us have internalized not only the terror of those times, but also rage about what happened. According to Wineman, when we become activated in the present moment, we may engage in "desperate efforts at self-protection" that are driven from a place of feeling powerless.[22] This is an individual human response to trauma that can also be evoked on the collective level. Israeli officials attempt to evoke our collective response of powerless rage, so that we channel these feelings into support for an aggressive fight response by the state, which claims to speak for all Jewish people.

This subjective experience of helplessness often prevents us from any awareness of how we are wielding actual power. In Wineman's words, "When internalized powerlessness is paired with objective dominance, it creates a lethal dynamic in which we unwittingly respond to our own victimization by oppressing others."[23] We see this playing out in terms of rhetoric around the October 7 attack on Israel. When Israeli officials present Israeli citizens as if they represent all Jews under attack from Nazis—rather than acknowledging the attack is coming from Hamas, who represent a people living under siege and occupation—they are consciously evoking trauma from the Nazi Holocaust to generate feelings of powerless rage that get directed at Palestinians. This reversal of power dynamics—Israel claims to be under threat of genocide while it enacts a genocide—only makes sense through trauma's distorting mirror.

The Upside-Down World of Zionism

In her book *Doppelganger: A Trip into the Mirror World*, cultural critic Naomi Klein provides an incisive framework to help us understand this vertigo-inducing doubling that happens when Israeli state officials claim to be victims while enacting unspeakably violent oppression. Klein argues that contemporary culture is rife with this kind of doubling, which can occur on both the individual and collective level. For example, in the world of social media, we create idealized virtual doubles of ourselves, while we project "the unwanted and dangerous parts" of ourselves onto others in order to sharpen the boundary of our identities.[24] Klein widens this out to the realm of international politics by arguing that "It is not only an individual who can have a sinister double; nations and cultures have them too."[25]

Klein builds off the argument of Caroline Rooney, a professor of African and Middle Eastern studies, who coined the term "doppelganger politics" to describe the state of Israel's relationship to Palestine. According to Rooney, Israel engages in doppelganger politics in two related ways: the first is that in creating the state of Israel, Zionist Jews mimicked the militant nationalism of the Europeans "that oppressed them for centuries."[26] The second is through "projecting all criminality and violence onto the Palestinian other, lest the state's own foundational crimes be confronted."[27]

In chapter 5, I discuss how Israel imitated the violent nationalism and colonialism of Europe in creating the state of Israel, but for now I want to focus on the dynamic of the Israeli state claiming to fight terrorists as justification for terrorizing Palestinians. Since 2005, when Israeli forces withdrew from the Gaza Strip thirty-eight years after capturing it from Egypt, Israel has attacked Gaza in five major incursions. Before the genocidal assault in the fall of 2023, the deadliest attack, Operation Protective Edge, took place in 2014 when Israel bombed Gaza for fifty days, killing 2,251 Palestinians, and injuring 11,231.[28] Sixty-six Israeli soldiers and five civilians were also killed.[29] In spite of killing and injuring civilians and destroying homes, the Israeli government claimed that Israel was under attack by terrorists, conflating the entire Palestinian population with Hamas.

Since beginning the attacks on Gaza on October 7, 2023, Israeli officials have openly declared their intention to commit genocide, while claiming that Israelis are under threat of genocide.[30] The first step toward enacting genocide is the use of dehumanizing language to describe the Other. On October 8, in announcing that Israel would cut off fuel, electricity, and food supplies to Gaza, Defense Minister Yoav Gallant claimed, "We are fighting human animals, and we will act accordingly."[31] Netanyahu described Palestinians as "an abominable enemy, human beasts who celebrate the murder of women, children and the elderly."[32] In a chilling address to the country, Netanyahu vowed, "What we will do to our enemies in the coming days will reverberate with them for generations."[33]

In December, South Africa brought charges of genocide against Israel to the United Nations International Court of Justice (ICJ) to demand that the court order an emergency suspension of the military campaign. In January, the ICJ found the claim "plausible" and declared that Israel must take action to prevent acts of genocide by its forces in Gaza.[34]

In spite of stating their intentions and then carefully implementing this genocidal attack, Israeli officials used two main tactics to combat the accusation. Not surprisingly, the first is to claim that the reverse is true; the Israeli government is the one trying to stop a genocide. After the first day's proceedings, Netanyahu said, "We are fighting terrorists, we are fighting lies. Today we saw an upside-down world. Israel is accused of genocide while it is fighting against genocide."[35] The second is to claim that the accusation itself is antisemitic. Israeli government spokesperson Eylon Levy went so far as to describe South Africa's case against Israel as "blood libel." Blood libel refers to historical antisemitic accusations that Jews engaged in ritual murders in order to use the blood of their victims in religious rituals. In medieval Europe, accusations that Jews used the blood of Christian children in making *matzah* (unleavened bread) for Passover often fueled violence against Jewish communities.

By evoking the specter of violent antisemitism, defenders of the Israeli state suggest that Israel couldn't possibly commit genocide because the state, as a stand-in for the Jewish people, is always and forever only a victim. Even as it becomes increasingly obvious that the state has tremendous political and military power, its spokespeople emphasize its precarity. Yossi Klein Halevi, an author and fellow at the Shalom Hartman Institute in Jerusalem, argued that the case was "a deep blow to the Zionist aspiration of normalizing the Jewish people and turning us into a nation among nations."[36] Instead, he claimed, "What we're feeling today is that we're the Jew of the nations."[37] In this formulation, the state of Israel is on trial not for its genocidal violence but for its Jewish character—even though the majority of Jews in the world live elsewhere.

Reclaiming Jewish Trauma Healing in a Political Frame

How do we heal from the traumatic history of antisemitism—which includes, but is not limited to, the Nazi Holocaust—when this trauma is being manipulated to justify the violent oppression of Palestinians? Even though I work as a body-based trauma healer, I've noticed my own confusion since October 7 about how to mourn Israeli deaths, or even how to acknowledge that my own traumatic history is being activated. I have been reluctant to draw attention to Jewish trauma when we urgently need to stop the genocide of Palestinians in Gaza. It has felt particularly hard to grieve Israeli deaths when Jewish suffering and pain are being used as a moral cover for Israel's genocidal assault on Gaza.

Klein's *Doppelganger* suggests that such avoidance or distancing is part of a reactive pattern of behavior on the political left. In the mirror dance of polarization between the political left and right, the right often picks up on areas where the left has been unable to hold complexity. Once the right picks up an issue, according to Klein, "It seems to become oddly untouchable by almost everyone else."[38] For example, during the height of the pandemic, once the right began to focus their hatred and paranoia about Covid vaccines onto Bill Gates, the left abandoned our critique of Gates. In our haste to promote masking and vaccines, we ignored how Gates sided with drug companies to protect corporate profit over public safety. But dropping these issues is actually quite dangerous because fascism and conspiracy thrive in the places where we fail to engage. When we refuse to engage with issues that the right has appropriated, we allow the right to define the public conversation about these issues.

We can also apply this to Jewish trauma, fear, and grief. The state of Israel appropriates Jewish historical trauma to justify state violence against Palestinians. If we cede the conversation about Jewish grief and trauma to the right, we leave Jews who are confused and frightened nowhere to turn except rightward—where their feelings will be validated (and manipulated). Instead, we have to find new ways to talk about Jewish grief and trauma that don't reinforce Israel's narrative but do make room for our full range of feelings.

While paying attention to power differentials and holding firm to a politic of ending the Israeli state's immoral occupation of Palestinian land, we can't fall into the trap of dehumanizing Israeli citizens. Dehumanization is not a tool of liberation, but a symptom of this legacy of colonization and violence. Dehumanizing anyone is out of alignment with the value of protecting and caring for all of life. We can't let the Israeli government rob us of our ability to feel sorrow in the face of all human suffering.

To create space for Jewish healing, we need to offer a liberatory framework for working with Jewish grief and trauma that helps people move through the traumatic histories held in our bodies. While every Jew is situated differently in relationship to the history of antisemitism—which includes exile, displacement, and genocide—many of us have not grieved, processed, or healed from this intergenerational trauma. When trauma hasn't been integrated, digested, or released, we end up reliving these traumatic experiences from the past as soon as we are activated by events in the present.

Body-based healing can help Jews move from a past that overshadows our present, to a present informed by, but not determined by, our past. When Israeli officials evoke the trauma of the Nazi Holocaust, Jews who are stuck in a trauma response struggle to distinguish between a history of powerlessness and current access to power. The present simply becomes a repetition of our history. Body-based healing helps us release some of the terror and helplessness that is frozen in our bodies. This offers us the ability to differentiate past trauma from current reality and make choices that align our values with our current context. By holding a political framework for healing, we can offer compassion for Jewish fear, while helping to build understanding of the current power dynamics that pit Jewish safety against Palestinian freedom.

Centering in Our Anti-Zionist Jewish Collective Body

Knowing how isolated, scared, and overwhelmed so many anti-Zionist Jews were in the fall of 2023, my colleague Dona and I led several drop-in online practice spaces for this community. We designed each space, attended by hundreds, to draw strength from our collective anti-Zionist Jewish body. As individuals, we were all struggling with the emotional pain of a genocide being enacted in our names. Many of us were also experiencing heartbreaking and frustrating rifts with friends and family because of our politics. We could not and cannot process the intensity of this moment alone because it is too overwhelming for any one body and singular nervous system. We created a collective container to help us connect with each other, ourselves, and our commitment to stop the genocide.

As facilitators and activists who were also running a separate ten-week anti-Zionist healing group in the fall, both Dona and I noticed how easy it was for so many of us (including ourselves) to feel caught up in the urgency of the political moment. It was hard to focus on anything else once the genocidal attack began; every day the news from Gaza got worse: from surgeons being forced to operate without anesthetic to Palestinians being told to flee south and then getting bombed on their way.

Week after week, we were consuming social media and the news, tracking Signal threads to coordinate efforts, organizing rituals and protests, and taking part in direct actions. In overwhelming moments like this, it's easy to dissociate from our bodies and move into action from a numb place where we lose connection with our feelings, sensations, and emotions.

As an invitation to return to our bodies, we led a centering practice to feel the three-dimensionality of our bodies and the container of our collective body. Imagining that we were all trees in a grove, we rooted down into the ground and extended up the length of our spines while feeling for our inherent dignity and the dignity of all life—especially Palestinian life. As we breathed into the width of our rib cage, we felt for our comrades in the global Palestinian solidarity movement to which we belong. After we invited in the strength of our ancestors at our backs, we looked toward the horizon to envision a future when Palestine is free, and Israelis are no longer occupiers. When we center inside what we care about, including our vision for the future, we can access more presence and aliveness. Even when we are physically alone, we can remember we are connected to an anti-Zionist Jewish collective that propels us toward a different future.

We also felt into some of the many contradictions surrounding this moment, including the instruction to not look away from this genocide. Many activists were interpreting the slogan "We won't look away" literally as a command to stay glued to social media and the endless cycle of horrific news, keeping us in a perpetual state of hypervigilance and distress. But witnessing is actually a collective effort from which each of us can take breaks. As a collective of engaged people not in Gaza, we are witnessing and acting against this violence, but each of us can and should take breaks to resource ourselves.

To embody this practice, we guided the group in collective witnessing taught to us by our supervisor, Jennifer Ianniello. We instructed half of the participants to set a boundary between themselves and their screens by extending their arms in front of them and then looking away from the screen or even closing their eyes. The participants who looked away were then encouraged to allow their eyes to rest back in their sockets, to let their shoulders drop down away from their ears, and to take deep breaths into their bellies. We reminded them that the other half of the group was continuing to bear witness so they could rest.

After encouraging participants who continued to look at their screens to also take some deeper breaths, we asked them to allow some of the tightness and energy in their eyes to sink down lower into their hearts and then all the way down to their bellies. Our eyes are not able to process all the violence that they hold. Our hearts and our bellies can be allies to help us metabolize what we witness. Instead of overextending through our eyes, we encouraged people to notice each other, to notice that even when we bear witness, we do not have to do so in isolation. Bearing witness can be a collective act that deeply connects us to each other.

After everyone took a turn continuing to bear witness and temporarily turning away, many participants said it was the first time they had been able to experience a moment of relief or relaxation in their eyes since the genocide began. Some noticed how painful it felt to look away because they immediately felt flooded with grief and rage and terror.

I had a similar experience when I first tried looking away. When Jennifer led us through this practice in a training group, hot tears immediately sprung into the corners of my eyes. I had a moment of deep grief and then anger at being asked to do this practice. I worried that if I felt even a fraction of the intensity of my feelings, I wouldn't be able to sustain my weekly activism. Moving away from numbness often feels painful because, as writer Toni Morrison reminds us in her novel *Beloved*, "Anything dead coming back to life hurts."[39] I had been justifying my constant consumption of news from Gaza as a way to stay connected to the suffering of the people in Gaza, but it became a method to numb and avoid the fullness of my emotions—including my rage and sorrow.

Witnessing the intensity of this genocidal moment is truly horrifying, haunting, and also humbling because of how difficult it has been for me to stay present in my body and connected to what I care about. I, too, am easily activated right now. I haven't lived through an Israeli assault on this scale, and most of my friends and loved ones are also struggling to find balance and stay present. I am approaching this book in this moment not only as an anti-Zionist practitioner who has facilitated individual and collective transformation for over two decades, but as someone on a healing journey of my own. While I will describe how I work to support people's transformation in this book, I will also recount my own such experiences to break down some of the walls between healers and healing. Healers need healing too, especially in moments like these.

During this time when I have been holding healing and ritual spaces for many people, I have been blessed to have people holding space for me as well, reminding and encouraging me to return to the wisdom and presence of my body. Being present in our bodies, even at this harrowing time, offers us a way to take action that is connected to our feelings, emotions, and deepest values.

Activism as Healing

As I will demonstrate throughout this book, speaking out and taking action against the Israeli government's violent oppression of Palestinians are integral to healing Jewish trauma and challenging Zionism. Whenever we do the work of showing up in solidarity with Palestinians and other people experiencing oppression, we heal our isolation by reaching for connection beyond the borders of our identities.

Since October 7, in the midst of my grief, rage, and terror about Israel and Palestine, I also experienced moments of hope and connection at protests demanding an immediate and permanent ceasefire, an end to the siege of Gaza, and an end to Israeli occupation and apartheid. Our chapter of JVP jumped into action on October 13 by staging a sit-in at Washington Senator Patty Murray's office in the federal building, where we insisted that Murray meet with us to hear our demand for a ceasefire. With linked arms, we sang Hebrew peace songs of resistance until several of us got arrested. Our protests grew bigger every week as we held rallies outside the building, occupied the lobby with chants and songs, and finally shut down the entrance to the building for several hours.

All of our actions have taken place in the context of a global movement for Palestinian liberation led by Palestinians fighting for their lives. As Jews across the country and across the world, we have been shattering the idea that Israel speaks in our name. We have been marching; occupying elected officials' offices; filling up our representatives' voicemails; shutting down bridges, train stations, and highways; and just as importantly, having hard conversations. The Israeli state is telling us that the Jewish future belongs to those who bomb and displace civilians, destroy schools, and kill thousands of children, but we insist—through our protests, actions, and words—that the Jewish future belongs to those of us who refuse to dehumanize others. To those of us who know that our own liberation is inextricably intertwined with Palestinian liberation.

Many of our rallies included mourning rituals, so that we could express our grief about the loss of life in a way that couldn't be coopted to justify more violence. Reclaiming our Jewish traditions that extend back thousands of years before Zionism, we offered prayers of mourning, the opportunity to stack and place stones, and a moment to breathe together with our hands on our hearts. During this grieving ritual, I reminded us that in this space, we had permission to feel the jumble of overwhelming emotions in our hearts—including grief, shame, outrage, and fear. I asked folks to look around at this community of mourners and feel the love in our hearts— for each other, for Palestinians, and for our traditions—that motivates us to come together week after week to take action, cry out, pray together, and say, "No more" and "Never again."

I was inspired and moved by Just Vision's Palestinian outreach associate, Fadi Abu Shammalah, who spoke on independent news program *Democracy Now* about how people in Gaza feel less alone when they witness the solidarity protests around the world. In this episode, he refers to protestors as people of conscience whose hearts are still "alive."[40] When we feel our emotions and come back into our bodies, we combat numbness and hopelessness in the face of this genocide. When we feel our emotions and come back into our bodies, we can move into action that is grounded in the love we hold for our collective humanity and the earth to whom we all belong.

Through participating in these rituals, many of us were finally able to experience some of our contradictory, painful, and unwieldy feelings. Several participants told us that they were able to cry or scream at one of our rituals for the first time since October 7. At the end of an outdoor rally that was also a Shabbat (שבת) service, a man with kind eyes approached me to thank us for leading the service. He told me that part of our service reminded him of a passage from the *Quran,* and asked if he could read me the blessing. After he was done, we touched hands for a moment, looked into each other's eyes, and both cried. I can no longer recall what passage he read, but I hope to never forget what it felt like to cry together and witness the rawness of each other's hearts alive with pain.

On November 19, 2023, our chapter led a protest that shut down the iconic Seattle Space Needle. While we sang Batya Levine's song "We Rise," we launched a forty-foot banner with the message "Ceasefire Now," which soared in front of the Needle, buoyed by orange helium balloons. Workers at the Space Needle walked out of their jobs and joined us. Groups of tourists picked up signs to participate in our program of singing, poetry, and ritual. As folks linked arms to block the entrance, Black, Indigenous, Palestinian, and Jewish speakers described how our intersecting struggles led to our refusal to remain silent in the face of genocide. We put forward a vision for Palestinians and Israelis to live full and free lives by addressing the root causes of Israeli military occupation and apartheid backed by US funding of over $3 billion every year.[41]

With this protest, we expanded the frame of possibility for our communities by showing how our overlapping and separate histories and struggles led us to solidarity with Palestine. We read the words of an anonymous psychologist from the Aida refugee camp who asked that we save ourselves from participating in genocide because our global humanity is at stake. As a collective, we insisted that stopping the genocide is only the first step in changing course. As a global community, we are poised at a crossroads. Will we choose the path of apartheid, colonization, and ethnic cleansing or the path of freedom and self-determination for all people?

Just a few weeks later, on the eighth night of Chanukah, we were one of eight JVP chapters who shut down eight bridges across the country to disrupt business as usual. With giant banners calling for a ceasefire and proclaiming "The whole world is watching," we shut down the University Bridge in Seattle for several hours while we chanted, sang, and celebrated Chanukah. The word *Chanukah* means "rededication," and on the eighth night we rededicated ourselves to fighting for justice. Artists constructed an eighteen-foot-tall olive tree menorah puppet operated by a team of nine folks to show solidarity with Palestinians, whose olive trees represent Palestinian resistance and steadfastness.

When we lit the menorahs on the edge of the dark bridge, we offered a reframing of the story of Chanukah. We explained how the festival of Chanukah commemorates the victory of the Maccabees, a Jewish Hasmonean priestly family, over their Greek oppressors in the second century BCE. Their oppressors outlawed Judaism and ordered the Jewish people to worship Greek gods. After two years of battle, the Maccabees won their battle of resistance. When they went to rededicate the desecrated Temple in Jerusalem, rebuild its altar, and light its menorah, there was only enough oil to last one day. But when they lit the fire, a miracle occurred and it lasted for eight full days.

Some say that this story underscores a powerful truth: even in the bleakest of times, oppressed people will somehow find the strength to continue their struggle. However, I pointed out that when most people tell the Chanukah story, they end it with the Maccabees winning the war and lighting the menorah to rededicate the Temple.

We shared the rest of the story: after the miraculous oil burns out, our heroes become doppelgangers of their own oppressors, using violence to force others to convert against their will. This Hasmonean period of one hundred years, which began with the story we celebrate during Chanukah, was actually filled with bloodshed and repression. It can serve as a cautionary tale that our story never ends when the battle is won. The trauma of oppression impacts us for generations. If we don't consciously heal from trauma and oppression, we can and have scrambled for power, taken revenge, and harmed others in the exact ways that we have been harmed. But another path is always possible if we choose healing.

To keep the energy going as it grew dark and cold out on the bridge, we started chanting "Up, up with liberation" as we pumped our hands into the sky, and "Down, down with occupation" as we bent toward the ground. Our friends from a Klezmer band spontaneously provided backup, punctuating our chants with music. Pretty soon all of us on the bridge, including the nine-person menorah puppet, were dancing so hard that we could feel the bridge swaying back and forth underneath us. For a brief interlude, we rejoiced in raising our voices together in a community of resistance, reclaiming our Jewish traditions, and imagining a future of liberation. Although I know that the trauma from this time will reverberate for generations, I also hope and believe that the beautiful expressions of solidarity, of reaching for connection beyond the borders of our identities, will reverberate into a future of healing.

CHAPTER 2

JEWISH LONGING AND BELONGING

Longing is the impulse that started the process of creation. Not G-d's will, but G-d's desire. So I understand longing as a language that is hardwired within us, who were made in the image of G-d. Longing is how we communicate with Source, the way we bring the energy of creation into the world.[1]

—RABBI NADYA GROSS

My journey to become a body-based healer grew out of my longing to belong to a Jewish community rooted in justice. I grew up in a predominantly Christian suburb of Columbus, Ohio, where I could count the number of other Jewish families on one hand. I can remember only snatches of Hebrew songs that I learned from attending Saturday school as a toddler for about a year in the neighboring Jewish suburb. When my family of eight could no longer afford the fees associated with membership, we stopped attending. Without any extended family or Jewish community nearby, we assimilated into the Christian-dominated culture that surrounded us and retained just a few remnants of Jewish culture. I absorbed a smattering of Yiddish words: my dad affectionately referred to our cat as *ketzel* and insisted that we shouldn't wear shirts that revealed our *pupik,* or belly button. We lit candles for Chanukah, which we celebrated on Christmas. One year, my sister's boyfriend delivered us a "Chanukah bush," a pine tree that we proceeded to top with a Jewish star crafted out of aluminum foil.

As an adult, I moved to Seattle, where I shivered in the freeze of the Pacific Northwest's Scandinavian-influenced culture. For many years, I hungered to connect to my Jewishness without knowing how to follow this longing. Most of my efforts hit dead ends until finally, in my thirties, some queer Jews invited me to a series of Shabbat dinners where we lit candles, broke bread, and shared how we learned about Palestine/Israel from our families. Thrilled to be included, I struggled to hide my shame about not knowing the Hebrew blessings for the candles, wine, and challah. Over shared food, many of us discussed the turmoil we experienced from being told that Israel was "our" safe haven, while watching Israel perpetrate violence against Palestinians.

Eager to learn more, our informal group morphed into a study group on the history of Zionism, the political ideology that led to the founding of Israel. Through reading articles and books, we learned the horrifying details of Israel's founding, which displaced over 750,000 Palestinians from their homes.[2] Appalled by the disparity between what we had learned from our families about Israel and what we were studying, we decided to become more politically active as a group. Several of us formed the Seattle chapter of Jewish Voice for Peace, a national grassroots organization inspired by Jewish values to transform US policy toward justice and equality for Palestinians. Our chapter of JVP was born out of queer Jewish relationship, ritual, and study.

As I became more politically active around Palestine, I also longed to become more rooted in my Jewish spiritual learning and wider community. I soon began attending Friday night services at a queer-friendly congregation that some of my friends attended. When I told the rabbi about my activism around Palestine, he proclaimed that different political perspectives on Palestine/Israel were welcome there, "As long as we still love each other at the end of the day." In my longing for Jewish knowledge and acceptance, I took him at his word and assumed that I had found my new spiritual community and home.

In 2006, not long after joining the synagogue, Israel attacked Lebanon and Gaza with air strikes. My JVP comrades and I showed up to protest Israeli military aggression at a Stand with Israel rally on Mercer Island, just east of Seattle. We carried signs that proclaimed "Israeli aggression betrays Jewish values," and "As a Jew, I cannot support bombing civilians." The police tried to keep us out of the rally, and irate Jewish attendees yelled at us, calling us "Nazis" and "Kapos." This was my first experience of vitriol from Jews who did not share my political perspective, and it shook me.

The intensity of the summer continued to ramp up. Just five days later, an armed man who proclaimed he was "angry at Israel" shot six women at the Jewish Federation in Seattle. Shocked and disoriented, my JVP comrades and I consoled each other, but we didn't receive much support from our non-Jewish activist community. Because the shooter mentioned Israel, they didn't know how to respond. Most of them didn't speak out to condemn the violence, which made us feel alone and isolated. We also didn't feel comfortable mourning with our larger Jewish community. Many of the organizations who sponsored the Stand with Israel rally were now the ones holding memorial spaces.

Recognizing the need to create our own space for both mourning the shootings and speaking out against Israeli apartheid, we created a *Tashlich L'tzedek* (תשליך לצדק), a social justice casting-off ritual. On the shore of Lake Washington, we led a ritual taking responsibility for the violence being enacted in our names as Jews by the state of Israel and asking our community to grapple with antisemitism.

A friend and fellow JVP member and I decided to write about our ceremony for our synagogue newsletter to introduce other members to Jewish Voice for Peace. Naively, we thought it was just another article in a newsletter filled with updates about the lives and interests of our fellow members. Not surprisingly (although it surprised me at the time!), we were immediately attacked by a congregant who wrote a lengthy email to us, the board, and the rabbi. She demanded a response to a barrage of questions, including "Are you aware that Muslim families rejoice in the death of their young people in suicide attacks?" and "Is there a possibility that anti-Israel Muslim nations have exploited the 'Palestinian refugees,' encouraging them to remain in refugee camps because it serves the Muslim political agenda?" She announced that at best, we were ignorant about "Muslim hatred for Jews," and, at worst, we fueled antisemitic violence, like the shootings at the Federation. When we tried to talk to the rabbi about our deep concern with her language, he dismissed our concerns, asking us, "What did you expect?" He also told us, "She made some very powerful points about Israel's right to defend herself against Muslim countries."

I was hurt and startled by his endorsement of Islamophobia and began reckoning with the unthinking nationalism and racism pervasive in the place where I had hoped to build a Jewish home. In retrospect, the pushback we encountered about our politics seems tame compared to the name-calling, attacks, and exclusions I have faced over the years because of my activism. I have received countless violent threats on social media, a death threat mailed to my home address, and numerous sexual assault threats. I have been told more than once that my head would be cut off in Muslim countries because of my queerness. But at the time, my very tentative sense of belonging in my congregation began to erode. I was deeply hurt by the accusation that my friend and I were promoting antisemitism, and I was disappointed by how few fellow congregants were willing to speak out against Israel's attacks.

I was reminded of this history when I read a beautiful sermon written by Rabbi Alissa Wise when she was leaving JVP as a staff member. In this piece, she reflects on the cost of developing a thick skin to protect herself from the unceasing harassment from other Jews because of her politics. Like so many of us, she tried to block out the persistent name-calling, exclusions, and threats by ignoring them and focusing on her work.[3] But Wise slowly came to realize that not only had they seeped in, but that she had failed to attend to the wounds they left, which were festering. In her words, "The thick skin turned from being protective to being corrosive."[4] To survive these attacks she had become numb, which distanced her from the pain, but the pain didn't disappear. Eventually, the energy it took to suppress the pain led to exhaustion and burnout. She warns us, "We don't want to let our skin be so tough that we don't recognize the pain that is there. Let's feel our pain *and* feel our power."

Wise offers us a gift as she links feeling pain with feeling power because—as the world of body-based healing tells us—when we start numbing ourselves to any difficult feelings, whether pain, grief, or anger, we also cut ourselves off from all feeling, including joy, satisfaction, or happiness. Developing a thick skin can protect us from others' judgments, but if it becomes too impermeable, we lose the ability to feel our own aliveness. We are no longer able to connect to ourselves and others, and we can't rejoice in our wins, revel in our solidarity, or feel inspired by our purpose. No wonder we burn out.

In her interview with *Jewish Currents* in 2021, Wise mentions that she wouldn't have been able to speak so freely about this dynamic if she wasn't leaving her job at JVP because she didn't want to center Jewish pain in her role as an ally to Palestinians fighting for a free Palestine.[5] Palestinians are the main targets of violent oppression by the state of Israel. However, Jews can't sustain ourselves in our political commitments if we don't start addressing how Zionism also harms Jews. In fact, this is what motivated me to become a body-based healer.

Beginning with the rally on Mercer Island, I learned firsthand how Zionism creates violent rifts in our communities, and how these divisions live inside our bodies. As Jews, we long to belong to each other, but many of us are told that we can only belong if we demonstrate support for the state of Israel. The extremely narrow range of acceptable political opinions is itself partially the result of historical trauma, which needs our attention and healing.

Jewish Healing through the Body

About eight years into my organizing for a free Palestine, I started training to become a body-based healer. My goal was (and is) working with other Jews to heal trauma in service of collective liberation. Doing activism around Palestine with other Jews taught me that Jews need healing from historical and current trauma in a politically relevant and spiritually grounded container. We need healing to end the political oppression enacted by the state of Israel against Palestinians. We need healing to end the enforcement of political conformity in our communities. We need healing to begin living into a liberated Judaism.

Body-based healing offers an effective healing path for Jews because it addresses the impact of trauma that is held in our bodies. Unlike some forms of traditional psychotherapy, which work primarily through our intellect, body-based healing integrates the wisdom of our minds, bodies, and spirits in the service of our healing. In many Western cultures, we have inherited a Cartesian split or mind–body dualism popularized through the work of seventeenth-century French philosopher René Descartes. Descartes not only promoted the separation of the mind and body as two independent entities, but he elevated the mind as the source of consciousness, thought, and perception. In his paradigm, the mind controls the body, which acts like a machine to serve the commands of the mind. This split has contributed to a persistent focus in Western mainstream cultures on the rational and cognitive aspects of human experience at the expense of emotional, embodied, and spiritual experiences. It's important to note that various communities, including many Indigenous ones, have protected and passed on cultural practices of spiritual embodiment; however, here I focus on how Western mainstream culture has promoted disembodiment.

Descartes's philosophy not only *emerged from* a period of European colonialism, but also *reinforced* colonialism by emphasizing the superiority of European rational mind-based cultures over non-European cultures, which were characterized as primitive. Europeans had supposedly emerged out of the bestial body and progressed into the mind, which was associated with culture or civilization. To justify stealing land and resources, Europeans posited that humans who lived close to the land, more in sync with its rhythms, were inferior because they hadn't yet learned to control and exploit the land. Colonialism was meant to reinforce European superiority by dominating both the people and the land.

Coming back into our bodies is inherently a political act because of the colonial legacy of disembodiment. The current systems of domination that grew out of this oppressive legacy—including capitalism—promote and rely on disembodiment and objectification of both people and land. When we can't feel ourselves or each other because we are disembodied and disconnected, we are more likely to accept treating each other—and our living environment—as objects. These objectifying behaviors support racialized capitalism in its efforts to profit from human labor and extract resources from the land. When we can feel and experience our interdependence with each other and the land, we become more resistant to the logic of racialized capitalism.

The world of politicized somatic healing insists on the impossibility of separating our bodies from our self or from the world around us. We are fundamentally intertwined with the natural world; shaped by cultural, historical, and natural forces. Our selves (including our minds, bodies, and spirits) are informed by the ways we have adapted to the world, including both its life-giving and oppressive forces.

Bringing together somatic healing and Judaism results in potent medicine partly because Judaism is rooted in embodiment. Unlike some forms of Christianity, Judaism does not view the body as a hindrance or obstacle to be overcome in order to release our spirit.[6] In Judaism, our bodies are made in G-d's image, and we access our spirit *through* our bodies, not through leaving our bodies. Instead of serving as an empty dwelling place for our soul, the body is the site of the soul.[7] Body and spirit are intimate and inseparable partners in Judaism. Accessing spirit *through* our bodies instead of through *leaving* our bodies helps us avoid a "spiritual bypass"—which refers to using spiritual beliefs, practices, or concepts as a way to escape or avoid facing the messy, difficult, and uncomfortable aspects of the world.

Of course, there are as many ways to be Jewish as there are Jewish people in the world. I am approaching Judaism as a queer, non-binary, feminist, disabled, white Ashkenazi (Eastern European) anti-Zionist Jew who accomplished the vast majority of my intentional learning about Judaism as an adult. I have reverence for the wisdom passed down to us by our ancestors through Jewish texts and oral histories, as well as a healthy skepticism of the patriarchal method through which we received traditional Jewish wisdom. I am aware that the voices of marginalized people—including disabled people, women, trans, and non-binary people—have not always been recorded in the traditional texts of Judaism, such as the Torah and the Talmud, and I honor the many feminist methods of recovering these voices.

Judaism is a multifaceted system of beliefs, cultural practices, and traditions that has evolved over thousands of years and continues to evolve through each generation. In *Loving Our Own Bones: Disability Wisdom and the Spiritual Subversiveness of Knowing Ourselves Whole,* queer feminist disabled rabbi Julia Watts Belser names how she engages with traditional texts that have caused harm to so many of us—in particular, disabled people. She tells us, "I claim this tradition and am claimed by it. I shape it and am shaped by it. I hold it close, and I am held."[8] Like Watts Belser, I am claiming these Jewish traditional texts by putting them in conversation with other sources of queer, antiracist, feminist wisdom.

All Jews come to healing from different places, because Jews are a diverse people with a range of political opinions, gender identities, abilities, class backgrounds, religious and cultural practices, and racial and ethnic backgrounds. Jewish ethnic groups include Eastern and Western European and Russian (Ashkenazi); Middle Eastern, North African, Central Asian, and Balkan (Mizrahi); Ethiopian and Ugandan (African); and Spanish and Portuguese (Sephardi). There are mixed-race Jews whose ancestors include non-European peoples, as well as white people and people of color who have chosen (or whose parents, grandparents, or ancestors chose) to convert to Judaism. Ethnically diverse Jewish communities exist all over the world.

In 2021, I began facilitating a Jewish body-based healing group called Ruach (רוח), which means "breath" or "spirit" in Hebrew. With Ruach, I bring together Jews of different ages, races, cultural backgrounds, gender identities, sexual orientations, and abilities who identify as anti-Zionist. By centering anti-Zionist Jews, I have purposefully created a space where anti-Zionists are not merely included but are instead held as the beating heart of the collective. The intention of Ruach is to foster a sense of belonging to each other, to Judaism, and to our ancestors. We use the words *spirit* and *G-d* in Ruach to indicate the creative source of life that emerges from the natural world, whose spark exists in each of us.

Longings Guide the Way

Just as my journey of becoming a healer began with my longing for Jewish community, our collective journey into body-based healing begins with the possibilities of *Olam Ha-Ba* (עולם הבא), or "the world to come." Unlike some forms of psychotherapy, somatics does not ask those seeking healing to start from a place of failure, deficit, or diagnosis of a problem. Instead, we ask ourselves, "What do we long for in our lives and communities?" and "What compels us toward the future?" These questions guide us toward our longings for both *who* we want to be in the world and *how* we want the world to be. We discover our longings by becoming present in our bodies through noticing and identifying our bodily sensations. When we notice how we feel in our bodies, we are not looking back on how we once felt or anticipating how we might feel in the future. We are listening to the language of our bodies in the current moment. Our longings, yearnings, and desires emerge from this ability to feel, and make meaning of, our bodily sensations.

Our longings move each of us toward the purpose that helps direct our lives. As we come back into our bodies to feel our longings, we learn how to differentiate between the goals we unknowingly inherited from our families, communities, and institutions; and our longings that come from deep within our beings. Once we can identify what we truly long for, we can move forward on a path toward who we want to become in the world. At the same time, we can discover what kind of world we long to live in. Because we are interdependent with the world around us, when we experience our longing for change in ourselves, we simultaneously experience our longing for change in our communities, our institutions, and our world. We can think of this as longing for Olam Ha-Ba, the world that simultaneously comes into being as we align with our visions.

For example, as Jews, many of us have inherited Zionism: the belief that Jews deserve a Jewish state, and the related notion that the state of Israel is the answer to our longings for Jewish safety, liberation, and freedom. As we learn more about Israel and question Zionism, we also develop a longing for

31

a different world. As a nationalist ideology that drove the founding of the Israeli state, political Zionism developed as one response to antisemitism in Europe in the late nineteenth century. Some Jews proposed the creation of a Jewish nation-state in historic Palestine. This proposal gained global support after the horrors of the Nazi Holocaust came to light, and the state of Israel was established in 1948. I will go into more detail about Zionism in chapter 5, but I define it here for the sake of understanding how our longings for ourselves intersect with our longings for the world in which we live.

As I discussed in the first chapter, many Jews identify as anti-Zionists, which means we oppose the political ideology of Zionism as a nationalist colonialist project that resulted in the dispossession of the Palestinian people. We support the Palestinian right of return, which would allow Palestinians (and their descendants) displaced during the founding of the Israeli state to return and be compensated for their homes and land. As a means of holding Israel accountable, we also support the Palestinian-led movement for Boycott, Divestment and Sanctions (BDS), which aims to pressure Israel to comply with international law and end its colonization of Palestinian land. In 2005, a coalition of Palestinian civil society organizations initiated the BDS movement, which calls for boycotting Israeli companies and institutions complicit in Israeli apartheid; divesting from companies that profit from the Israeli occupation; and imposing economic, cultural, and diplomatic sanctions on Israel until it complies with international law.

Some of us who inherit Zionism from our families and communities begin to recognize that what we were taught about Zionism as a liberatory ideology is not truly liberatory because it is based on the oppression of Palestinians. We must unlearn what we were taught and begin to redefine ourselves and our place in the world. In other words, as we come into our longing for *who* we want to be as Jews, we come into our longing for *how* we want the world to be—a world of interdependence, Palestinian freedom, and collective liberation.

This questioning is similar to the process of coming into queerness. As queers, we learn to challenge what most of us were taught about our identity, gender, sexuality, relationships, and family. As we long for and create new identities for ourselves, we also long for and help create communities that resist the societal norms and structures upheld and enforced by oppressive institutions. Because many queer people, particularly queers of color, are disproportionately targeted by state violence and oppression—including anti-trans legislation, police brutality, and discriminatory laws—we also learn to interrogate state power.

This means that many of us also begin to question Zionism as we engage with our desires for ourselves, each other, and a new world. In her beautiful memoir, *Push the Water,* queer Jewish filmmaker Irit Reinheimer writes, "For me, being Jewish and queer means being part of two diasporas—so many of us felt a need to leave home. Our sense of alienation gave way to a kind of desire. I found that when we embraced this feeling of strangeness and when this strangeness developed into a desire for each other, we figured out how to survive."[9] Leaving home can mean questioning the Zionism, homophobia, and heteronormativity of the communities in which we were raised.

Black lesbian feminist writer and activist Audre Lorde also speaks to the power of desire in her essay, "The Uses of the Erotic." She redefines our erotic power, our deepest longings, as an assertion of our life force, which has been limited and distorted by oppressive systems. Although she is specifically referring to women in this essay, I think most humans impacted by oppressive systems need to reclaim the power of our desires. When we reconnect with the erotic in our longings, Lorde writes, "We begin to live from within outward," so that our inner power impacts our outer world.[10] Experiencing and following our deepest desires helps us combat the numbness of late capitalism, and "Our acts against oppression become integral with self, motivated and empowered from within."[11]

Our longings are the source of our agency, choices, and aliveness. When we pay close attention to the stirrings of our longings, we start to feel the chasm between where we are and where we wish to be. Looking into the gap can awaken in us a fear that we won't ever arrive on the shore of fulfillment. Sometimes we become afraid to declare or share our longings for fear of being embarrassed and disappointed if we don't fulfill them. But when we shut down our longings, we curtail our life force.

In my favorite novel (and film) about queer Jewish desire, *Call Me By Your Name* by André Aciman, one of the main characters, Elio, has just been left by his lover, Oliver. Heartbroken, Elio tries to numb his pain by minimizing his feelings about their connection. In a tender and unusually supportive conversation with Elio, his father reflects on the cost of shutting down the pain of heartbreak. His father warns:

> We rip out so much of ourselves to be cured of things faster than we should that we go bankrupt by the age of thirty and have less to offer each time we start with someone new. But to feel nothing so as not to feel anything—what a waste! Right now, there's sorrow, pain. Don't kill it. And with it, the joy you felt.[12]

As I mentioned earlier, we can't just shut down access to one feeling, like sorrow, without shutting down access to all our feelings, such as love, connection, and belonging. When we can live into and sustain our longings—whether for connection with another person, G-d, or a more just world—we remain engaged, awake, and alive. We also open ourselves up to heartbreak—the possibility that our longings won't be met—but this too is an experience of our aliveness.

Longings and Prayer

Longings spur us toward healing, and they also fuel our prayers. I am defining Jewish prayer broadly as any practice or process that we undertake by first turning inward in the service of widening outward, to meet a holiness larger than our individual lives. That holiness might include nature, spirit, purpose, or community. I'm not only referring to the conventional Jewish prayers in Hebrew or Aramaic that we recite at home or during services, but they are certainly included in this definition of prayer.

While Jewish prayer is a different technology than embodied healing, it shares a similar goal of helping us understand ourselves on a cellular level, so that we can transform ourselves to become more aligned with our purpose in this world. So many of us have been cut off from the traditions of Jewish prayers meant to be passed down from our ancestors, whether due to antisemitism, assimilation, or oppressive dynamics within Jewish institutions and communities. Reclaiming prayers for ourselves can include reconnecting to traditional prayers, creating new prayers, and redefining our sacred healing practices as prayers.

In a special issue of *CrossCurrents: God, the God of Unmet Desire*, Zisl, the pen name of a non-binary queer Jewish writer, offers us a queer Jewish framework for the centrality and importance of longing in our prayers by reinterpreting "Shacharit" (שחרית), the Jewish morning prayers. Zisl starts with an irreverent reinterpretation of a line from the central Ashrei (אשרי) prayer, which is conventionally recited three times a day in Jewish liturgy. Instead of translating the text as thanking G-d for providing living beings with what they desire, they read it as thanking G-d, who "provides every living being *with desire*."[13] Desire is conceived here as central to who we are as people.

In this interpretation of Ashrei, Zisl emphasizes the importance of determining which longings we should follow. Not all of our desires are meant to be enacted, particularly if they impinge on someone else's agency by enacting power over others through domination, control, or oppression. On our path of discernment, we must determine which longings need consent. Zisl points out that right after we thank G-d for endowing us with desire, we ask G-d to help us hold justice in our minds and kind love in our deeds. In Zisl's words, "G-d wants us to be close to Them and one another—but not in any way or at any cost. Only with truth, justice, and kindness—that is the closeness that G-d Desires."[14] Fulfilling our desires should never impinge on someone else's sovereignty. We hold this framework to ensure that we respect each other's desires, even as we delve into our own.

If desire is what fuels our aliveness, then the dearth of desire is a kind of numbness or death of our soul. Whereas longings and prayers are a beginning, as Zisl explains, Zionism is an ending. Zionism tells us that we have already arrived home, that the establishment of the state of Israel can and should fulfill our age-old longings. But to arrive, we must deaden our feelings because we are denying and erasing the fact that this land, this place, was and is already a home for the Palestinian people.

Too often in this current world built on colonialism and exploitation, the fulfillment of some people's desires relies on the suppression of others. Zionism implemented Jewish people's desires without even acknowledging, let alone honoring, the desires or the dignity of the Palestinian people. When we close the gap between having and wanting, without truth in our minds or loving-kindness in our deeds, we often cause harm. We need to slow down and notice the foundation of what is propelling our desire.

Zisl reminds us never to trust "an ideology that tells you that you can get whatever you want. It is one of the most seductive and dangerous lies that is told, and it is a denial of the fundamental human condition of precarity, shared struggle, and yearning."[15] We should never feel fully satiated; when we fulfill certain longings, others will appear, because that is the nature of being alive. We must learn to linger in the sensations of longing itself as the source of our aliveness.

In supposedly ending our exile, the founding of the state of Israel made us forget our own struggles; they became something to overcome, no matter what the cost, instead of a commonality that we share with other vulnerable people. When we stop longing, we become numb, disembodied, and disconnected. Ignoring others' desires as we reach for our own leads us away from G-d, feeling, and the beautiful entanglement of our lives with all that surrounds us.

Finding Our Longings

In the numbness that late capitalism encourages, we often can't feel what we truly long for. We can be fooled into thinking that our true desires can be met by accumulating more things or gaining more accolades. Many of us can't feel our longings outside of what our cultures dictate for us, or what we have inherited through our families. If we have experienced individual or collective harm, violation, or violence, we can end up hiding the things we care deeply about—including our desires. We might reasonably fear that our longings will be used against us.

As we become more embodied, it becomes easier to feel the tug of these longings inside our sensations. We start by developing our somatic awareness, our ability to name and live inside of our sensations—including three guiding sensations: temperature, pressure, and movement. As we develop our ability to feel ourselves from the inside out, we learn how to experience our sensations and corresponding emotions without a need to shut them down or take immediate action. When we can tolerate more feeling, we encounter our longings.

For example, I recently discovered that I had been shutting down a longing for connection to the wider Jewish community. Because of my history of being attacked and rejected by Jews who don't share my politics, when I meet a new Jewish person, whether at synagogue or a party, I often brace myself for political misalignment around Palestine. This attempt to protect myself makes sense, given my history; however, my approaching all Jews from this hardened place disempowers me, and forecloses on the possibility of connection.

To understand this pattern, I had to drop into the sensations, emotions, and story that arose in this situation. Most recently, when I met another Jewish person at a dinner party, I noticed that my breath became shallow, my throat clenched; and my chest and stomach tightened. Imagining the worst about their political beliefs regarding Israel, I expected a conflict and braced myself for its impact. When I slowed down and breathed into the contraction in my chest, my heart felt sore and swollen. Underneath the bracing, I discovered the painful tug of a longing to be accepted by other Jews. Fear arose because admitting to this longing, even to myself, made me feel quite vulnerable. I am embarrassed that I still long to be accepted by a community that has repeatedly rejected me. Acknowledging this longing brings up the painfulness of this history of exile from Jewish communities, as well as the possibility of relating to it differently.

Creating a Kavanah

Once we can feel our longings, we channel them toward creating a *kavanah* (כוונה) ("intention") statement to declare our commitment around our healing. In generative somatics, we call these "commitments," but in Ruach, kavanah (or intention) carries more resonance. The root of kavanah is the verb *kaf-vav-nun,* meaning "to straighten or direct." We create a kavanah statement that helps us direct our healing toward what we care about. These statements are a promise to our future selves—they help guide us toward who we want to become. While not grammatically correct, we frame them as "I am a kavanah to..." because we want to embody or become the person who can live into this kavanah.

Our kavanah statements serve as a compass for our healing path. To arrive at our statements, we ask these questions:

- For the sake of what change are we declaring this intention?

- What longing are we moving toward around belonging, connection, or purpose?

- How might our lives feel different if we embody this kavanah?

- What is the change we want to see in ourselves, in our communities, in our world?

In my process of shifting how I relate to other Jews and Jewishness, I created this kavanah statement: "I am a kavanah to trust that as an anti-Zionist Jew, I belong to the Jewish people, and they belong to me." This kavanah anchors me in my Jewish identity, so I can connect with other Jewish people from a steady place of political commitment and openness. The long-term intention is to help transform Judaism from within, hasten the end of Zionism, and forward collective liberation.

We measure the progress we make toward embodying our kavanah by creating conditions of satisfaction or milestones that help us track our growth. One condition of satisfaction for this kavanah is: "When I meet new Jewish people, I am able to connect to them from a centered and open place most of the time." To create these markers of our progress, we can ask ourselves questions about how our lives might feel different when we embody this kavanah. What resources will we be able to draw on? What actions might we take? What will be qualitatively different in our connections to self, spirit, and community? For this kavanah, I created two more conditions of satisfaction: "I will feel more relaxed in my belly when I meet new Jewish people," and "I will discuss my beliefs around Palestine with new Jewish people without getting defensive."

To live into our intention, we also need new practices. In the world of body-based healing, we insist that we become what we practice. We are always practicing something, but we often practice unconsciously. In other words, we might have developed habits by adapting to difficult or oppressive dynamics inside our families, communities, and/or institutional and social structures. While we respect how these practices have protected us, we also need to develop new habits that are more aligned with our intentions. For example, my practice of constricting upon meeting new Jewish people did protect me. It allowed me to stay strong in my beliefs and activism when I first came into my anti-Zionist politics. However, after twenty years of anti-Zionist activism, I no longer need this constriction; it diminishes my ability to feel steady and connected to myself and others.

Now when I meet new Jewish people, I practice softening the front of my chest and breathing into my diaphragm and stomach to help me stay open to connection. This doesn't mean I'm going to avoid political disagreement, but I don't have to close myself off or shrink in the face of difference. Other practices for this kavanah include singing Jewish songs upon awakening and before going to sleep and tending to my ancestor altar every day, to keep rooted in my inherent belonging inside Judaism. I also practice centering, one of the core practices of somatic healing that I learned through generative somatics.

Finding Center

The centering practice serves as a foundation for all the other body-based practices. Centering helps us become more awake, alive, and feeling. We center inside ourselves to become less numb and to feel *more*, not necessarily to feel good or calm. The goal of centering is to become more connected to ourselves and our intention, inside of any emotions we are experiencing. When we center, we increase our awareness of the sensations of aliveness that flow through us as organic beings who are part of the natural world.

Instead of only thinking our way into our intention, we start to embody our kavanah through our full three-dimensionality. Centering helps us create a home base inside of ourselves to come back to when we are under pressure or face stressful situations.

The first part of our centering practice is a body scan. By feeling our sensations and corresponding emotions, we bring ourselves into the present moment before we try to change anything. We can center in any position—seated, lying down, standing. As we have learned from disability justice, we don't want to practice self-domination, which means forcing our bodies into certain positions based on ableist norms. If it works for our bodies, we center with our eyes open in a soft gaze because we want to be able to stay attuned to the world while we feel ourselves deeply. If our vision is impaired, we practice staying attuned through our other senses.

We become more present by consciously deepening our breath and tracking temperature, pressure, and movement throughout our body. We might notice the temperature of the air where it meets the surface of the skin on our hands, and then feel the temperature somewhere deep inside us, perhaps in our belly. To notice pressure, we find the contracted places in our bodies. Many of us hold tightness behind our eyes, in the hinge of our jaw, in our shoulders, and our hips. We can use our breath to meet these tense places and simply acknowledge all that they are holding. After we feel for constriction, we also find places in our body that are open or spacious—where our breath has room to move. When I'm feeling particularly tense, I try to notice whether one small part of my body—for example, one of my fingers or toes—is already relaxed, and I send my breath there.

Finally, we feel movement by first noticing how the rhythms of life move through our bodies: the pulsing of blood and the flow of breath through our nose, mouth, diaphragm, and lungs. We can also bring our attention to more subtle cadences of vibrating, humming, or tingling. Once we identify these rhythms, we also notice the places that are quiet, still, or numb. After feeling for temperature, pressure, and movement, we identify how these sensations help create a mood and story about how we are in this moment. The body scan is a glimpse into how we are doing in this moment, before we try to change anything.

After the body scan, we fill into our three-dimensionality (length, width, and depth) and our kavanah. We start by locating our center of gravity, which is one to two inches below the belly button. Placing a hand there, we can direct our breath and attention to this place, which holds what we care about. Because our energy follows our attention, when we bring our attention to a specific place in the body, we also direct our energy there. To extend into our length, we move our focus and our energy down from our center into the earth by tracing our breath down through the belly, pelvis, thigh bones, lower legs, and feet. We then allow our muscles to relax into gravity as we send gratitude to the land and respect for the first peoples of the land where we are centering. When I extend down into the earth, I like to imagine my roots reaching for nutrients from the mycelial network and the soil.

Once we establish this magnetic base of connection with the earth, from our center we extend up in the opposite direction, to the sky. From center, we breathe up our spine, imagining more space and light between our vertebrae as we lengthen out through the crown of our heads. I imagine my branches reaching up to the light of the sun and the moon to offer gratitude. When we expand into our length, we embody our inherent worth and dignity. As we send respect to all that is alive, we acknowledge that we also deserve respect because we include ourselves in the circle of life that surrounds us.

After lengthening, we broaden into our width from side to side. We start by softening our gaze to take in more on either side of us with a wide peripheral vision. This wide focus helps us widen and soften across the width of our faces. We breathe from the midline of our bodies out to our edges across the span of our jaw, between our shoulders, across our ribs, and across our hips. We expand across the width of each leg and foot from the inner to the outer edge. The metaphor for width is connection. When we bring our presence out to the edges of our being, we feel our interdependence with others. The goal is to widen enough to feel the people, animals, and land to whom we belong. We can imagine our beloved humans, flora, and fauna surrounding us, and then widen enough to feel their presence. I like to imagine that I am one tree in a grove of trees, inherently connected to my community through the underground network of mycelium.

Maintaining our length and width, we invite depth by waking up the back of our bodies. We might notice where our clothes touch the back of our body to awaken this back plane. Then we might feel the back of our head, the space between our shoulder blades, and the backs of our knees and heels. We often spend more time in the front body—on screens and socially—so we have to practice feeling for the wisdom that lies farther back. With depth, we are working with the metaphor of time. We can imagine that our history—everything that has come before this breath—is at our backs. To feel resourced by this history, we can imagine opening up the pores on the back of our bodies.

As we reach for our past, we access the wisdom we have gained in our own lifetime, and we offer gratitude to the generations that came before us. Imagining a wide "V" extending out and back from our bodies to include our ancestors, we feel for all the beings—human and more-than-human—who made our lives possible. This includes both our *ushpizot* (אושפיזות), "ancestors," of blood and our ancestors of craft or calling. I often feel for my radical left Jewish ancestors who helped create the path I'm on, including the queer anti-Zionist writers Leslie Feinberg and Melanie Kaye/Kantrowitz. They both devoted their lives to working for justice, including Palestinian liberation, through their activism and writing. I often lean back a little onto my heels or sit bones to imagine that I'm resting into their supportive presence.

This wide "V" represents a river of life behind us, which we can allow to flow through our bodies—from back to front—to help us experience our depth. We can feel the flow of energy from the back to the front of our hearts, from the back to the front of our rib cages, and from the back to the front of our bellies. In our thickness, we access our interior landscape, where many longings reside. Finally, we wake up the front plane of our body from our eyebrows to our collarbones to our toes. As we gaze out toward the horizon, we orient ourselves toward the future: our next breath, our kavanah, and the generations yet to come. We try to find this balance from back to front and front to back. We don't want to be stuck in the past, nor do we want to lean so far forward into the future that we lose connection to our history.

We are invited to stay connected to time beyond linear time through being present and balanced in this moment.

From this place of three-dimensionality and fullness in our length, width, and depth, we place one hand at our center of gravity and one hand at our heart and feel for our kavanah. As we bring our focus to the emotional center of our heart and the intuitive center of our belly, we imagine what it might feel like to be embodied in this kavanah. If it were one year from now and we were living into this kavanah more fully, what would that feel like in our bodies? What adjustments will help us create more space for our kavanah? We might notice that we need to soften our shoulders or lengthen our spine or widen across our hips. Then we speak our kavanah out loud while we feel our sensations.

Centering as Prayer

Centering is a holy offering that we can do before we pray or as an embodied prayer. Like centering, Jewish prayer is informed by our kavanah: when we pray with kavanah, we pray with hopefulness, intention, and focus. Both centering and our prayers are meant to transform ourselves and the world around us. In *Davening: A Guide to Meaningful Jewish Prayer*, Rabbi Zalman Schachter-Shalomi tells us that we practice prayer with a deep intention behind it, so that "when you are in trouble, you shall find the words."[16]

In other words, an iterative process of praying with an intention (saying the same set of blessings on Friday nights or holidays) allows the prayers to become part of our embodiment or muscle memory. This means we can easily access them. If we have a consistent practice of praying, when we are activated or upset about something, we still remember how to pray because the prayers live in our muscles, tissues, and bones. If we only pray when we're in crisis, the prayers won't help us come back to ourselves. Rabbi Watts Belser writes that the power of prayer is embodied by her consistent practice of lighting Shabbat candles. She explains, "My hands can lead me when my heart is closed. Sometimes the gesture is enough to guide me home."[17] This is also why we practice centering. If we have practiced centering enough, when we are activated or under pressure, we can find our way back to our center, our home, and our kavanah.

It becomes easier to find our center by consistently doing the practice over time. I try to center every day without being too rigid about it. I also like to use individual pieces of the practice when I need them. For example, I might take some deep breaths and feel the ground underneath my feet before a stressful conversation. When I am activated, I try to remember to breathe into the back of my body and invite in the wisdom of my ancestors. I might also breathe into the width of my ribs to remember my connections and feel my center of gravity. When under stress, I also can remember my kavanah to remind myself what I care about or ask a friend to help remind me.

Rabbi Zalman argues that the goal of prayer, like centering, is "to get to the place where we, like the needle on a compass, will naturally swing around to align ourselves with our inner core of kavanah."[18] In somatic language, when we become embodied in our kavanah, we will take actions that align with our values, even under pressure. This is how we define somatic transformation. We can live into our intentions even under duress.

Now, when I meet another Jewish person out in the world, I notice my activation as it appears in bodily sensations. I remind myself that these sensations and corresponding stories make sense based on my past experiences, but that I don't know how the interaction with this new person might unfold. I center in my length to embody the dignity of my political stance. I soften at my sides to feel my belonging inside of Jewish community, and I use my depth to connect with the history of Jewish people who resisted nationalism and racism. When I center inside my kavanah, I remind myself of my shared Jewish history with the person in front of me—a history that extends back centuries before Zionism. I envision how we might connect after the end of Zionism.

I don't always succeed in coming back to my kavanah of trusting that I belong to Jewishness and my people belong to me. But when I do, it leads to interactions that feel more empowering and relational. When I feel secure in my own sense of belonging, I am more open to connection, less quick to anger and judgment, and better able to deeply listen as the basis for connection.

We begin Jewish body-based healing by finding and following our long-ings for who we want to become, as we create the world we are calling into being. Our longings help us find our kavanah, our anchor that steadies us in rough waters. Holding our kavanah in the center of our bodies helps us develop a body-based place to return to when we are feeling activated. As we follow our longings toward healing, we have to tend to our unhealed trauma, which threatens to pull us off our path and away from our bodies, our centers, and our *kavanot* (plural of *kavanah*).

CHAPTER 3

THE EMBODIED TRAUMA OF ANTISEMITISM, RACISM, AND ASSIMILATION

If slavers, invaders, committers of genocide, and inquisitors can beget abolitionists, resistance fighters, healers, and community builders, then anyone can transform an inheritance of privilege or victimization into something more fertile than either.[1]

—AURORA LEVINS MORALES, *MEDICINE STORIES: ESSAYS FOR RADICALS*

On a tour of the Auschwitz death camp, the guide asks Jewish students packed in the cattle car of a display train to feel the terror of being ripped away from their families, not knowing what horrors await them upon arrival at their destination. On these tours, students undergo an intense curated experience of the concentration camps during which they are encouraged to imagine the trauma of the camps as though they are living through it themselves. The harrowing trips actually traumatize many students, who are encouraged to seek comfort in the present by wrapping Israeli flags around their shoulders while they sing the Israeli national anthem.

On the *Birthright* blog, American Jared Sapolsky, an alum of the Birthright program, which fosters young Jewish people's connections to the Israeli state, describes wearing the flag as he "knelt by the memorial stone next to the ruins of the gas chambers in Auschwitz-Birkenau, where nearly a million Jews perished during the Holocaust."[2] He describes how he promised his ancestors to do everything within his power to protect his people. The goal of these trips is to trace a straight line from the trauma of the gas chambers to their antidote—the triumph of the Israeli state. The state of Israel is both the reward and the solution for Jewish suffering, which must constantly be defended against.

Zionism freezes Jewish people's fears, rooted in historical trauma, so that they remain stuck in a perpetually traumatized state. Throughout our diverse histories as a people, Jews have collectively experienced periods of being integrated into local cultures and economies, as well as various forms of historical trauma related to antisemitism. As I discussed in chapter 1, both individual and collective trauma send us back in time so that we react to the present through the prism of past feelings. This confusion between past and present is compounded by the ongoing confusion about the relationship between Jews and power. On the one hand, antisemitism promotes the myth that Jews are all-powerful, wielding a disproportionate influence over the world. On the other hand, Zionism portrays Jews as perpetually on the verge of victimhood.

Originating in European Christianity, antisemitism includes discrimination, violence, or dehumanizing stereotypes directed at Jews simply for being Jewish. The Jewish people—who are religiously, racially, ethnically, and politically diverse—are treated as a single entity. Antisemitism then blames "the Jews" for all of society's problems, particularly economic inequality. Before European colonialism, Jews in the Middle East, North Africa, Central Asia, and the Balkans lived as one religious minority among many. They lived with restrictions and were sometimes targeted for violence as non-Muslims, but they mostly were not singled out for persecution. That changed beginning in the nineteenth century, when European Christian colonizers in the Middle East and North Africa (MENA) granted Christians and Jews economic privileges denied to the larger Muslim population, who grew resentful about their status. European antisemitism and the tensions of colonization caused Jews to become targeted by violence in moments of societal upheaval.[3]

Different strands of antisemitism have emerged since the Middle Ages, interacting with historical and cultural trends. In the nineteenth century, antisemitism converged with scientific racism, which was used to justify colonialism, slavery, and antisemitic policies. Scientists and intellectuals claimed that non-white races, including Jews, were biologically distinct and inferior to white European Christians. One of the most prominent examples of this was Arthur de Gobineau, a French aristocrat and diplomat who published his book *An Essay on the Inequality of the Human Races* in the mid-1800s.[4] Gobineau argued that the Jews were a non-European, Semitic race, which he claimed was responsible for the decline of European civilization. In the early twentieth century, these ideas were adapted to support eugenics—a movement intended to "improve" the human gene pool by encouraging reproduction among those considered to have "desirable" traits and discouraging reproduction among those considered "undesirable." Eugenics was used to justify racist and ableist policies in North America from forced sterilization of disabled people to segregation and restrictions on immigration. This included the Immigration Act of 1924, which limited immigration from Asia as well as from Southern and Eastern Europe, where many Jews lived.[5]

Starting in the early 1930s, the Nazi regime used eugenics to justify their genocidal policies of sterilizing and murdering Jews, queers, Roma people, communists, and people with disabilities in order to keep the white Aryan race "pure." Eugenics lives on in the ideology of white nationalism, which emerged out of the system of white supremacy—a system of exploitation and domination rooted in the false belief of the biological superiority of white people. White supremacy includes the legacy of institutions and ideologies that emerged from Europe to justify colonization, ethnic cleansing, and slavery. White nationalism, an ideology that gained increased traction in the era of Donald Trump, is a post–Civil Rights Era movement that seeks to expel people of color and non-Christians to create an all-white Christian ethno-state. Antisemitism is an ideological cornerstone of white nationalism.

The "Jewish conspiracy theory" strand of antisemitism promotes the myth that Jews have outsized power and secretly function as puppet masters running the world—including the media, banks, government institutions, and even social justice movements. We witnessed the convergence of this conspiracy theory with eugenics at the August 2017 white nationalist rally and march in Charlottesville, Virginia, when white nationalists chanted, "Jews will not replace us."[6] This antisemitic and racist "replacement theory" claims that Jews are trying to displace and pollute the white population through pushing immigration, intermarriage, and racial justice movements. For example, the gunman behind the Tree of Life massacre in 2018 told law enforcement officials that he had targeted the synagogue because it was a hub for the Jewish community's efforts to aid refugees and immigrants.[7]

As one response to antisemitism, Zionism promotes its own myth about Jews: we were once powerless victims of the diaspora who now must vigilantly protect our safety and access to power, which is entirely dependent on the state of Israel. Like antisemitism, Zionism lumps all Jews together no matter where we live or what our politics. By claiming to represent all Jews, Zionism erases the vast differences in our widely varied embodied experiences as diverse Jewish people. I will go into more detail about the ideology of Zionism in the next chapter, but for now I note how both the trauma of antisemitism, and Zionism as a response to that trauma, make it difficult to assess our current positionality or access to power.

Defining Trauma

As generative somatics founder Staci Haines explains in *The Politics of Trauma*, we define trauma somatically as "an experience, series of experiences, and/or impacts from social conditions, that break or betray our inherent need for safety, belonging, and dignity."[8] We all need material and physical safety: access to protection from the elements, and protection from physical, emotional, and sexual abuse. We also need connection: to feel a sense of belonging in our intimate relationships, our communities, and to the land where we live. Finally, we need dignity: to be treated with respect.

Trauma breaks these three needs apart and often pits them against each other. We see this play out on every level, from the intimate to the collective. In my own childhood, in order to ensure some measure of safety in a nuclear family with a violent father who struggled with his mental health, I had to give up my inherent dignity. I had to do whatever my dad requested, hide my feelings, and apologize for whatever he decided was my fault. As a young adult navigating friendships and relationships, I was willing to collapse my dignity for the sake of safety and connection. As I grew a bit older, I swung in the opposite direction, refusing most forms of intimacy because I understood them as preceding a threat to my dignity. I had to relearn—and am still relearning—how to expect and invest in relationships where I am inherently safe and can feel belonging without being asked to give up my dignity. This does not mean relationships where there is no conflict, but rather relationships where the goal is to navigate conflict with respect.

Throughout history, Jews were often forced to give up our dignity for the sake of temporary safety. In many places where Jews were targeted for our differences, it was safer to assimilate or try to fit in and jettison the dignity of our Jewish practices and rituals that marked us as Other. For example, the Jewish Reform movement responded to antisemitism in Germany in the mid-1800s by seeking to modernize Jewish practices, rituals, and beliefs, in an effort to assimilate into the larger culture and counteract the stereotypes associated with Jews. Promoting the idea that Jews should be German citizens first and Jews second, the movement altered Jewish worship to look more like church worship, complete with organs, sermons, and prayers in the vernacular language of local communities instead of Hebrew.

As a different response to antisemitism, Zionism attempts to restore Jewish dignity with the creation of a "Jewish state," where we won't be subject to antisemitism, but it does so by cutting us off from the rest of the world. In other words, temporary safety and dignity are prioritized over connection. We are told that we can only belong when we have our "own" nation-state that keeps other people out with borders, walls, and checkpoints. This attempt to uphold Jewish dignity comes at the cost of Palestinian dignity. When we attempt to bolster our dignity by oppressing others, we are denying the inherent dignity of all people, and thus ultimately compromising our own.

Trauma is a force that breaks apart our needs for safety, dignity, and connection. It can be caused by a wide range of disturbing and distressing experiences that overwhelm our ability to protect ourselves and process those experiences. These include but are not limited to physical, sexual, and emotional violence and abuse (on the intimate, communal, and/or state level), witnessing violence, neglect or abandonment, accidents, medical interventions, natural disasters, war, discrimination, and oppression.

Too often, mainstream healing modalities have ignored the ways that our individual experiences of trauma always occur in relation to traumatizing systems of oppression that perpetuate collective trauma. Collective trauma means that an entire group of people is targeted, harmed, and threatened. Institutional or systemic trauma—the violation, exploitation, and oppression of groups of people by the state or institutions—is a form of collective trauma. Collective and systemic trauma are often intergenerational, meaning each generation of people inherits the traumatic effects of genocide, slavery, war, and forced migration from previous generations.

In 2005, the Atlanta-based Kindred Southern Healing Justice Collective coined the phrase *healing justice* to center the need for healing from intergenerational trauma inside of social justice movements. In their book *Healing Justice Lineages: Dreaming at the Crossroads of Liberation, Collective Care, and Safety,* activists and writers Cara Page and Erica Woodland describe Healing Justice as a lens and movement created by Black, Indigenous, and mostly Southern queer, trans, and disabled people to include healing as an integral part of leftist culture. They wanted to "intervene and respond to collective trauma, burnout, and violence in our lives and our movements," so that we can heal from the trauma of oppression even as we work to end oppression.[9] They specifically invoke returning to and revitalizing ancestral healing methods to help Black, Indigenous, and people of color (BIPOC) communities heal from intergenerational trauma.

One of the pillars of healing justice, transformative justice (TJ) insists that we remove the state from our healing. According to Page and Woodland, TJ is "an abolitionist framework that seeks to address harm, violence, and abuse without relying on interventions based on carceral strategies—punishment, retaliation, policing, surveillance, and prisons."[10] I will discuss more about transformative justice in chapter 9, but TJ is essential to healing justice because it insists that our healing framework should never reinforce state power. I honor the lineage of healing justice, which is vital to the work many of us are doing to integrate culturally specific healing into our political movements, and to bring a political framework into our work as healers.

The Original Wounds of North America

We can't talk about healing in North America without talking about the original wounds of settler colonialism and slavery that live on in our individual and collective bodies. If you are reading this book in another part of the world, I invite you to consider how systemic trauma from colonialism and slavery is woven into the history and culture where you reside. These are global wounds that impact all of us differently depending on our location. Because I live in the US, I'm looking at the US relationship to the traumatic wounds of attempted genocide of the Indigenous inhabitants of this land and chattel slavery of people originally from Africa.

Thousands of generations of Indigenous people were living in a reciprocal relationship to this land when European Christian settlers from England, Spain, France, the Netherlands, and Sweden attempted genocide against these first peoples, aiming to destroy Indigenous life. European settlers murdered Indigenous people, burned down their dwellings, stole their land, forced them onto reservations, and forced them to assimilate. Settlers stole children from their families and placed them in abusive boarding schools where they were forbidden to speak their Native languages, practice their spirituality, or engage in any aspect of their culture. In response to the devastating impacts of colonialism, Indigenous peoples have always resisted and continue to resist European American colonization—both politically and culturally.

While Indigenous communities were and are living most directly with the traumatic results of these devastating attacks on their cultures, settler colonialism has impacted all our relationships to each other and the land. Colonialism separates humans from one another and from nature by promoting the idea that humans have the right to command, control, and extract resources from the land. Settlers from Europe treated the Indigenous peoples of Turtle Island (a term used by some Indigenous peoples to refer to the continent of North America) as inferior because their relationship to the land wasn't one of ownership or domination. By stealing their land and enforcing this worldview of "civilization" to create profit, settler colonialism has been devastating for Indigenous communities, the land, and our collective humanity. In North America, many of us have inherited a legacy of disconnection from ourselves, from the earth, and from one another.

The first wound was stealing the land and attempted genocide, and the second wound was slavery. In *Liberated to the Bone: Histories. Bodies. Futures*, healing justice practitioner Susan Raffo describes chattel slavery as "The movement from owning land to owning people, the turning of complex breathing human beings into objects to be bought and sold, to be traded as a commodity, to provide stolen labor."[11] The institution of slavery was a form of traumatic control enacted first on the Indigenous peoples of North America and then on people stolen from Africa. The legacy of this institution lives on in systemic anti-Black racism that pervades our culture and institutions. Generations of white people and those with institutional power continue to perpetuate anti-Black racism by continuing to encode anti-Blackness into our structures and institutions.

It is important to name these systems of trauma, which impact all of us, but are often overlooked in the narrow focus of individual healing.

Whatever our identity or history, when we live in the US, we develop a relationship to the land and each other that is informed by this history and the continued perpetuation of harm through white supremacy. Those of us who do not have Indigenous or Black heritage may choose to turn away from consciously acknowledging these historical wounds, but we all live in relationship to these wounds—which need accountability, healing, and repair for the sake of our relationships with each other and the land. Indigenous, Black, and other people of color—including Jews of color—are simultaneously navigating structural and systemic racism and harm inside of this system, while they are at the forefront of movements, like healing justice, that point the way toward healing from these ruptures.

European Jewish Assimilation

As Jews who landed in North America as settlers, many of us also live with the generational trauma of antisemitism and the ways it intersects with these original wounds. A defining moment for the intersection between antisemitism and racism was the early twentieth century, when European Jewish immigrants assimilated into US culture, often by adopting the culture's anti-Black racism. While there is a complicated history of coalition, conflict, and power differences between Blacks and Ashkenazi Jews (and, of course, there are Black Jews) in North America, for now I'm focusing on the role of racism in Jewish assimilation into whiteness. I am not trying to reinforce Ashkenazi-centrism (continuously recentering the stories of Ashkenazi Jews as the standard in Jewish culture). However, the sections that follow will focus on how Ashkenazi Jews became white in the United States because this process is closely related to this book's larger conversation about the formation of Zionism. I speak more about Sephardic and Mizrahi experiences in chapter 6.

While many Ashkenazi Jews in North America adopted the racism of the mainstream culture in an attempt to escape from antisemitism, the founders of Zionism in Europe responded to antisemitism by emulating European nationalism and colonialism with the creation and eventual implementation of Zionist ideology. Because this historical and cultural context is crucial to our understanding of Jewish healing around Zionism, this chapter will focus on North America, and chapter 5 will focus on Jews in Europe.

As a descendant of European Jews from Russia, Poland, Romania, and Lithuania, I also locate my lineage inside this history, including my family's journey into whiteness. Part of the work of healing—in which I am both a participant and facilitator—is facing, acknowledging, and making repair for the ravages of these histories.

As people who often migrated to cities, Ashkenazi Jews and Black people were linked tightly together in US consciousness at various times, including and especially between the World Wars. The large-scale immigration of Jews from Europe in the late nineteenth century was followed by the Great Migration of Black people northward. Jews were fleeing antisemitic violence and pogroms, the violent riots against Jews in Europe. Black people were fleeing lynching, segregation, and limited job opportunities. In 1913, Leo Frank, a Jewish factory manager in Georgia, was convicted of raping and killing a white woman who worked in his factory. He was found guilty despite flimsy evidence. In 1915, Frank was kidnapped from prison and lynched by a white mob in much the same way that thousands of Black people were subjected to racial terrorism.

In the wake of the Frank trial, many Jews recognized the danger of being associated with Black people who were (and still are) subjected to racist state violence. Jewish immigrants began trying to reposition themselves as white, with limited success. Jews were being held responsible for a variety of issues that troubled people in the US including communism, immigration, and the rising tide of war in the 1930s. Articles about "The Jewish Problem"—which often referred to antisemitic conspiracy theories that Jews wielded too much economic or political power—proliferated in the press, and quotas and restrictions were enacted to limit the number of Jews allowed into universities, clubs, and neighborhoods.

Not surprisingly, during this time European Jewish immigrants developed a contradictory relationship to Black people in the US. As Jewish Studies Professor Eric Goldstein explains in *The Price of Whiteness: Jews, Race, and*

American Identity, Jews longed to experience "what it was like not to be the focus of national hostility and resentment" as they were experiencing in Europe.[12] At the same time, many Jews identified with the suffering of Blacks in the US and continued to display empathy for them as a persecuted, diasporic people. The most emphatic statements of Jewish identification with Black people in the US occurred in the Yiddish press where non-Jewish readers could not chance upon them. The Yiddish press roundly condemned racism by comparing race riots against Black people in the US to pogroms, and white mobs to "Cossacks"—the people known for perpetuating pogroms.*

On June 2, 1921, when news of the Tulsa Race Massacre reached New York, Yiddish daily newspapers covered the story in great detail. The socialist newspaper *Forverts* reported "heartrending" scenes in which Black people "were dropping like flies."[13]

Becoming White through Blackface

As Professor Michael Rogin documents in *Blackface, White Noise: Jewish Immigrants in the Hollywood Melting Pot,* this relationship was further complicated because Jewish identification with the struggles of Blacks in the US sometimes took the racist form of either cultural or literal blackface as Jews attempted to become part of US culture by taking on Black-derived music, along with plantation nostalgia (an idealized vision of plantation life in the Southern US before the Civil War).[14] This kind of nostalgia for the era of slavery erased its brutal realities. Popular Ashkenazi Jewish entertainers, including Eddie Cantor, George Burns, and Sophie Tucker, all performed in blackface in the early to mid-nineteenth century. It is also important to note that many Jewish artists and activists spoke out against blackface, including the Yiddish theater actor and director Maurice Schwartz, as well as the Jewish composer and lyricist Harold Arlen.

---

* In Jewish folklore, literature, and historical memory, Cossacks are often depicted as symbols of oppression, violence, and fear.

The most famous example of a Jewish actor in blackface, *The Jazz Singer*, was one of the first "talkie" films to come out in 1927. The film's central character, Jakie Rabinowitz, the son of a cantor (a leader of congregational singing), is expected to follow in his father's footsteps by becoming a cantor at their synagogue in Manhattan's Lower East Side. Rabinowitz, however, wants to sing jazz, which enrages his father, who, in turn, disowns him. After running away from home, Jakie Rabinowitz changes his name to Jack Robin, acquires a Christian girlfriend, and becomes a singing success on the stage, often performing in blackface. The actor Al Jolson (born Asa Yoelson), also the son of a cantor, defied his father by becoming a blackface performer.

The Yiddish press downplayed the degrading aspects of blackface in the film by focusing on Jewish identification with the struggles of Black people, emphasizing the movie's tagline: "The son of a line of rabbis well knows how to sing the songs of the most cruelly wronged people in the world's history."[15] Of course, he is not singing the songs of Black people, but participating in the white culture's imitation of Black songs in their nostalgia for slavery. Jews in the New World attempted to escape their shtetl pasts and try on new identities by literally painting on the racism of mainstream white culture by performing in blackface and stereotyping Black people.

When I was in my mid-twenties, I was on the phone with my Mom, telling her what I had learned about Jewish blackface. She told me, "I remember my father leaving the house in blackface to perform at the local Jewish community center." In response to my jaw-dropping silence, she continued, "They just didn't know what it meant back then." Her announcement hit me like a fist. As a Jew whose grandparents immigrated to the US around the turn of the last century, I hadn't felt directly implicated in the US legacy of slavery. However, I immediately began reshuffling our family history in my head, as I tried to reconcile the fond memories of my jovial PopPop with this haunting image of him performing racial minstrelsy.

In my attempt to understand more about this era, I watched *The Jazz Singer* and tried to learn more about my grandfather Maurice's experiences. In the film, Jack's father represents Jewish cultural difference because, as a title card suggests, he "stubbornly held to the ancient traditions of his race," while Jack has moved away from his Jewishness to become a jazz singer.[16] The first time we see Jack in blackface, he is backstage with his girlfriend before dress rehearsal. His mother arrives to inform him that his father is sick and begs him to take his father's place at services to sing "*Kol Nidre*," a solemn song performed on the eve of Yom Kippur, the holiest of Jewish days. Torn between making his debut on Broadway and his mother's request, Jack tells his girlfriend that he is moved by hearing "the call of the ages—the cry of my race."[17] This is the first time we witness Jack's longing for his culture, portrayed as a race, and it occurs while he is in blackface.

While very few movies at this time made by Jews represented Jewish themes, *The Jazz Singer* tells the very Jewish story of assimilation. However, it obscures the forces of antisemitism and racism by displacing them onto intergenerational differences. After visiting his sick father, Jack forgoes an opening night appearance on the Broadway stage, to fill in for his father at the synagogue. In a melodramatic scene, his sick father hears him singing, forgives him, and dies. The film ends with Jack performing "My Mammy" in blackface at the Winter Garden Theatre (where Al Jolson often performed) to his mother, who is weeping in the front row. Jack can only express his sadness about leaving his cultural motherland (the Lower East Side and Eastern Europe) through a Black-white racial lens by equating his Jewish mother with a Southern "mammy."

Many of the Jews who performed in blackface, including Jolson, began their careers as Jewish comedians and turned to blackface as their urge to assimilate made it less desirable to do comedy about Jewish themes. Assimilation meant both separating from Jewish culture and participating in white racist nostalgia. The Mammy stereotype grew out of the violent reality that Black mothers were often forced to nurse enslavers' children (and then, post-slavery, forced to take care of them as servants) often at the cost of their relationships with their own children. This history was encoded into the stereotype of the happy, loyal, desexualized Mammy, whose happiness encouraged white people to feel that slavery was actually a benevolent institution.

In moving to America, my grandfather Maurice was cut off from his mother and his culture. His father Max (my great-grandfather) came to the US by himself from Warsaw in 1900 as a shoemaker. Max didn't want to bring over his wife Cecilia and six-year-old son (my grandfather Maurice) from Poland, but he was pressured to do so by his family. When they did arrive, Max was embarrassed by Cecilia's Old World Yiddish-speaking ways and began isolating her. He wouldn't give Cecilia any money, he restricted her food, and he didn't want her to learn English.

The family story is that he drove her "crazy," and then put her into what they referred to as an "insane asylum," where she lived out the rest of her life. It's unclear how much English Cecilia could speak and how much of her supposed mental illness resulted from being an isolated immigrant with limited language skills. Max then put Maurice and his sister Dora into a Catholic orphanage for several years, until he remarried. Al Jolson also spent some of his childhood in a Catholic orphanage after his mother died when he was ten years old.

During my mom's childhood, her father Maurice—always quick with a joke—never spoke about his childhood and told my mom that her grandmother (Cecilia) was dead. Only after Cecilia actually died when my mom was an adult did the secret come out that her father and aunt used to visit their mother at the asylum. I wonder how or whether my grandfather's own sadness about the loss of his mother and motherland played into this performance as he attempted to become a white North American. Was Maurice singing in blackface about his own longing for his mother? As part of his own assimilation, Maurice obscured his family history by refusing to even let his children meet their grandmother.

Both Al Jolson and my grandfather immigrated to the US as children around the turn of the last century. Both families escaped Europe because of antisemitism, and in the United States they were encouraged to become citizens by leaving behind their differences and participating in US nostalgia for an even more racist past. As Professor Goldstein observes, Jewish blackface became a means for people to express pain and sorrow that they could not express as Jews—including the pain of antisemitism and exile. Blackface obscured these performers' Jewishness through stereotyping Black people, blending identification with Black suffering with a deeply racist performance.

My grandfather Maurice certainly faced antisemitism in his life while he also perpetuated racism. For many years, he worked for MetLife, a large insurance company, never getting promoted. When he confronted his boss about his lack of promotions despite his hard work, his boss admitted that Maurice would never get ahead because he was Jewish. So, he started his own company and sold insurance primarily to Italian and Jewish immigrants, as well as Black people who often faced higher premiums or outright denials from the larger insurance companies. My mom says that his clients loved him because he would sometimes make their payments for them, so that their insurance policies wouldn't lapse. He would take her to visit his friends in the mostly Black West Ward neighborhood of Easton, Pennsylvania, where he knew almost everyone, and they called him "doc," as a term of endearment. This is a classic dynamic: because of antisemitism, Jews often had limited options for employment at this time, though they certainly had many more options than Black people had due to anti-Black racism. They often took on these "middle manager" roles as the visible face of capitalism, while the white Christian power structure remained invisible.*

His father Max's siblings stayed in Poland, and all but one of Maurice's cousins died in Auschwitz, probably around the same time that he was performing in blackface. Jews in the US were willing to accept the conditions of assimilation—adopting white racism—in part because in Europe they were being persecuted and then killed as a "race."

As a young man performing in vaudeville shows, Al Jolson, the first openly Jewish man to become an entertainment star in North America, also faced antisemitism and fought racism. Although he was one of the highest-paid performers in the US in the 1920s, Jolson was frequently referred to with antisemitic slurs by audience members—who even attacked him once after a show. He was known for promoting Black performers, including Ethel Waters, and fighting discrimination and segregation on Broadway and later in Hollywood. In 1927, Jolson succeeded in getting a hotel in Miami, Florida, to admit Black guests by threatening to cancel his show.

---

* For more on the middleman dynamic, see "Understanding Antisemitism: An Offering to Our Movement," Jews for Racial and Economic Justice, accessed March 15, 2024, www.jfrej.org/assets/uploads/JFREJ-Understanding-Antisemitism-November-2017-v1-3-2.pdf, 26–29.

While at least some resistance to racism appears to be part of Al Jolson's story, as well as my grandfather's, that doesn't negate their racist performances. It does shine a light on the complexity of their identification with Black suffering, even as their performances afforded them some distance from this suffering. They were both active participants in a process through which Ashkenazi Jews became white that wasn't solidified until the period of economic prosperity following World War II.

One of the key factors in becoming white, according to Professor Karen Brodkin Sacks, author of *How Jews Became White Folks and What That Says about Race in America*, was the government-sponsored GI Bill of Rights, which provided educational and economic opportunities to World War II veterans. While the bill was intended to benefit all veterans equally, in practice it was often administered in ways that excluded or disadvantaged people of color, including Black and Indigenous people. It ended up serving as a form of affirmative action for white men, including European Jews. With access to free education, low-interest home loans, and job training, European Jews began accruing the material benefits accorded to whiteness.[18] Many European Jews in North America agreed to this bargain just as the horrifying details of the Nazi Holocaust came to light.

In *Medicine Stories*, writer and historian Aurora Levins Morales offers an invaluable framework for understanding our ancestors' choices to cut themselves off from others' suffering. As Levins Morales writes, "Without a vision of a society that could provide for all, they narrowed their interests and provided for themselves."[19] In the late nineteenth and early twentieth centuries, many Ashkenazi Jews who fled antisemitism in Europe were attempting to survive in a culture of domination that pitted people against each other. Their path to survival was paved with the dominant culture's racism, particularly anti-Black racism.

As their descendants, we are left holding the jagged shards of these broken relationships. When we can look at these shards with clarity, we can begin the process of repair, healing, and accountability. Levins Morales reminds us that "knowing, honestly examining, and taking full responsibility for what our ancestors left us is both a spiritual and a political practice of integrity and authenticity, empowering and radical and strategically essential."[20] She invites us to examine the specific debts and assets of our lineage, so that we can transform our ancestors' legacies. While we can't change their actions, *we* can take reparative action. For Ashkenazi Jews, this can include everything from supporting reparations for Black and Indigenous people in North America to funding Black-led organizing and fighting racist state violence both here and in Palestine. In the next chapter, we will consider how trauma is held in our bodies, including this history of antisemitism and racism.

CHAPTER 4

THE SHAPING
OF TRAUMA

*Everyone must have two pockets, with a note in each pocket, so that he or
she can reach into the one or the other, depending on the need. When feeling
lowly and depressed, discouraged, or disconsolate, one should reach into
the right pocket, and, there, find the words: "For my sake was the world
created." But when feeling high and mighty one should reach into the left
pocket, and find the words: "I am but dust and ashes."*[1]

—RABBI SIMCHA BUNIM BONHART

The impact of individual and collective trauma lingers in our bodies because
our survival reactions become stuck at the time of the trauma, prompting
us to relive patterns of behavior from our past. When humans experience
dangerous or threatening situations, we activate our innate and automatic
survival reactions: fight, flight, freeze, appease, and dissociate. Designed
to keep us safe, these built-in reactions are part of the sympathetic nervous
system's response to danger, and they occur without any conscious thought.
These reactions trigger a range of physiological changes in our bodies, often
including an increase in heart rate, blood pressure, and breathing rate to
prepare us for immediate action and allow us to respond quickly to potential threats.

Our sympathetic nervous system also triggers the release of adrenaline and stress hormones to provide energy to our muscles and tissues. It directs blood flow to the muscles and away from the digestive and immune systems. The adrenal glands release cortisol, which helps to break down stored energy in our fat cells and muscles, providing additional energy for use in response to the threat. Our bones release calcium and other minerals to support muscle contractions in preparation for responding. This mobilization of energy in our muscles, tissues, and bones is meant to be a temporary reaction that subsides when the danger is over; and the parasympathetic nervous system takes over to slow down our heart rate, lower blood pressure, and direct the blood flow to the digestive and immune systems—promoting relaxation, rest, and recovery.

In traumatic situations, when we are unable to fully protect ourselves (and possibly other people) through escape or resistance, the increased energy is never fully discharged. The parasympathetic response is suppressed or inhibited, and we store the incomplete reaction in our bodies. Our sympathetic nervous system may become overactive or chronically activated, leading to ongoing symptoms, such as hypervigilance (constantly being on alert). This intense frozen or stuck energy can also manifest as anxiety, insomnia, and even panic attacks based in feelings of powerlessness, terror, and rage.

A part or parts of ourselves and our psyches (at whatever age we experience the trauma) become trapped or frozen inside of us along with the stuck survival reaction. We all have different parts, or aspects, to ourselves according to the methodology of Internal Family Systems (IFS) therapy, developed by Dr. Richard Schwartz. These discrete parts hold different aspects of our personalities, beliefs, and motivations. Emerging from our life experiences, our parts carry the emotions and memories from these experiences and often serve a protective function of shielding us from overwhelming, painful feelings. Depending on our internal and external landscape, parts may collaborate, conflict with each other, or even take over.

IFS theory emphasizes the concept of the *Self*, also referred to as the adult self, as the core essence in each of us. The Self provides a compassionate and curious perspective from which to relate and understand our various parts. The goal of IFS therapy is to help us develop self-awareness, self-compassion, and self-leadership by integrating the parts into a balanced system led by our Self.[2]

In somatics, we also look at where these parts live in our bodies. The parts that are frozen in time because of traumatic experiences often retain the thoughts, emotions, beliefs, and behaviors associated with the age when we experienced the trauma. When these parts are activated, we often act from a part of ourselves that is stuck in a reaction to the past in the present moment. When our survival reactions do not complete their cycle, they can become habitual generalized responses to pressure in our lives that can show up as younger parts of ourselves unconsciously taking over control. Each reaction lives inside us differently, but there are general patterns to how they show up.

Trauma Reactions

Flight refers to the built-in response that tells us to flee, escape, or move away from danger that can become attached to a younger part of the self. If we repeatedly mobilized a flight response but didn't get to complete it by fully escaping from harm as, for example, a teenager, then this protective strategy can become the predominant way we approach any pressure or stressful situation. Without consciously choosing to, this teenager part might prompt us to leave any relationship when things get uncomfortable or difficult, or we might avoid uncomfortable situations altogether. In relationships, we might pull a part of ourselves back and away from connection. When a flight response is stuck in our bodies, we might experience excessive energy in our legs or arms and feel the need to compulsively exercise. We might often feel restless, fidgety, or trapped, which results in constant movement.

Fighting means automatically becoming aggressive or confrontational under threat. When the fight response becomes our generalized mode of responding, we can get defensive, argumentative, or go on the attack when we feel activated. Experiencing chronic irritation, frustration, or hostility, we can explode in anger and lash out at others physically or verbally. If fighting was something we learned as a toddler, that part may act out under pressure. Easily provoked, that young part might encourage us to throw tantrums, blame others, hold grudges, and seek revenge. We tend to take up more space with this reaction: we might puff out our chests to get bigger and speak louder. With the chronic fight reaction, we might find that we automatically say "no" to most requests or offers and distrust most people. We often feel tightness in our jaws, a clenching in our hands or legs, and the urge to punch, kick, or attack when we are activated.

Appease refers to placating whoever or whatever is threatening us by making ourselves smaller and less threatening with the hopes that the threat will dissolve. Whenever our predominant reaction is appeasement, we might find ourselves unable to express our needs or set boundaries with others. A chronic appease reaction might show up by always agreeing with others, even before we know what they mean. For example, we might find ourselves nodding as someone is talking without even tracking what they are saying because appeasement or appearing to agree is such a familiar response. We might get smaller by shrinking our height, tilting our heads, and pulling in tightly at our edges, so that we take up less room.

Freeze refers to entering a state of immobilization to avoid being detected or attacked. In a freeze, we often cannot move or use our cognitive skills. This tends to happen when all other options feel too risky, and we feel trapped and overwhelmed. We see this reaction when opossums "play dead" to fool predators into not eating them by freezing and emitting a rotting stench. When the freeze response is stuck in our bodies, we often feel numb and opt for less stimulation (avoiding conflict or even excitement) for the sake of feeling less. When we experience something activating, our brains might freeze or go blank; we might hold our breath or breathe shallowly. Freezing often comes with a feeling of heaviness, stiffness, or coldness in our limbs, a decreased heart rate, and a sense of dread. A collapse is a type of freeze response that occurs when we become so overwhelmed by trauma that we lose the ability to function or make decisions. When we collapse, we tend to experience a profound sense of hopelessness or helplessness.

Dissociation tends to occur in combination with all these survival reactions. Dissociation means that we leave a traumatic situation without physically leaving it. In other words, when a traumatic event is too disturbing for our consciousness, we disconnect from our thoughts, feelings, sensations, and surroundings. We abandon part of ourselves to absorb the trauma. This protects our conscious self from being overwhelmed by the intensity of the experience, but a younger part will retain the experience. Often people who are physically trapped (for example in an abusive relationship or in an abusive institution like prison) will dissociate to check out mentally and survive their physical environment.

When dissociation lingers in our lives, we might experience anything from a slight fuzziness in our brains to a foggy confusion about where we are in time or space to a sense of fully floating outside our bodies. We might lose track of time, feel like we are in a dreamlike state, or have difficulty focusing. Sometimes dissociation happens right before or after another survival reaction kicks in. For example, when we feel activated by someone who is not respecting our stated boundaries, we go numb or vacant and then start a fight. Or we freeze under the pressure of a disagreement and then appease the other person by apologizing.

While dissociation is a brilliant survival strategy, it also splits us off from ourselves. Our conscious selves leave the situation while it is happening, but our nervous system and the younger parts of ourselves will continue to hold the trauma. This split in our consciousness often leads us to oscillate between numbness and activation. For example, we might routinely tell the story of a traumatic event without noticing any emotions or sensations. At other times, we might suddenly experience a body memory of the pain and terror associated with a trauma without consciously noticing that we have been activated. Because I grew up with a lot of violence in my household, certain loud noises can activate intense anxiety and a shrinking response for me, though I have no conscious memory of what is being evoked. Some people can find themselves reexperiencing the sights, sounds, and smells of a traumatic event without remembering the event itself.

These body memories can be deeply distressing, and we might feel "out of control," "haunted," or as if our body is turning against us, because we don't understand what is happening. We often feel that we can't survive the intensity of the sensations and emotions related to these memories and flashbacks, so we double down on contracting or numbing ourselves. However, the stored energy from these survival reactions needs to move through us; therefore, it will keep showing up in fragments of memories, sensations, or flashbacks. Those younger parts do not want to be left to carry the trauma on their own. They call our attention back to our past because these wounds need tending, and these survival reactions need to complete and integrate, so we aren't stuck.

To successfully move out of this cycle of intense feeling followed by periods of numbing, we have to turn and face our trauma, so that we can release the stuck energy inside of us. Somatic healing can help us understand, appreciate, and honor the wisdom of our survival reactions. We do not want to eradicate these survival strategies, which have kept us alive for so long. Instead, we want to develop more choice in employing them. Through a series of practices that we will explore in the following chapters, we can support these stuck survival reactions in completing their cycle of protection. This completion helps the frozen energy of these reactions to release or integrate. As insightful as we might be, we cannot think our way out of frozen energy that is stuck inside us; we need body-based practices to help us physically move this energy.

Each of us has access to all these survival reactions, though most of us rely on some more frequently than others. Which strategy we use also depends on context. For instance, our reactions that show up in intimate relationships can differ from our reactions in community. As a young person, I tended to appease in intimate relationships because that is what I learned in my family, but I developed more of a fight response in organizing contexts, and a freeze inside of community conflict.

Social context—including race, gender, class, and other aspects of our identities—influences which survival strategies are encouraged, accepted, or discouraged by those around us, including our families, communities, and institutions. For example, race and gender norms often dictate who is encouraged to enact a fight response (mostly white cisgender men) or who will be punished for it (everybody else) or who has been awarded for appeasing (women, femmes, and non-binary people) and who will be reprimanded for doing so (often cis white men). Many of us with less social power are encouraged to appease people with more power, whether because of race, gender, class, or another social context. We might make a conscious choice not to appease, but we are still reacting to the cultural norms of white patriarchal capitalist ableist culture.

Reacting to the Present from the Past

When pressure in the current moment reactivates our past trauma, we will often automatically default to whichever survival strategies appeared to work the best to keep us alive, even when they were not completely success-ful in protecting us. When these reactions become mobilized unconsciously, the sticky fingers of time yank us back into the feelings and sensations of the original trauma. There are certainly times when we need to mobilize survival reactions, but when we are activated by past trauma, we cannot accurately assess whether our present situation warrants this response.

In other words, the shock and helplessness associated with traumatic and oppressive experiences cause us to travel back in time. Because our survival reactions could not be completed at the time(s) of the traumatic events, they start to drive our behavior. On an unconscious level, we are constantly preparing for harm because we believe it could happen again at any time. From this hypervigilant place, it is extremely difficult to take in current information, and therefore impossible to respond to the present moment from a centered place.

When past trauma is ignited, we often feel helpless, regardless of our actual agency or power in the current moment. As I discussed in chapter 1, in *Power-Under*, Steven Wineman argues that trauma often leaves us feeling enraged about our past helplessness. Because we were unable to successfully protect ourselves from harm at the time of the traumatic event, we internalize not only the terror, but also rage about being overpowered. When we reexperience feelings of helpless terror from our past, we can lash out in rage at those around us.

Because we can only perceive our powerlessness in these moments, we lose awareness of how we are impacting others. When we subjectively feel powerless, but have access to objective power, we can respond to the feeling of being oppressed by oppressing others. In a world organized by domination, we often express resistance to our own oppression by directing our rage toward those who hold less power than us, rather than at those who have oppressed us. In our desperate, adrenalized attempt to find someone to blame for our own suffering, we cannot see the ways we might be causing harm.

Wineman uses the metaphor of someone drowning to explain the expression of powerless rage. Like a person who is drowning, a survivor flails about, convinced by the past that they are in a desperate fight for their lives. From this place, they cannot possibly assess the impact of their actions or understand how they could endanger someone else.

Wineman calls this dynamic "power-under" because we can feel subjectively powerless, even when, objectively, we might be causing harm to anyone we encounter.[3] Time compresses here; historical trauma from the past perpetuates more harm in the present, where we enact our powerless rage on those around us. Ultimately, one goal of somatic healing is to become subjectively more powerful, while becoming objectively less powerful so that we don't dominate others. We need healing to help us redirect our traumatic rage *away* from those with less power and *toward* fighting the structures of power that perpetuate oppression and domination.

Somatic Contractions and Shaping

All our stuck survival reactions, including traumatic rage as a chronic fight response, are held as contractions—a tightness in our muscles, tissues, sinews, and bones. Contractions include our physical and energetic patterns of tension, holding, or constriction that can appear as stiffness, pain, or tightness in the body. We contract around the discomfort of stuck energy from our incomplete survival reactions. These contractions are accompanied by emotional and mental patterns of constriction, avoidance, or defensiveness. When we hold these contractions in our bodies for long periods of time, those areas of our body might even become numb, slack, or frozen; we might not be able to feel them at all.

These contractions become an integral part of our "shape" or part of how we physically embody our history, thinking, and values. Our current physical shape includes our posture, gestures, actions, and movements. This physical manifestation of our shape represents our internal world. Our shape also includes our habits—what actions we commonly take and those we don't take—and our emotional range, including what we can feel and express, and how we relate to others. Like all aspects of ourselves, our shapes are impacted by our relationship to power, privilege, and oppression.

Body-based healing transforms our shape over time, so that we can inhabit a shape that embodies what we care about. When we heal enough to allow our stuck survival reactions to complete, integrate, and release, then the contractions in our bodies also begin to soften. This helps us slowly shift our shape to allow more life and energy to flow through us, so that we can respond to the present moment without so much weighing on us from our histories.

My client Liza provides a good example of someone who experienced a significant shift in her physical shape, which represented a transformation in her internal world. A white Ashkenazi Jewish cis woman who survived sexual assault as a teenager, Liza was struggling in her social justice work and her relationships. When she first came to see me, she tucked her pelvis under her spine to protect herself and slouched her shoulders forward. Her voice was constrained by a contraction in her throat; she frequently acquiesced to others and had a hard time knowing or saying what she wanted or needed. This pattern of appeasement led to a simmering resentment, which showed up in passive-aggressive behavior and even entitlement. Because Liza felt like she was already working very hard to be "good," whenever she was challenged about her behavior, including patterns of racism, she would freeze, get defensive, and then collapse.

She wanted to inhabit a shape that made it easier to set boundaries, communicate her needs, and accept feedback from a centered place. In our work together, we discovered that a thirteen-year-old part of Liza was trapped in this pattern of appeasement and resentment that covered up a deep rage at the violation she had experienced at that age. Liza was holding a lot of frozen and stuck energy from flight and fight responses that never came to completion when she was trapped in an abusive relationship as a teenager. Through body-based practices, including bodywork, Liza moved this energy, so it could be released and integrated. Over many months, we also practiced setting boundaries, making requests of others to support her needs, and receiving feedback. Liza's younger self needed help understanding that feedback wasn't harmful and learning that her current adult self knew how to hear feedback without collapsing. She learned how to be centered and accountable regarding the impacts of her actions.

The combination of allowing her survival reactions to complete and learning new skills helped Liza transform her shape. She currently stands up straighter with her shoulders back, an open chest, and her pelvis in a neutral position. This new physical shape corresponds with an ability to set boundaries that protect her dignity but are permeable enough for her to also be self-reflective. Her voice comes from lower in her throat, and she has learned how to communicate more directly.

Just as each of us individually inhabits a shape, our communities inhabit "collective shapes," which refer to the shared physical and emotional patterns and tensions held within a group. A collective shape is formed by the community's culture, history, and responses to trauma. Like many other communities, Jews have experienced collective trauma, and have also participated in perpetuating trauma. Collective trauma necessitates collective healing from the larger historical forces that shape our communities.

The Shaping of Antisemitism, Racism, and Assimilation

For Ashkenazi Jews in the US, this history of antisemitism, assimilation, and racism that I discussed in the last chapter shapes us in complex ways. As an example of what this can look like, I am going to explore the embodied impact of learning about my grandfather Maurice's participation in the racist performance of blackface.

While I intellectually understand the era and context of his choices, every time I think about him doing blackface, I experience a whirlwind of shame, contract against it, and then collapse and dissociate. The cyclone swirls in my stomach and diaphragm, and a prickly heat rises up through my chest and lands on my cheeks. Overwhelmed by the intensity, I squeeze my diaphragm, contract my throat, and clench my jaw. A magnetic force sucks my inner arms toward my ribs. The shame can't entirely be contained, and I start to give in; I slump over my diaphragm, my face goes slack, and my arms and legs feel wooden and heavy. It becomes so unbearable that I float out through the top of my head to gain some distance. I want to watch TV, find a snack, scroll on my phone—do anything but feel this shame. But the healer and activist in me knows that numbing never leads to the kinds of changes we want to see in ourselves and in the world.

We cannot numb ourselves to our grief or shame or rage about our histories without experiencing numbness in our current relationships with ourselves, each other, and the land. These original wounds need tending, but dominant culture always encourages dissociation and promotes amnesia regarding the past that still lives in our present. If all I do is tighten, collapse, and dissociate in response to my individual lineage, then I am cutting myself off from the possibility of repairing these ruptures. If Ashkenazi Jews collectively refuse to face the complex legacy of our lineage in North America, we perpetuate even more harm by refusing to account for the messy truths of our histories.

White supremacist capitalist culture relies on our disembodiment and numbness, so that we can't perceive our connections to each other or our relationship to the natural world. Cultures of domination promote these separations by pitting us against each other, and then encouraging us to prioritize our individual safety and dignity over our connections. In the history of European Jewish assimilation into US culture, many of us lost our kinship with the people being targeted in North America by the same kind of racist state violence that we narrowly escaped in Europe.

Disembodiment is both created by trauma and part of a system of violence that perpetuates trauma and oppression. This is why body-based healing is so important: it helps us feel our connections to each other and the land. When we feel these attachments, it brings into relief the history of violent separations that have harmed all of us and our living environment. As Jews, we need to feel and grieve the harm caused to us by antisemitism as well as the harm that we have caused others by participating in colonialism and racism. When we can truly acknowledge this painful history, we also can feel the possibility of making relational repair within and outside of ourselves.

As white Ashkenazi Jews in North America, we gained many of the privileges of the dominant culture, but we also experienced incalculable losses: of culture; community; and an interdependent relationship with Black people, Indigenous people, people of color, and the land. We acceded to the terms of the dominant culture that slotted us into its racial hierarchy, while pressuring us to give up our Jewish difference that made us inherently unworthy.

When I respond to the vortex of shame by tightening around this image of my grandfather performing minstrelsy, I feel as though I'm protecting my family from a threat. Intellectually, I know that the very definition of privilege is that it relies on someone else's oppression. However, this image of my grandfather evokes so much shame about the racism we enacted along the journey to becoming white that I fear we are just "bad" people. In response, I cling even harder to my privilege to protect my family's dignity. The US culture in which my ancestors became white didn't respect their dignity as Jews; it made their dignity dependent on assimilation. I can practically feel my ancestors telling me to hold onto my privilege, so that we don't once again sink to the bottom like we did in Europe. They ask me, "Haven't we lost enough already?"

Right underneath my tight grip is a collapse. In this case, I am collapsing into shame about my ancestors' choices with a defeated resignation. My limp and weighted limbs make action feel impossible. I let the history dominate me, as though what happened was inevitable, and there's no other option moving forward. From a collapsed state, I withdraw from the possibility of connection—both to myself and the broken relationships that arise from this history. Then I start to dissociate, so that I don't have to feel the shame of giving up. I'm teetering between these two poles: gripping around the privilege to protect my family's dignity or collapsing from shame and dissociating.

Neither the tightening nor the collapse/dissociation aligns with my commitment to collective liberation. However, body-based practices can help me come back into feeling and recenter myself, so that I can get wide enough to hold the many contradictions of this history and access my agency to take responsibility and shift course. When I am neither rigid nor collapsed/dissociated, I can look squarely in the face of this history and say, "Yes, this is the bargain we made, but I do not have to accept its terms any longer." Showing up in solidarity for racial justice as Jews in both the US and Palestine is both inwardly and outwardly healing. We can use the privileges that we gained at the cost of others' dignity to turn around and say, "No more," or in the words of Aurora Levins Morales, "This time it's all of us or none."[4]

Embodied Healing and Contradictions

A body-based healing practice around contradictions can help us face the complexity of our identities and histories. In North America, Christian hegemony promotes a moral binary system that divides everything into "good" or "bad" categories. Activist and writer Paul Kivel describes Christian hegemony as "the everyday, pervasive, deep-seated, and institutionalized dominance of Christian institutions, Christian values, Christian leaders, and Christians as a group."[5] Kivel reminds us that while some of the influences of Christianity in our culture are more overt, some are nearly invisible because they have become "commonsense" filters for perceiving the world. Some of these Christian filters include the ideas that humans are superior to and thus have dominion over nature, that only one Truth exists, and that time is linear and finite. One of the most damaging overarching concepts is binary thinking, which encourages us to think of ourselves and others as either good or bad, victims or perpetrators, right or wrong. As part of the culture of white supremacy, binary thinking contributes to divisions, hierarchies, and domination.

Because of the prevalence of binary thinking, when we are faced with contradictions, many of us feel pressured to choose one side or the other. However, when we do so, we flatten the depth and richness of our histories and our lives. Rabbi Bonhart suggests in the epigraph that we should hold one of two seemingly contradictory ideas about our significance at a time: the world was created for us *or* we are but dust and ashes. But what if we could hold both truths simultaneously without trying to resolve the tension between them? As Ashkenazi Jews grappling with our history of assimilation, we tend to focus either on our history of "overcoming" antisemitism, ignoring the role of racism; or we focus only on our complicity in racism and refuse to acknowledge the impacts of antisemitism. The goal is to be able to widen our capacity, so that we can hold both truths.

When we hold this tension between the two poles instead of choosing a side, we make space for multiple truths, including the many facets of our histories and our lives. We have inherited many models for embracing contradictions inside Judaism, including *pilpul* (פלפול), a method for studying the Talmud—a collection of Jewish law and tradition.* Pilpul refers to a scholarly debate for and against different interpretations of Talmudic passages.[6] The goal of pilpul is not to arrive at a single "correct" interpretation,

---

* The Talmud consists of two parts: the *Mishnah* (compiled in the second century CE) and the *Gemara* (compiled over several centuries following the *Mishnah*).

but rather to explore the nuances and complexities of the Talmudic text without resolving the contradictions. Differing opinions are uplifted as sacred. Indeed, even when majority opinions became the accepted legal ruling, minority opinions were preserved in the Talmud because they contribute to the depth of Jewish discourse.

In one of my somatic training sessions, I decided to practice widening inside this contradiction about my grandfather and the history he represents. I practiced with two other people, each of whom represented one side of the contradiction. I instructed the person on my right to represent the viewpoint that my grandfather was just a bad person. She gently tugged on my right arm and said: "Your grandfather was racist," "He did blackface," "You should be ashamed," and "He was bad." The person on my left represented a more accepting view of my grandfather. While tugging my left arm, she said, "He faced antisemitism himself," "He was an immigrant doing his best," "He was struggling to survive," and "He paid the cost for you to be here."

To begin the practice, I stood between them facing forward while each of them gently tugged on an arm and started talking at the same time. Embodying the two sides of the contradiction, they often talked over each other, their voices competing for my attention. For the first round, I just noticed what happened in my sensations, emotions, and narrative. Upon hearing and feeling the competing voices, I immediately shifted my weight to the right and tuned out the phrases coming from the left. I latched onto all the phrases about my grandfather representing something bad, and I felt myself tighten and tuck away beneath my ribs, so that I could hide from the shame. I felt defeated, and the story became, "Just don't feel; there's nothing you can do about this anyway."

For the second round, I noticed my responses again, but then centered myself with a particular focus on width. At first, I could hear both sides, but I got so overwhelmed by the dissonance that I started to shrink toward the midline of my body and tune out all of their words. Looking off into the distance, my face became very still, and I started to imagine what I was going to make for dinner. When it came time to recenter, I came back into my body with some deeper breaths, and I sent my energy down into the earth. I lengthened into my inherent dignity, evoking my grandfather's dignity as well. Then I widened into feeling connected to my many friends who also hold intense contradictions in their lineages. As I noticed the tingling and warmth at the back of my body, I felt gratitude to my ancestors who crossed the ocean with the threat of antisemitism at their backs. I moved that warm energy through the depth of my heart and imagined passing on a different legacy of Jewish solidarity with other vulnerable peoples to future generations. Finally, I felt into my kavanah around belonging and my longing for a different Jewish future.

After coming into my full dimensionality and remembering my kavanah, I was able to hear both sides without trying to shut out one or the other. I felt how all these statements were and are part of my lineage. Yes, my grandfather faced antisemitism, participated in racism, and assimilated into dominant US culture. He made what he felt were the best trade-offs to be safe and relatively dignified. He was fully responsible for his choices, and he was encouraged to make these choices inside of his cultural and historical context. I took another breath from the midline to the outer edges of my arms, hips, and legs while imagining the width of the Salish Sea. I recognized that I had space to hold all these truths inside this vast expanse. I could feel compassion for my grandfather, while being accountable for the legacy and impact of his choices.

I can't change the actions that my grandfather or other ancestors took, but when I get wide in the face of that history, I am able to hold the complexity behind their choices. This helps me decide how to transform that history, so that a different set of values can be passed down to future generations. What if we don't have to give up our Jewish difference or separate ourselves from others to feel safe? We can stay rooted in our Jewishness to reclaim the pieces of ourselves that were lost to assimilation, even as we reach out to repair and reconnect with the relationships we severed in our attempts to survive.

While we grapple with this complex history, Jewish folks also need healing to allow our stuck survival responses from centuries of antisemitism to integrate, even though antisemitism is still a force in the world. Many of us have found myriad ways to heal. However, one dominating force in modern Jewish life, Zionism, makes healing from the past difficult because it thrives on eliciting a collective shape of fear and aggression in Jewish communities around the globe to justify the need for a Jewish state.

CHAPTER 5

SURVIVING ZIONISM

Between the Jew as victim and the Jew as military hero, the ideal of the Jew as a normal human being has begun to disappear. A legacy of powerlessness becomes the justification for the exercise of power.[1]

—DAVID BIALE, *POWER AND POWERLESSNESS IN JEWISH HISTORY*

When Israeli students return home from visiting the Nazi death camps in Poland, they make statements such as "We need to wipe out the Gaza Strip," and "We need to destroy anyone who hates Jews."[2] Many of them channel their helpless rage about the Nazi Holocaust toward the people whose land they are occupying. After being activated into a state of adrenalized terror rooted in historical trauma, they are encouraged to embrace its supposed antidote, military strength. This was also true after the October 7 Hamas attack. Israeli officials like Likud MK (Member of Knesset, Israel's parliament) Moshe Saada not only said, "It's clear to everyone that all Gazans should be exterminated," but also proclaimed that he was speaking for Israelis across the political spectrum.[3] Zionism has evoked a collective fight as the only appropriate survival reaction to the activation of historical trauma.

Political Zionism developed in the late nineteenth century as a response to antisemitism in Europe, but it reinforced and continues to reinforce the same logic of domination inherent in antisemitism. Following the French

Revolution and the spread of liberalism, Jews in Europe made some gains in economic and political power; however, they became disillusioned about the possibility of full integration into European society because of the persistence of violent antisemitism. This included an increase in pogroms that resulted in the loss of life and property for Jewish communities, the rise of scientific racism that categorized Jews as an inferior race, and the wrongful conviction of Alfred Dreyfus, a French Jewish officer, for treason in 1894.

European Jews at this time responded to antisemitism in various ways, including assimilation, emigration, and Zionism. Those who coalesced around political Zionism proposed the creation of a Jewish state in historic Palestine, modeled after European settler colonialism. Cultural Zionism, in contrast, was a movement that emphasized the revival and cultivation of Jewish culture, language, and identity through creating a cultural homeland in Palestine. Its proponents, including the philosopher and theologian Martin Buber and intellectual Ahad Ha'am, were critical of the political Zionists' ethnonationalist proposal for a Jewish state. Insisting on the importance of respecting the dignity and rights of the current inhabitants of the land, they argued that the creation of a Jewish state would also damage the Jewish spirit. After an 1891 visit to Palestine, Ahad Ha'am, whose pen name meant "one of the people," warned that political Zionism, built on the myth of an empty land, made an empty promise of "a complete and absolute solution of the Jewish problem in all its aspects."[4]

In the late nineteenth century, political Zionism was just one idea among many for addressing antisemitism and was characterized by most European Jews as impractical and utopian. Members of the Bund, a Jewish labor group that was founded in Lithuania in 1897, were vehemently opposed to Zionism because they believed that Jews should fight for justice alongside a multiethnic community of workers in the countries where they lived. In their view, antisemitism was a tool the ruling class used to divert attention away from economic inequality and divide the working class. They advocated for workers' rights, supported labor movements, and sought to address economic disparities. Uplifting the concept of *doikayt*, the Yiddish word for "hereness," the Bund promoted preserving Jewish culture, language, and traditions wherever Jews lived—as opposed to immigrating to Palestine.

While the Bund saw economic inequality as the cause of antisemitism, Theodor Herzl, the charismatic founder of political Zionism, and his political allies argued that it was caused by the presence of Jews in predominantly non-Jewish societies. Therefore, Zionists at the time called for the exodus of Jews from Europe not to combat antisemitism itself, but to remove Jews from Christian countries.

Instead of turning their anger about antisemitic violence toward European Christians, from the beginning Zionists emulated European nationalist movements and utilized antisemitism to implement their political aims. They appealed to the bigotry of European leaders, making the case that creating a Jewish state elsewhere would help expel Jews from Europe. In his foundational pamphlet, *Der Judenstaat,* Herzl argued that "The anti-Semites will become our most dependable friends, the antisemitic countries our allies."[5] He wasn't interested in *eradicating* antisemitism, but rather in *mobilizing* it to launch the colonial project of Zionism.

With the rise of fascism and Nazism in the 1920s and 1930s, political Zionism started to gain more traction given the extremely precarious and dangerous situation of European Jews.[6] Cultural Zionism never really found its footing because it would have required a slower pace of Jewish integration into the land of Palestine. Meanwhile, the leaders of political Zionism galvanized support for the creation of a Jewish state, garnering backing from influential world powers. Witnessing the conflation of ethnonationalism and Zionism, in 1929, Buber presciently warned, "Let us be careful not to commit ourselves what has been committed against us."[7]

Tragically, by the end of World War II, the majority of people in the Bund were wiped out first by Nazism and then Stalinism. As Bund scholar Molly Crabapple writes, "Once, thousands of Jewish communities were laid like lace across the map of Eastern Europe. They had made the 'here' in the Bundist concept of Hereness. By 1945, this world had vanished, along with its inhabitants."[8] After Nazism decimated the Jewish population in Europe, global support for Jews going "there" to the state of Israel increased exponentially, in part because Europe and the United States didn't want to absorb the Jewish refugees stuck in Displaced Persons camps at the end of the war. As Naomi Klein describes in *Doppelganger,* Zionists seized the moment after World War II to reframe the quest for equality "not as the right to be free from discrimination, but as the right to discriminate. Colonialism framed as reparations for genocide."[9] Just as European Christians relied on the concept of *terra nullius,* a Latin term that means "empty land," to justify European colonialism, Zionists embraced the phrase "a land without people for a people without land" to erase and displace the Palestinian people.*

Even after the founding of the Israeli state, cultural Zionists and members of the Bund who were still alive continued to be critical of political Zionism. In Buber's article, "Zionism and 'Zionism'" published May 27, 1948, just two weeks after the establishment of the state, he criticized the treatment of Palestinians in the name of "collective selfishness" and asked, "Where do truth and justice determine our deeds...?"[10] Like Zisl, whom I wrote about in chapter 2, Buber argued that impinging on other people's sovereignty was immoral, unjust, and corrosive to the soul of Jewishness. In his essay "Politics and Morality," he also argued that driving Palestinians from their homeland could never be justified by "pleading values or destinies."[11] In 1948, the Bund, which had reconstituted itself the year before as a small global network based in New York, called for Jews to renounce the goal of a Jewish state and demanded the right of return for all Palestinian refugees expelled by Israeli forces.[12]

Nonetheless, political Zionism prevailed. Under the charged atmosphere of the recent Nazi Holocaust, political Zionism directed the powerless rage of Jewish people toward the Palestinian people, as though they were the ones responsible for anti-Jewish violence. Instead of seeing Palestinian resistance to Jewish encroachment on their land as an anticolonial

---

* "A Land without a People for a People without a Land," Jewish Virtual Library, accessed March 19, 2024, www.jewishvirtuallibrary.org/quot-a-land-without-a -people-for-a-people-without-a-land-quot-diana-muir. Christian Restorationist Alexander Keith actually coined the phrase in *The Land of Israel According to the Covenant with Abraham, with Isaac, and with Jacob* in 1843.

struggle for self-determination, political Zionists framed Palestinians as anti-Semites, like the Nazis, who needed to be crushed with the kind of military force that Jews had no access to in Nazi Europe. From the start, they dehumanized Palestinians by enacting the same forms of violence and displacement that were used against Jews.

In forming the state, Zionist forces inflicted widespread terror between 1947 and 1949, when they destroyed most Palestinian towns and expelled the majority of Palestinians from the land that they claimed for the state of Israel. Over five hundred Palestinian localities were destroyed; 15,000 Palestinians lost their lives, and more than 750,000 residents were expelled or fled in terror and were not allowed to return to their homes.[13] The Israeli government continues to violently oppress Palestinians, destroying their ancient homes and olive groves, killing and arresting and detaining Palestinians of all ages—including children—with no due process. Zionism separates families through checkpoints and walls; separates farmers from their fields; and restricts access to healthcare, jobs, and education.

While Zionism causes great harm to Palestinians, there has always been and continues to be Palestinian resistance through organizing, activism, and cultural work. Many Palestinians determinedly hold onto the keys of their pre-1947 homes. As eighty-four-year-old Palestinian Abu Salah Al Hilo said, "This key and Koshan (land title), I inherited from my parents, means my dignity and my identity that I will never give up . . . even if I die before returning back, I will bequeath it to my sons."[14] Every day, Palestinians reject the political ideology of Zionism through their activism, their thriving culture, and their refusal to be uprooted from their daily lives. Because the founding of the state of Israel was based on the idea of a "land without people," Palestinian existence itself is a form of resistance.

The Collective Shape of Zionism

Zionism, itself partially a response to Jewish trauma, has obviously become a deeply traumatizing force for Palestinians, but it has also been harmful for Jews. Zionism teaches Jews not to build connections wherever we are, but to barricade ourselves inside the borders of a "Jewish state." We are taught that we can't have safety and connection simultaneously. Zionism tells us we are constantly in danger and under attack, just like we were in the past, so that we are willing to condone an aggressive fight response to protect ourselves. However, this feeling of powerlessness and rage gets directed *not* at the European Christian power structure that enabled the Nazi Holocaust or the current right-wing perpetrators of antisemitic attacks in the US, but at Palestinians who have less political power than we do.

The Israeli government and Israel advocacy organizations around the world simultaneously whip up fears about antisemitism and deflect criticism of the Israeli state by conflating any such criticism with antisemitism. American Israel advocacy organizations, such as the American Jewish Committee (AJC), the Jewish Federations of North America, and the Anti-Defamation League (ADL) among others, promote the dangerous idea that anti-Zionism is a form of antisemitism. In this equation, anyone who critiques the political ideology of Zionism can be accused of antisemitism.

Under its guise as a civil rights organization, the ADL uses its supposed moral authority to shield the Israeli government from criticism, while offering the public misleading information about antisemitism. Every time there is an antisemitic act, almost every major US news outlet turns to the ADL for "statistics" about the seemingly continuous rise of antisemitism, but the ADL inflates these numbers by including anti-Zionism as a form of antisemitism. They also regularly change their reporting methodology and often present isolated incidents of antisemitism as representative of a broader trend.[15]

In their 2022 report on antisemitism, they include a range of incidents from assaults and vandalism to "harassment"—which includes everything from antisemitic slurs to anti-Zionist graffiti. One example references stickers found on public property near the Hillel building at the University of Texas at Austin that read "Free Palestine. End the occupation."[16] This exaggeration and distortion around antisemitism makes it more difficult to understand and combat actual instances of antisemitism as part of our fight for a more just world.

Zionism uplifts an extremely aggressive fight response as the only way to combat antisemitism. In *Unheroic Conduct: The Rise of Heterosexuality and the*

Invention of the Jewish Man, scholar and historian Daniel Boyarin shows how this defensive shape grew out of a response to antisemitism, colonialism, and Jewish anxiety about gender.[17] Prior to the end of the nineteenth century, the ideal of Ashkenazi Jewish masculinity was that of a quiet, self-deprecating, nonaggressive, non–physically active scholar. Violence, he argues, was antithetical to Jewish masculinity and generally not highly regarded in Jewish culture. At this time antisemitism, nationalism, and the development of the two categories of heterosexuality and homosexuality converged. Fearful of Jewish masculinity being associated with homosexuality, Zionism rewrote the Jewish ideal of masculinity in Europe as aggressive, muscular, and violent. According to Boyarin, "The Jewish male, vilified for hundreds of European years as feminized . . . set out to reinstate himself as manly in terms of the masculinist European culture that had rejected and abused him."[18]

Boyarin argues that Zionism functioned as the fulfillment of assimilation, so that Jewish men could prove their similarity to white Christian Europeans by becoming colonizers and recreating a mini-Europe in historic Palestine. One of the founders of political Zionism, Max Nordau, famously called for a "muscle Jewry," in opposition to Jews of the diaspora whom he characterized as passive, weak, and feminine in this deeply sexist paradigm.[19] After the Nazi Holocaust, Zionist rhetoric expanded this characterization of Jews to blame them for their supposed passivity in the face of Nazi violence, and advanced this militarized "masculine body" as the necessary shape of Zionism.

Zionism freezes Jews in a reaction to the history of the Nazi Holocaust—both in its characterization of diasporic Jews as passive and in its valorization of a collective aggressive, masculinized national shape with rigid boundaries that must be protected. In this deeply patriarchal Eurocentric and colonial paradigm, Zionism continuously manipulates Jewish trauma to keep us afraid of our present and ashamed of our past. This combination of *feeling* subjectively powerless in the present while objectively *wielding* the power of a massive state is a truly deadly combination. When we feel rage and shame about our past powerlessness and supposed passivity, Zionism urges us to find Jewish pride in a continual fight response that terrorizes the Palestinian people.

Jews who are critical of Zionism risk not only being excluded from Jewish communities but also coming under attack by establishment Jewish organizations. Many synagogues, Jewish institutions, and even Jewish community centers make support for Zionism a prerequisite to belonging. For example, in North America, Hillel, whose mission is to support all Jewish students on campuses, specifically excludes individuals and groups who support BDS.[20] In May 2022, ADL Director Jonathan Greenblatt went so far as to conflate Palestine solidarity groups such as JVP, Students for Justice in Palestine (SJP), and the Council on American-Islamic Relations (CAIR) with white supremacists and January 6 insurrectionists. Calling them "the Radical Left, the photo inverse of the Extreme Right," Greenblatt claimed that "these radical actors indisputably and unapologetically regularly denigrate and dehumanize Jews."[21] He promised that the ADL would apply "more concentrated energy toward the threat of radical anti-Zionism" through lawsuits, research, and lobbying.[22] The ADL is waging war on the "threat of anti-Zionism."[23]

While the ADL hides behind its image as a civil rights organization, it promotes this kind of inflammatory rhetoric that encourages vicious attacks on anyone organizing for a free Palestine—particularly Palestinians. By suggesting that the threat of antisemitism on the left is just as dangerous as antisemitism on the right, the ADL obscures the fact that almost all the perpetrators of deadly antisemitic incidents with known political motives, such as the 2018 shooting at the Tree of Life synagogue in Pittsburgh and the 2019 shooting at the Chabad in Poway, California, have been linked to the white supremacist right.

American Zionist Institutions Reinforce State Violence

I'm going to look at how the local branches of two national Jewish institutions, the ADL and the Jewish Federation, advance reactionary politics both locally and globally by reinforcing this collective shape of Jewish fear coupled with aggression. In June 2017, in the same week that Seattle police shot and killed Charleena Lyles, a pregnant Black mother of four, after she called to report a burglary, the Jewish Federation of Greater Seattle planned to honor former Seattle Chief of Police Kathleen O'Toole and the Seattle Police Department (SPD) with its Tikkun Olam (תיקון עולם) ("repairing the world") award.[24] Outraged by this injustice, individual Jews and Jewish grassroots groups in Seattle organized a protest and petition, signed by over seven hundred people, to demand that the award be rescinded. Under pressure, the Federation postponed presenting the award, but quietly gave the Tikkun Olam award to O'Toole and the SPD later that year.

What kind of world does the Jewish Federation imagine could be repaired by an inherently racist and violent institution? The primary function of the police in the US is and has always been the protection of white wealth and property. As Alex Vitale argues in *The End of Policing,* the origins of the police as representatives of the state were tied to "three basic social arrangements of inequality in the eighteenth century: slavery, colonialism, and the control of a new industrial working class."[25] In Southern cities, the police grew out of patrols to prevent revolts and stop enslaved people from escaping to the North. Beginning in the 1830s, police in northern US cities functioned to protect property, quell riots, and break up strikes, while police in the Southwest—such as the Texas Rangers—worked to expand white colonialism by killing Indigenous and Mexican people and pushing them off their lands. The police continue to target, harass, and kill Black, Indigenous, and other people of color as they continue to protect the interests of the powerful. In fact, for over a decade from 2012 to 2023, the SPD, like many other police departments, was under investigation by the Department of Justice for its use of excessive force and racially biased policing.[26]

Establishment Jewish institutions like the Federation imagine a world in which the most powerful Jews can perpetually claim a righteous victimhood. In this world, the precarious safety of Jews must continuously be defended by promoting state violence that harms others. The Federation justified their decision to award SPD by pointing to the police department's participation in two programs: one focused on hate crimes and another called "Law Enforcement and Society: Lessons of the Holocaust," a collaboration between the ADL and the United States Holocaust Memorial Museum.[27] This focus on hate crimes goes hand in hand with turning our gaze back to the Nazi Holocaust. Hate crime laws reinforce the power of the state to target and punish vulnerable communities, including communities of color, but do nothing to address the root causes of violence and oppression that contribute to hate. Focusing solely on the Nazi Holocaust turns our attention away from the history of racism in North America, including the racist legacy of policing in this country, as though they are totally separate histories. In fact, in *Hitler's American Model: The United States and the Making of Nazi Race Law,* James Whitman explores how Nazi leadership explicitly took inspiration from US racism of the late nineteenth and early twentieth centuries.[28]

One goal of establishment Jewish organizations is to evoke Jewish fears around our past powerlessness, in order to justify current state power—whether by the police in the US or the IDF in Israel. For years, the ADL sponsored police exchange programs where police from the US (including SPD) exchanged oppressive tactics with Israeli police officers and Israeli army officers.[29]

The "Lessons of the Holocaust" training teaches officers about police collaboration during the rise of the Nazi regime and encourages officers to think of themselves as "guardians against mass crimes against humanity" by locating these crimes of police collaboration securely in the past.[30] The training embodies a contradictory relationship to state power by presenting Jews as both historical victims of the state, and as current-day subjects who rely on the state's protection to stave off victimhood. While focusing on past injustices, this program is training police officers who represent the state's current assault on humanity: killing, surveilling, harassing, and oppressing Black and Brown people—including Jewish people of color, and other vulnerable communities.

Another goal of legacy Jewish organizations is to represent the Nazi Holocaust as one stream in a timeless river of antisemitism. The regional ADL website describes how Pacific Northwest Director Hilary Bernstein presented educators with "A History of Antisemitism" in 2016 by encouraging them

> To "flip" their thinking: rather than seeing antisemitism as one element of the Holocaust (along with the politics, economics, nationalism, etc., of that time period), they should help students see the Holocaust as one horrific chapter in the very long story of antisemitism which continues to rear its ugly head today.[31]

Such ahistorical framing exceptionalizes Jewish history and invisibilizes other victims of the Nazi Holocaust, including queers, disabled people, Roma, and political dissidents. If the Nazi Holocaust is disconnected from historical trends like nationalism and colonialism, then it stands outside of history with no relationship to other forms of oppression.

Jewish healing from past trauma is necessarily threatening to the project of Zionism, which depends on Jews being easy to manipulate because we are perpetually activated around the Nazi Holocaust. We are encouraged to feel as though we directly experienced what happened to our ancestors. While the state of Israel and its supporters constantly reference the Nazi Holocaust as if it were still happening to Jews, they are outraged and horrified by any comparison of it to other historical or ongoing genocides, including the genocide in Gaza that began in the fall of 2023. To truly heal from the historical trauma, we must situate the Nazi Holocaust securely inside of its historical context. One way to do that is to understand the atrocities of the Nazi Holocaust as the continuation of centuries of genocide and racialized violence in the Americas and Africa that were then turned inward.* Hitler simply modernized colonial methods, and he explicitly stated how he drew inspiration not only from British colonialism but also from the racial

---

* Many writers suggest this framework for understanding the Nazi Holocaust, including Aimé Césaire in *Discourse on Colonialism* and Hannah Arendt in *The Origins of Totalitarianism*. Arendt argues that the expansionist and racist ideologies that fueled colonialism were turned inward during the Nazi era, leading to the implementation of genocidal policies.

hierarchy pioneered in North America, including Jim Crow segregation and the ethnic cleansing of Indigenous peoples.

How we perceive our history is integral to how we perceive ourselves. When we portray the Nazi Holocaust as a singular event that sits outside of history, we also cast Jews in a frozen state of perpetual victimhood. But if we contextualize the Nazi Holocaust as inextricably intertwined with a history of colonization, then we can understand how this piece of Jewish history intersects with the history of other peoples.

The ADL's training program can focus on past state repression of Jews and simultaneously reinforce state violence against other communities because this version of history separates and elevates antisemitism above other oppressions. In turn, the Federation can award a racist police department for "repairing the world" because they focus only on the fracturing force of antisemitism, as though it were disconnected from every other form of domination—including structural racism. Seeing white supremacists and Nazis marching with swastikas and confederate flags in Charlottesville in 2017 should be enough to make us rethink this separation.

How do we challenge this history of Jewish trauma that reinforces a sense of internalized powerlessness and encourages us to grasp for any power within our reach? We need to tell a different story about our history that helps us recognize when we are being manipulated and activated around our past trauma. A more complete story can help us relate differently to the past and feel our subjective agency in the present. When Jews gain a sense of our own complex agency—both the real power many of us hold and how our history is being manipulated—we can refuse to exercise the power of domination over others, thereby pulling ourselves out from the stranglehold of traumatic reenactment.

When Jews in Seattle protested giving an award to the police department, we used our agency to insist that authentic Jewish safety doesn't come from a gun pointed at someone else, but from working in alliance with other vulnerable communities. We separated ourselves from the collective shape of Zionism by refusing to elevate and separate Jewish suffering outside of history. By situating the Nazi Holocaust as a continuation of the history of colonization, we can take our rightful place in the current fight against all forms of racism, oppression, and colonization—including Zionism.

One Alternative History

In *Medicine Stories,* Aurora Levins Morales explains how colonial regimes always install a "replacement origin myth, a story that explains the new imbalances of power as natural, inevitable, and permanent. . . ."[32] This myth presents a distorted version of history to demonstrate that our current reality is the only possible outcome of our past. As a colonial ideology, Zionism has created a narrative of overcoming past Jewish powerlessness through the creation of the state of Israel, but this distorted story is dependent on placing Ashkenazi Jews at its center. When we center other Jewish histories from around the globe, different histories and possible futures emerge.

Zionism has been specifically harmful to Mizrahi and Sephardi Jews whose ancient communities were disrupted by the founding of the Israeli state. For thousands of years Jews were living mostly integrated lives in the Arab world and North Africa, sharing community, language, and customs with Muslims and Christians. Zionism disrupted and attempted to erase these histories, while it destroyed entire communities.

In her thought-provoking piece "Antisemitism, Palestine and the Mizrahi Question" in the anthology *On Antisemitism: Solidarity and the Struggle for Justice,* JVP Managing Director Tallie Ben Daniel demonstrates the role of Zionism in perpetuating trauma for Mizrahi Jews.[33] She critiques the role of Ashkenazi-centrism in this colonial narrative that traces an intractable and cyclical history of discrimination from ancient times to the Nazi Holocaust. This Eurocentric model ignores the diverse history of Jewish communities around the world, positions antisemitism as the basis for all other oppressions, and serves as justification for the creation of Israel as an answer to this unending history of oppression.

To shift our viewpoint, Ben Daniel offers an alternative narrative that centers the experience of Jews in Iraq who flourished for thousands of years in urban areas while maintaining their own cultural and religious identity.

After World War I, British colonialism exported anti-Jewish sentiment to the region, which led to an anti-Jewish riot in Iraq. Once Israel was founded, the Israeli government made a secret deal with the Iraqi government, which then expelled Jews from Iraq so they could immigrate to Israel. Upon arrival, they were put in refugee camps, marginalized, and discriminated against because of their culture. Like Jews from Yemen, Egypt, Syria, Iran, India, Morocco, and other Middle Eastern and North African countries, Iraqi Jews were and are subjected to racism and discrimination in Israeli society. The Israeli government not only pressured Mizrahi and other Jews of color to assimilate into Ashkenazi culture, it also violently separated children from their parents. Some of these children were stolen and adopted by Ashkenazi families, and some were placed in the equivalent of Native American boarding schools where they were taught Hebrew and Ashkenazi cultural practices at the expense of their own cultural heritage.

By centering the experience of one group of Jews from the Middle East, Ben Daniel allows an alternative history to sprout between the cracks of the dominant story of cyclical antisemitism. In this story, Mizrahi Jews lived in relatively peaceful coexistence with their neighbors until the arrival of European Christian antisemitism and the traumatizing force of Zionism, which forced many Mizrahi and Sephardi Jews out of their homelands. Once in Israel, these Jews faced and continue to face a racist Eurocentric state into which they were forced to assimilate.

Ben Daniel concludes that even analysis on the left, including April Rosenblum's popular zine, *The Past Didn't Go Anywhere: Making Resistance to Antisemitism Part of All Our Movements,* can reinforce a Eurocentric analysis that lets white Jews off the hook for participating in white supremacy.[34] Rosenblum argues that antisemitism functions differently than other oppressions by making its target look powerful and thus diverting anger from the ruling classes to the Jews who become the target for people's anger about class exploitation.

But Ben Daniel points out that this model can ignore how some Jews gain access to power and privilege by assimilating into white supremacy. In Ben Daniel's words, "It is one thing to say that Jewish power is a myth of antisemitism; it is something else entirely to say that powerful Jewish people are a symptom of antisemitism."[35] She argues that this model normalizes instead of challenges how racism, white supremacy, and classism manifest themselves within Jewish communities. As part of telling a different story about our history, we have to acknowledge that Jewish people—like other people who gain class and race privilege—are just as capable of misusing power as we are of working for liberation.

Ben Daniel is admittedly telling just one story among many, but we need to tell more of these stories to map the varied streams of Jewish history that disrupt the funneling of all Jewish history through the Nazi Holocaust. A more nuanced understanding of history can help us situate antisemitism relative to other oppressions, including the original wounds of the United States. Finding a dynamic and shifting sense of ourselves in history can help us move toward a collective shape of Jewish solidarity that allows us to feel our kinship with others instead of shutting them out. This shape includes permeable boundaries, a commitment to redistributing power, and a leveraging of the power that we do hold for the sake of collective liberation. In the next chapter, we will learn about practices that help us return to center after our survival reactions are activated.

CHAPTER 6

REDEFINING JEWISH SAFETY

The state's carceral safety robs our communities of the conditions and nutrients that would allow true safety to grow, forcing us into the position of constantly reaching for more security from the very institutions that make us collectively less safe.[1]

—MARIAME KABA AND ANDREA J. RITCHIE, "RECLAIMING SAFETY"

Were there no Israel, there wouldn't be a Jew in the world who is safe.[2]

—PRESIDENT JOSEPH BIDEN, WHITE HOUSE CHANUKAH RECEPTION, DECEMBER 2023

In December 2023, seventy members of Congress called for the firing of three college presidents for supposedly not keeping Jewish students safe on their campuses: University of Pennsylvania President Liz Magill, Harvard President Claudine Gay, and MIT President Sally Kornbluth. Pro-Trump Republican Representative Elise Stefanik's combative questioning of the presidents near the end of the five-hour hearing went viral because she ambushed them with yes/no questions that equated calling for an end to the genocide in Gaza with calling for the genocide of Jews. Questioning President Gay, Stefanik asked, "Will admissions offers be rescinded or any disciplinary action be taken against students or applicants who say, 'from the river to the sea' or 'intifada,' advocating for the murder of Jews?"[3]

The question itself is misleading because Stefanik falsely equates chants calling for Palestinian freedom with demands calling for the genocide of Jews. The word *intifada*, which means "uprising," or more literally, "a shaking off" in Arabic, is a call to resist Israel's violent military occupation and apartheid system. In 2011, it was also used to describe the uprisings against corrupt leaders in Egypt and Tunisia. The second half of the other phrase Stefanik references, "From the river to the sea," proclaims that "Palestine will be free"—a call for Palestinian liberation from the Jordan River to the Mediterranean Sea. According to Palestinian-American writer and political analyst Yousef Munayyer, the phrase is "a rejoinder to the fragmentation of Palestinian land and people by Israeli occupation and discrimination."[4] As such, it promotes freedom, not violence. As Palestinian-American Representative Rashida Tlaib said about her use of the phrase, it is "an aspirational call for freedom, human rights, and peaceful coexistence, not death, destruction, or hate."[5] In fact, there has never been an official Palestinian position calling for the genocide of Jews or the removal of Jews from the region.[6]

Instead of contesting the logic of the question, Gay replied, "As I have said, that type of hateful, reckless, offensive speech is personally abhorrent to me."[7] The other presidents replied to Stefanik's questions with similarly tepid legalistic answers. Because they never refuted the validity of the questions themselves, they appeared reluctant to condemn genocide *against Jews* in the middle of a genocide *against Palestinians*. Under pressure, both Magill and Gay ended up resigning from their positions, and the mainstream press castigated them for their supposed failure to keep Jewish students "safe."

Under the guise of combating antisemitism and advocating for "Jewish safety," Israel's promoters have attempted to quell the surge of student activism calling for a ceasefire and an end to US support for the genocide in

Gaza. In the fall of 2023 at Columbia University, two student groups, Students for Justice in Palestine (SJP) and JVP, were suspended for the term and accused of "threatening rhetoric and intimidation" for holding an "unauthorized event" calling for a ceasefire in Gaza.[8] Following suit, Brandeis and George Washington University suspended their campus chapters of SJP in the fall, while MIT suspended SJP the following February.

On April 17, 2024, hundreds of student protestors set up a Gaza solidarity encampment at Columbia University to draw attention to the genocide and pressure their university to divest from companies with ties to Israel. The next day, at the request of Columbia President Minouche Shafik, the New York Police Department (NYPD) charged in with riot gear to arrest more than a hundred students. On May 1, they arrested three hundred students and destroyed the encampment. This set off a wave of global student protests and countless solidarity encampments on campuses across the country and the world.[9]

At the forefront of the movement, students have been demanding that their universities disclose their investments and divest from companies and organizations profiting from the genocide in Gaza. Jewish students have been an integral part of the encampments, many holding Passover seders and Shabbats in solidarity with Palestinians. Nonetheless, accusations of antisemitism have been used to justify bringing in the police. Student protesters, including many Jewish students, have faced police brutality, arrests, and suspensions—all under the guise of protecting Jewish students. As Robin D.G. Kelley wrote to President Shafik, "You are keeping no one safe, except for your donors, trustees, and Columbia's endowment."[10]

This squelching of free speech on college campuses in the name of Jewish safety is nothing new. In March 2014, Barnard College took down an SJP banner with a hand-drawn map of Palestine that read "Stand for Justice, Stand for Palestine," because pro-Israel students complained. The president of Hillel at the time said that the banner "threatens and makes many students on campus feel unsafe."[11] In 2014 when Brooklyn College hosted a BDS panel with Professor Judith Butler and Palestinian activist Omar Barghouti, the Zionist Organization of America filed a complaint alleging that Brooklyn College "tolerated a hostile environment for Jewish students."[12]

These are just a few examples out of countless incidents in which Jewish students' "safety" is used to justify limiting free speech and shutting down any protests, events, or even publicity in support of Palestinian rights on college campuses.[13] Students are encouraged to equate feeling uncomfortable about a political stance with feeling "unsafe" in order to pressure universities to censor or punish advocacy that supports Palestinian freedom. These organizations intentionally activate Jewish fears about safety for their own political agenda.

Trauma derails our sense of safety and our ability to assess whether we are safe or unsafe at any given moment. When our automatic survival reactions kick in, even when we are relatively safe, we can feel and act as though we are under threat. How do we define safety? We can break it down into physical, emotional, and spiritual components. We experience physical safety when our basic needs are met, including but not limited to food, clean water, shelter, health care, education, freedom of movement, and freedom from violence and oppression. Emotional safety encompasses but is not limited to our access to positive relationships with each other and our communities. Spiritual safety includes the ability to engage meaningfully with the land, our cultures, and our spiritual beliefs.

Currently, because of systemic oppression many of us—both individually and communally—don't have access to physical, emotional, and spiritual safety. However, we cannot wait until the world is completely safe for us to find our agency. As activists, we are working to change the material conditions in our communities and in the world, so more people can feel and be safe more of the time. In the meantime, even in a fundamentally unsafe world, an integral part of healing from trauma is rebuilding our internal sense of safety.

We build this competency by learning skills to take care of ourselves, our loved ones, and our communities. When we strengthen this internal sense of safety, we don't feel safe or calm all the time; safety is not a static state. Instead, we learn how to trust ourselves to accurately assess when a situation feels unsafe, and act accordingly. When we can trust our ability to notice threats and take appropriate action, we do not have to live in a constant state of hypervigilance—endlessly tracking for safety in our environment. By coming back into our bodies, we learn how to stay connected to ourselves (physically, emotionally, and spiritually), which helps us accurately assess our safety. As part of rebuilding an internal sense of safety, we also learn how to distinguish what matters to us and how to take actions and set boundaries that support our needs and wants.

Trauma impacts our experience of safety by pulling our attention outside of our bodies. Our sense of safety then becomes contingent on other people's behavior or on outside events. We start imagining that we *would* feel safe "if only" this person, event, or environment would provide exactly what we need or expect. This is ultimately disempowering because we cannot control other people or our environment—nor should we aspire to. Referring to the quote that opened this chapter, President Biden suggests that the seven million Jews who live in the US have to look to another country for safety because we cannot possibly find safety in our own. To defend the US government's military and financial support of a genocide, Biden evokes Jewish fear and antisemitic tropes of Jews as outsiders.

Sometimes trauma impacts our sense of safety by making us feel safe in what are actually dangerous conditions, or unsafe when we are in safe conditions. The forces of hierarchical domination that are rampant in this world teach us an upside-down version of what it means to be safe, both on an individual and collective level. For example, because I grew up in an abusive household, as a young person searching for connection, I only felt "normal" or safe when I was in a relationship with someone who was dangerously controlling. Because I was taught that love meant control, I felt unsafe when I was with someone kind and caring.

On the systemic level, Zionism teaches us that safety for Jews comes from walls, checkpoints, and surveillance when in fact this perpetual state of war against Palestinians makes all of us—including Israelis—less safe. As settlers, Israelis live in a militarized society with mandatory military service, streets patrolled by soldiers, and mandatory bomb shelters.

Because of the Israeli occupation, they live in fear of attack from those being oppressed by state violence. By claiming that the apartheid state of Israel represents all Jews, the Israeli government puts all Jews in danger by implying that we are all responsible for the violent oppression of Palestinians. Jews then become targets for people's understandable frustration with Israeli apartheid.

So how do we rebuild our trust in ourselves from the inside out, so that we can make grounded assessments about our safety, both individually and collectively? We have to first understand the mechanism of our individual survival strategies. As discussed in the last chapter, when trauma prevents our survival reactions from completing their physiological cycle, the stored energy of those reactions becomes stuck as contractions that live inside our younger parts. In order for these parts to release their grip on us when we are under pressure, we need to do two things.

The first is to meet these parts on their own terms with an understanding and an appreciation of their purpose. In somatics, this skill is called blending: acknowledging and honoring our survival reactions and shaping as intelligent adaptations that we make to find safety, connection, and dignity. We use the term *blending* here differently than in Internal Family Systems, which defines blending as unconsciously identifying and merging with a particular part of ourselves. In somatics, blending is a conscious process of affirming our shaping. The second is to build other strategies for taking care of ourselves—including learning how to set responsive boundaries, building supportive alliances with others, and returning to center after we have been activated around our trauma.

Blending with Survival Shaping

As we discussed in chapter 4, when we repeatedly activate unresolved survival reactions over time, they harden into contractions that become physical manifestations of our inner worlds. These contractions become part of our "safety shapes" or the ways we react under pressure to protect ourselves. We can think of these shapes as younger parts of us who got stuck at the age when we experienced trauma. These shapes become more pronounced when we feel threatened, but they can also show up in our everyday lives.

For example, as a child, I was frequently punished for being "too sensitive." My parents implied that if I didn't "toughen up," I wasn't going to make it in the world. They often disciplined me for expressing any "negative" emotion, including sadness and fear. If I started crying when my dad was yelling at one of my siblings, he would immediately turn his anger on me. I remember being scared most of the time because I never knew when he would erupt, and I was scared that my reactions to his rage would cause more trouble.

Fear of my father permeated all aspects of my life. As the youngest of six kids, I often became scared when our family watched cop or detective TV shows. If I appeared scared in any way, including crying, I was sent to my room while everybody else continued watching the show. In my room alone, I would replay the scenes that upset me. I can still remember the most disturbing episode of *Starsky and Hutch* from when I was eight years old. A mentally ill man lay on a dirty mattress all day, staring at a naked lightbulb dangling from the ceiling until he was enlisted to enact violence. It was terrifying to be alone with images like this running through my head, so I learned to hide my feelings and then dissociate, so that I could sit through shows without being isolated. I survived my family of origin by unconsciously constructing a shape that combined freeze and dissociation. I would suck all my energy inside and become very still (freeze) and then part of me would float away from the scenes of actual or depicted violence (dissociation). This is one way I "toughened up."

Before I did any healing as an adult, this shape made it difficult for me to reveal how I was truly feeling to anyone, including myself. I certainly couldn't access the full spectrum of emotions from rage to joy. When I felt activated or threatened, I retreated, froze, and dissociated. In conflict with others, I would retreat into this shell, unable to access any emotions or even stay present. As a kid, shutting down my feelings helped protect my connections and my safety, but as an adult, my safety shape made navigating intimacy and conflict quite challenging.

Blending with our safety shapes means understanding their logic on their own terms, so that we can honor the wisdom of our parts who created these protective patterns. When we blend with our safety shapes, we befriend them instead of trying to break them apart. We might be frustrated with the impacts of these shapes, but if we try to force them open, our younger selves will perceive this as a threat to our safety and double down in their efforts to contain the threat. In other words, the contractions will harden, and we will enter into an antagonistic relationship with ourselves.

Instead, if we metaphorically link arms with our younger selves, we support the shaping both physically and emotionally. We physically support our safety shapes by inviting them to contract. We verbally affirm the intelligence of our safety shapes by thanking them for taking care of us, often for a very long time. When our younger parts feel affirmed, they allow the contractions to loosen, so that the stuck energy can start moving through our bodies.

When someone first blended with my safety shape—withdrawing internally, freezing externally, and dissociating—my younger self felt seen and affirmed. During a somatic training, my practice partner asked me to shape my body in a way that felt familiar and protective. I sat on the floor with my knees bent, my arms circled around my legs with clasped hands, my chest collapsed, and my head bent down. I tucked my real self under my ribs in the back of my diaphragm and clenched my stomach. My heart had receded and was protected by my shoulders and arms, which felt rigid and stiff. My jaw was locked, my eyes vacant, my face still, and I could not feel my legs at all. I felt scared and braced for whatever was headed my way. Part of me had already drifted away. My partner sat next to me and took on a similar shape, clasping their arms around their legs.

My practice partner spoke directly to this younger shape, saying, "Good job hiding your feelings; they can't be used against you," and "Good job hiding; nobody can find you." At first, my arms just started to grip even harder because it felt embarrassing to be seen in my safety shape, but after I heard these affirmations a few times I started to notice a gradual loosening of my grip and a softening in my shoulders. When we checked in, I asked my partner to affirm the wisdom of this strategy by adding this phrase to the next round: "You won't be present for whatever happens." After they added this to the litany of affirmations, I felt my cheeks start to relax and my eyes began to soften; tears rose to the surface. My younger eight-year-old self was proud of how they had protected me.

As the shape started to relax I felt more fear, and my legs started to tremble. My partner directed me to slowly stomp each foot into the ground several times. As I stomped my feet, my face and chest heated up, and I started sweating. Energy began gently flowing from my diaphragm to my stomach, which also started to loosen and tremble. After a few rounds of stomping, my legs were shaking, and the soles of my feet felt heavy and connected to the earth. Once I stopped stomping, I suddenly became more aware of my surroundings and my partner.

My partner and I talked about how this frozen and dissociated shape had protected me for a long time, but also how it got in the way of being known and seen. When I'm in this shape, it is almost impossible to feel any connection to myself, to others, or to my aliveness. When this eight-year-old part of me felt affirmed, they could let go of their tight grip, and energy started to move through my body. As a child, I was trapped inside my house, where I could only escape by going inward or dissociating. The stomping helped shake loose some of the stuck energy from the trapped flight response. I actually began to *feel* what it might be like to complete the survival reaction of flight and run away from the threat.

Over time and many iterations, this practice of blending has given me tools to relate differently to my safety shaping. When I notice that I'm tucked away inside and my outer edges become rigid, I thank my eight-year-old self for helping me survive, and I allow myself a moment to curl inward even more. Once I have supported and blended with the contraction of this shape, I assess whether I truly need this protection in the present moment. I remind myself that I am not currently trapped. As an adult, I have more choice and the agency to set boundaries, to make requests, and to leave situations that feel unsafe.

Blending is an effective healing tool, which can be used in political contexts. When I work with clients struggling with Zionism, I blend with their survival shaping so that it will loosen its grip, and they can find different ways of responding to their fear. Many of my Jewish clients who are critical of Zionism are afraid to discuss their political differences with their families of origin. If I just insisted on how important it is to have this conversation with their families, their younger selves would see me as a threat and clamp down even more tightly. My clients might intellectually agree with me at the moment of our session, but this won't help them shift out of the safety shape when it arises. Most of my clients are afraid of losing connection with their families because of how political uniformity is enforced in Jewish communities.

My client Lex, a young white Ashkenazi Jewish non-binary person involved in environmental justice work, struggled with their father's unconditional support for Israel's military actions. Whenever their father talked about his politics, they would appease their father with a weak smile and then disappear from the conversation by leaving out the back of their head. Their mind would go blank, their stomach contracted, and they would find themself nodding along without really tracking what was being said until the conversation was over. I blended with this shape of appease and dissociate by acknowledging the ways it enabled them to stay connected to their father amidst disagreement. A much younger Lex had learned to agree with their father because they saw what happened when their mother disagreed with him. Their parents had fought continuously until their father moved out when Lex was six. He disappeared from their life for a few years, which was devastating. When he came back, they were continuously terrified of losing this relationship, so they learned to agree with most of their dad's opinions.

After months of my blending with Lex's survival shaping and practicing new skills to keep them safe—such as boundary setting—they were ready to articulate their political disagreement with their father. Blending doesn't mean encouraging someone to stay stuck in that shape, but instead acknowledging its inherent purpose and wisdom so that the shape can loosen. This time when Lex's father brought up Israel's "right to defend herself," Lex told him not only that they didn't support Israel's actions, but that they had been protesting Israel's attacks on Palestinians. When their father reacted with surprise and anger, Lex was able to listen to their father's concerns while remaining rooted in their own values. They made their father feel heard, but didn't waver about anything that they had said. Their father left the initial conversation angry and confused, but also willing to stay in this conversation. He agreed to read some of the articles that Lex sends him as long as Lex agreed to read some articles he sends. Their connection feels fraught, but still intact.

Now that the conversation has begun, Lex feels more in alignment with their political values. As they navigate these differences with their father, they sometimes find themself appeasing and dissociating—especially when they are tired and under-resourced. This is when our survival shapes often creep back in, but Lex has developed a different relationship with their safety shape, which allows them to understand it without berating themself when it appears. We never "get rid" of our safety shapes; they remain with us our whole lives. We learn different ways of relating to them, so that we have more choices for how we respond when we are activated.

Self-Protection and Boundaries

Another way we can rebuild our sense of safety is through learning to set boundaries. Traumatic experiences often prevent us from being able to successfully defend ourselves because we were overpowered at the time of the trauma. When it is impossible for us to set physical boundaries, we will shift into survival reactions. As a result of not being able to protect ourselves, we can develop an internal sense of helplessness that lingers in our lives. We often have to learn the skill of protecting or defending ourselves with embodied boundaries that take care of our own and each other's well-being. Learning to feel and say our embodied yeses, nos, and maybes is a powerful skill set for rebuilding our sense of agency.

When working with Lex around boundaries with their father, we also practiced saying "no." This was an integral part of learning to differentiate their political stance from their father's. Lex and I tried out several types of "nos." The most emphatic "no" is called the "push away." Representing Lex's father, I would walk toward them with both arms outstretched in front of me and say, "Of course, Israel is our home." In this practice, they would meet my outstretched arms with their hands as I approached, feel their center, and push me back and away with their arms while saying "no." The first time we did this, they froze and let me come too close to them before they were able to weakly push me. I only moved about a foot away from them. They also forgot to say the word *no*. This was very emblematic of how they struggled to stand up to their father.

We practiced "nos" for months. Lex practiced what it felt like to center inside of their political commitment, feel their kavanah at their center of gravity, and say "no" from that place. Over time, they were able to resource their "no" by centering inside their intention, values, and politics. They learned to push while simultaneously feeling their center, legs, and connection to the earth. When they were able to successfully push me away with an embodied "no," I felt the force of their differentiation, and it literally moved me several feet away from them. We both felt really excited when their "no" felt congruent through their body and their words.

There are other types of "no" that we practice, including an intimate decline in which we stay connected to the person in the midst of differentiation. We also learn what it feels like in our bodies to say and feel "yes" and "maybe." With a "no and redirect," we learn how to say "no" and then redirect and guide someone toward a different vision. For example, we might say "no" in response to someone's proposed solution to a problem, but then offer a different solution. In order to ask for what we want and need, we also practice making requests. Finally, we learn how to leave or quit a situation from a centered place. These are lifelong skills that we practice in order to build trust with ourselves, support our agency, and increase our internal sense of safety.

Allyship and Protection

My grandmother always told me, "Friends are nice, but you can only rely on your family." This sentiment grew out of her family's experiences of being abandoned under duress by their non-Jewish neighbors and friends in Lithuania. Because of antisemitic experiences like my grandmother's, many Jews learn to deeply distrust others—especially those who are not Jewish, and this distrust is reinforced by Zionist narratives. As my friend Rabbi Jessica Rosenberg reminds us, when we only retell stories of Jewish isolation and separation from other communities, we erase the "wide deep and nuanced aspects of Jewish life in the many different places and ways in which Jews lived over centuries and continents."[14] We start to believe that it is not possible for Jews to feel both safe and connected to other people.

Being left behind and isolated is traumatizing for us as social creatures meant to belong to a pack. We expect others to protect us from harm, so that we aren't left exposed and vulnerable. Because of this expectation, when the people around us don't offer protection, we experience a sense of betrayal that compounds our trauma. This impacts our sense of safety, belonging, and worth; and can lead to excessive self-reliance, distrust of others, and conflict in our relationships. We might find it incredibly hard to ask for help, and we can end up feeling like we have to do everything on our own. Even when we do ask for help, we might then push people away for not helping us in the exact way that we needed, reinforcing the idea that we can only rely on ourselves. When we practice allyship with each other somatically, we undergo an experience, possibly for the first time, of feeling safe and protected by others. Safety and connection are braided back together.

In my first year of training in somatics, I experienced a powerful allyship practice that helped heal some traumatic memories that kept appearing as recurring nightmares.* These felt related to the violence I had personally

---

* I originally published a version of this account in Tikkun magazine. Wendy Elisheva Somerson, "A Ritual Dismantling of Walls: Healing from Trauma through the Jewish Days of Awe," Tikkun 29 (3): 17–22, https://doi.org/10.1215/08879982-2713286.

experienced as a child, and the antisemitic violence some of my ancestors had experienced when, for example, their homes were raided during pogroms. I kept having one particular dream in which a man had broken into my bedroom. In this dream, his hands would circle my throat from behind and I would go rigid with terror, unable to speak or breathe. I would often dream that I woke up and he was still there, and then I would have to wake myself up again, but his presence would linger in the room. This nightmare was ravaging my days and nights—I was incredibly anxious, fearful of going to sleep, and experiencing insomnia.

Two non-Jewish friends, Elizabeth and Noah, with whom I was studying somatics, came over to my place to do an allyship practice around this nightmare to help me move through it. With the allyship practice, we time-travel to a moment in the past when we really needed allyship but didn't receive it. By offering support from the present to our past, we alter how this traumatic experience lives in our bodies. In this case, my friends were joining me in the experience of the nightmare, so that I didn't feel so alone with the trauma it represented. A strength of somatic healing is that we didn't need to remember or understand every detail about exactly what happened, or why I was having this nightmare. Instead, we worked with the bodily sensations, emotions, and story evoked by the nightmare—regardless of the details of the original trauma.

The first step of the allyship practice is to choose how we want our allies positioned around us by trying out different positions to determine what feels best to our bodies. We can explore what it's like to have someone stand in front of us, as though they are standing between us and the threat; behind us to have our backs and support us; and next to us, so that we can feel their presence shoulder to shoulder. Elizabeth tried out these positions with me, and I decided I felt most protected with her on my right side. It is surprisingly easy for most people to determine where it feels most supportive to have someone positioned. When Elizabeth was on my right side, I felt my right shoulder relax, and I felt comforted. Noah then asked me to evoke the feeling of the nightmare and to tell them what sensations I noticed. My chest was burning and tight with anxiety. My legs were twitching, and I started to feel an electric buzzing in the spaces between my fingers.

The second step is to determine what we want our support people to say or do that feels protective. The power of this practice comes from requesting and receiving the specific kind of allyship that we have been longing for. When I dropped into the nightmare, I had Elizabeth first stand on my right side, saying "Leave them alone" several times, directly to the man who had invaded my dreams. I immediately began crying and shaking, afraid to drag my friends into the undercurrent of the nightmare's terror, though their presence also gave me the strength to face it. After trying out various positions, the three of us ended up sitting on the floor facing my front window. I sat cross-legged in the middle with my knees touching my friends' legs, where I rested my hands. I felt their attentive presence as I sank into the nightmare. My legs trembled; my shoulders convulsed, and I felt energy streaming up and down my spine. There was a lot of movement, but there was little connection between the upper and lower halves of my body.

Then I had my friends simply say "We see this" several times, so that I could feel witnessed. In my head, I said to the man, "They see you. You can't hide from them." My friends also saw me. Their presence highlighted how alone I had felt with this terror for so long. Bringing my friends into the nightmare with me was both deeply satisfying and deeply vulnerable. I was grateful they were there, a little embarrassed by the intensity of my feelings, and sad for how alone I had felt with this terror for so long. I also felt some deep sadness for my ancestors whose homes were repeatedly invaded during the pogroms in Eastern Europe. My legs started twitching faster, bringing more movement and energy. My shoulders moved up and down, while warmth spread from my heart out through my arms and down to the tips of my fingers.

Henry, my Siamese cat, was fascinated by what we were doing on the floor; he came over to rub his cheek against our legs. My friends each held up one hand to prevent the man from coming near my neck, and they each put one hand on my sacrum, which responded with a pulsing movement.

"Go away," they said in rounds. "Go away. We won't tolerate your presence." The energy in my body sped up and widened outward, as my gaze encompassed the width of my living room.

I watched as the man's shadowy figure retreated into the corner. Henry chased after him, and his figure evaporated. "Don't come back. You don't belong here," my friends said. The two halves of my body clicked back together, making room for powerful tides to rush up and down through the widening canal of my pelvis. I felt my entire body vibrating, pulling in strength and connection from touching Elizabeth and Noah. My energy slowed to a rhythmic pulsing through my body, and we slowly completed the practice.

Sitting on the couch after the session, Noah asked me what this version of myself, still humming with aliveness, would tell the self who can't sleep at night. "You are not alone," I say. "You are not alone," he repeated slowly. This one practice of being supported by others through the isolation, impact, and imprint of personal and intergenerational violence changed my sense of safety, particularly at night. The nightmares became less frequent, and when they did occur, I often dreamed that I had the strength to push the man off of me. Even in my dream state, I feel more powerful. I stopped feeling so fearful, and I rediscovered a new sense of agency.

Traveling back in time helps us rewire our nervous systems. Instead of being yanked back in time by an activating event to reexperience the trauma, we intentionally revisit and receive support at a time when we felt alone and vulnerable. While I can't change the violence of my history that the nightmare represents, I can change how I relate to this past. My experience of this practice was both deeply physical because I experienced so much sensation in my body, and deeply spiritual because it reorganized something fundamental in myself. Experiencing non-Jews helping to protect me broke my isolation. Since that practice I feel more connected to others, even when I am physically alone. The healing also moved backward in time, offering my ancestors the experience of being protected by people who are not Jewish.

Returning to Center: Grab, Center, Face

In somatics, we refer to anything that activates our survival reactions as a "grab" that pulls our attention away from the present moment and into an activated safety shape—some combination of fight, flight, freeze, appease, and/or dissociate. When we experience a grab, we tend to remain stuck in our automatic reaction, unable to respond to the grab in a centered way. The practice of "grab, center, and face" helps us return to center after being grabbed, so that we can face the activation. As James Baldwin brilliantly observed, "Not everything that is faced can be changed; but nothing can be changed until it is faced."[15] When we face the issues that pull us away from center, rather than remaining stuck in our reaction, we discover more options for responding to the situation.

Because I'm working on a kavanah around Jewish belonging, I often practice responding to grabs that arise from conversations about Palestine with other Jews. One of my biggest grabs occurs when someone asks, "Do you believe in Israel's right to exist?" As a political talking point, this question doesn't tend to come from a place of curiosity. I have absolutely no love for the structure of nation-states and their boundaries; but in our current global economy, Israel does exist, and many Jews live there. Most anti-Zionists are not advocating for Jews to suddenly vacate the land of Palestine/Israel, but we are envisioning a multiethnic, multireligious land where Jews and Palestinians share equality, freedom, and self-determination.

This question about a "right to *exist*" is emotionally laden because it conjures up images of the Nazi Holocaust and the attempted extermination of European Jews. Because of its emotional weight, the question becomes difficult to answer. By implicitly conflating the state of Israel with Jewish peoplehood, this question hides a trapdoor that is easy to fall through. I can't agree that Israel should continue to oppress Palestinians. But if I respond "no" to the question, it registers as antisemitism, as if I were saying that I don't think Jews—my own people—deserve to be alive. The person asking this question doesn't have to take my concerns about Palestinian freedom seriously if they can dismiss me as a "self-hating" Jew because I don't care about the existence of my people.

To practice this grab, my partner moves toward me on my right side, asking, "Do you believe in Israel's right to exist?" When they reach me, they exert pressure by grasping my wrist with their left hand. I pay attention to the sensations, emotions, and stories that arise when I am grabbed. I also notice where my energy goes: does it move away from the person making the grab (flight), toward them (appease), against (fight), or do I freeze? Some combination of these shows up for me, and different reactions appear based on which side of the body I am being grabbed.

When my partner came in with that question from my right side, I first noticed myself clamping down: my right shoulder tightened up and thrust forward, my jaw squeezed shut, and my arm pulled away from them. Part of me felt like fleeing—I pulled my energy away and out through the left side of my body, but then part of me prepared for a fight. My face got hot, my body felt tight and rigid, and energy started to course down my arms. I felt angry, afraid, and dismissed.

When the grab came from the left side, I began to freeze and dissociate. I became very rigid and still, and my mind started to go blank. I couldn't quite remember what happened or whether or not they really asked that question. My energy started to float up out of the top of my head, and I vacated my whole arm on my left side. I couldn't feel most of my body. My mood was more distracted and diffuse, and I was no longer emotionally present.

We practiced the grab several times on each side because the two sides of our bodies tend to react differently. Each side holds our history differently based on past traumatic experiences and injuries. Grabs on the right side of my body tend to provoke a more intense reaction. I trace some of this to my childhood when my sister sat to my right at the dining table during meals. She was often in trouble with my dad, so I learned to contract and pull in the energy on the right side of my body.

These two main reactions track very closely to how I react when asked that question in a conversation. I might pull my energy away because the person I'm talking with doesn't seem open, and then prepare to argue with this person from a disconnected place. Sometimes, I go into a freeze and start to disappear because it feels safer to withdraw. I might give a perfunctory answer and then walk away because I decide that this person isn't worth talking to.

After I noticed my reactions to these grabs several times, the next time my partner grabbed me, I recentered and then turned to face the grab. When my partner grabbed me for this round, I first noticed that I had contracted in my body, disappeared part of myself, and also prepared for a fight. I thanked this reaction for protecting me, and then I purposefully started to come back into my body to recenter. I took some deeper breaths to wake up my center. As I also lengthened upward to the sky, I allowed my jaw and shoulders to relax down into gravity. I reminded myself of my own dignity, the dignity of my political stance, the dignity of the Palestinian people, and the dignity of the person in front of me. Finding my width by breathing across my diaphragm allowed me to imagine my connection to my circle of anti-Zionist comrades. As I breathed into the back of my body, I called in my ancestors for support in this conversation, and as I brought the energy forward, I tried to imagine a future where Zionism had ended its unsuccessful run. Finally, I remembered what I care about, my kavanah, which served to remind me that my belonging as a Jew is simply never in question.

When I felt centered inside my body and my kavanah, I turned around to look the grabber in the face. They were still gripping my wrist. When the person and grab were right in front of me, it was reactivating, so I centered myself again before I decided how to respond to this question. I managed to find some genuine curiosity about the grabber's experience, and I brought my breath and energy to the place where their hand touched my wrist in order to feel their presence. I imagined that if they weren't just trying to score a political point, they might have been feeling afraid. I decided to ask them what they meant by the question. This allowed me to hear more about their intention before I decided how and whether to engage with them.

If I never face this grab, I am allowing myself to stay stuck in reactivity, which hardly ever leads to a genuine exchange or connection, and also feels disempowering. This is common around fraught issues; each person is spinning around on their individual hamster wheel of activation and protection, unable to pause and be curious about the other person. If we can notice the activation, pause, recenter, and turn to face the grab, we can start to see each other's concerns, fears, or motivations. Turning and facing doesn't mean agreeing. It means that we allow ourselves to be impacted by the interaction and consider one another's full humanity. In this interaction, only one of us needs to be centered, and this can serve as an invitation to the other person to join them in a more grounded place.

I remember a poignant time when I was able to ask someone what he meant by this question about the right to exist. After I listened to him make some rote political points, he eventually told me about the fracturing impact the Nazi Holocaust had on his mother's side of the family and his deep desire for Jews to have a safe home. I was able to share that the Nazi Holocaust has also impacted my family, and that I share this same desire. Eventually, I was able to widen out the conversation to include the idea that Palestinians also deserve a safe home, which is something we ended up agreeing on. I'm not saying I convinced him of anything in this one conversation, but I managed to stay connected to myself and remain open to this person whose position on Zionism I vehemently disagreed with. At the very least, he didn't leave the conversation believing that this anti-Zionist Jew doesn't care about their people.

I wish I could say that I have the energy to do this every time a question like this comes up, but I don't. It takes quite a bit of effort and intention, so I have to gauge when it feels worth it. Like all the practices, grab, center, and face is a lifelong one. The path of least resistance is to let our automatic reactions and safety shapes dictate our behavior. It is easier to turn away from the situations that kick up our fear, but now I recognize that I don't have to shut down when I hear this question. Having returned to center from the grab, I have a felt sense of what it was like to turn and face this question, to differentiate feeling uncomfortable from being unsafe.

When we build an internal sense of safety through blending, practicing boundaries, learning to support and be supported by each other, and turning and facing our grabs, we develop our capacity to shift out of our safety shapes. We learn to unstick ourselves from the past and navigate the world through attunement to the current moment. Because our safety shapes live inside our muscles, tissues, and bones, the next phase of healing is to employ somatic bodywork to help these shapes and associated narratives loosen to allow new shapes and stories to emerge.

CHAPTER 7

HEALING TRAUMA THROUGH BODYWORK

When I use the phrase "healing justice," I am reflecting on how the systems we seek to change outside of our bodies are also carried within our bodies.[1]

—SUSAN RAFFO, *LIBERATED TO THE BONE*

One of my clients, Jaya, a South Asian trans femme academic, experienced medical trauma when she underwent multiple eye surgeries as a child. As an adult, Jaya managed to avoid her trauma by never slowing down; she was constantly juggling numerous collaborations, speaking events, and conferences. However, at night when she was trying to rest, Jaya experienced insomnia and restlessness in her legs. In talk therapy, Jaya didn't make much progress on her insomnia because she relied on her sharp intellect to justify the importance of her involvement in the many projects that kept the terror from her childhood at bay. She had many insights about her behavior, and why she overcommitted herself, but she never reduced her commitments. Her therapist suggested that she try more body-based work.

In our first few sessions of bodywork, Jaya's whole body started trembling, her throat constricted, and she saw an image of the perforated ceiling of the room where she underwent surgery. Trapped in an incomplete flight response to the medical trauma she underwent, Jaya's terrified younger selves were clamoring for attention, but until that point, she mostly ignored them or pushed them away, which is why they showed up at night in her unconscious. Doing bodywork allowed Jaya to bypass some of the intellectual barriers she put up to feeling the terror that needed to move through her.

Bodywork provides an effective method for working with trauma because we can work directly with the places in our bodies that hold the trauma instead of trying to approach them primarily through our intellect. After we have developed more trust in ourselves and our ability to assess safety and protect ourselves, somatic bodywork helps us undergo a fundamental shift in our shape. Somatic bodywork uses touch, breath, sound, narrative, and imagination to help release old patterns and stories to make room for new feelings, narratives, and possibilities. Skillful touch can help our survival reactions move through and get released or integrated, so that we can move from contraction and dissociation to more openness and an ability to stay present in our bodies. When the contractions soften, we can bring life to the places that have become numb or empty, and open the places that have been shut down, so that more aliveness can run through us.

In this chapter, I will frame the theory of somatic bodywork and then go into more depth with client examples, as well as my own healing, to offer a path into understanding the potential of bodywork and how it might intersect with political work. While all somatic practices are in some sense "bodywork" because we are practicing developing our somatic awareness and building body-based skills, the bodywork I refer to here includes using our hands to bring touch to the places in our bodies where we hold contractions. This usually involves a practitioner working with a client, but we can also make contact with our own contractions, often guided by a skilled healer.

Since the beginning of time, humans have used touch to support each other's healing. When I first experienced somatic bodywork, it felt like returning to a human birthright—to deeply feel, connect, and witness each other through touch. In fact, falling in love with the transformative possibilities of giving and receiving touch prompted me to become a somatic healer. When we contact someone else's life force through bodywork, we experience the harmonizing power of each person's *nefesh* (נֶפֶשׁ), or "embodied soul."

Through bodywork, I partner with each person to help them access the flow of life that wants to move through their body but might be blocked because of how they adapted to find safety, dignity, and belonging.

Unlike some forms of massage, we do not work on someone else's body while they simply relax or dissociate. We are encouraging them to be fully present by bringing their breath and presence to meet our touch and by noticing any shifts in their sensations. While muscles and tissues can and do relax during bodywork, the goal isn't a state of emotional calm, but a state of feeling more aliveness in our bodies. After noticing where energy is trapped in a client's body, we encourage the contracted places to gently relax and open. The muscles, tissues, and bones reveal which stories, associated images, and feelings need to move through that have been held back, contracted, or disappeared. We then offer these stories oxygen, space, light—and eventually, release or integration into a new story.

With somatic bodywork, we are inviting somatic opening or a disorganization of the shape we've been inhabiting, so that a new shape can emerge. Opening in somatic bodywork can look like trembling, vibrating, rocking, shaking, laughing, heating up, sweating, shouting, and crying. We tend to feel movement—tingling, streaming, pulsing—in our bodies that might feel like a release or a relief. Some of us will find the movement overwhelming, especially if we have been shutting down movement in our bodies for a long time.

While these are some general tendencies, each of us opens differently. Some people's whole bodies will shake in a seismic fashion, while other bodies will experience a small quiver—more like a body hiccup. We often experience an emotional release through somatic bodywork, but that isn't how we determine whether healing is happening. We make sure the opening moves through the muscles and fascia because lasting change takes place through the body, not just through releasing emotions.

Blending with Contractions

When we make contact with the tight places in our bodies, we get to discover what is being held there and how these contractions have supported and protected our survival. When we blend with contractions in bodywork, we literally help hold the contraction of the muscles and tissues with our hands (and sometimes with the assistance of sandbags or blankets). As we are holding these contractions, we also verbally affirm the wisdom of the contractions to allow the stories being held in those tight places to reveal themselves—whether through words, images, or sensations.

For example, I worked with Naomi, a Black Jewish cis woman whose shoulder band was contracted; her shoulders were in a permanent shrug up toward her ears, with a slight roll forward. This rigidity in her shoulders was out of alignment with the warmth and wisdom that otherwise came through her presence. In her leadership as an executive director of a nonprofit, Naomi was struggling to allow other people to help shape the important work of the organization. Through conversation and practice, we realized that she was embodying in her shoulders a story that she couldn't fully trust anyone else. While she delegated some tasks at work, she often ended up double-checking the work of her colleagues, who then felt micromanaged. Morale at work was especially low during the beginning of Covid, so instead of holding people accountable, she started taking on more and more of the work herself. Naomi is a beloved leader, but she was quickly burning out on the racial and economic justice work she was doing because she was shouldering so much on her own.

In the individualistic culture of late capitalism, many of us have learned that we shouldn't or can't rely on others or ask for help. Because of trauma and oppression, we often haven't consistently received the kind of help we needed. These experiences may have solidified into a belief held in the shoulder girdle that we don't deserve to receive support or care. When we blend with and support this contraction, we hear each person's stories or images of what it feels like to hold so much on their own.

Naomi and I worked on increasing her sense of interdependence through somatic practice, but we gained the most traction through somatic bodywork. Over many sessions, I blended with her shoulder contractions by gently cradling her shoulders from behind her head and lifting her shoulders slightly up off the table and toward each other. As I cradled her shoulders, I also verbally appreciated the wisdom of this protective strategy. I told her, "You're doing a good job making sure everything gets done. Nothing will fall through the cracks. Nobody will disappoint you. Good job doing it all on your own." Slowly, with both the physical support and the verbal affirmations, Naomi's shoulders started to relax.

In one of several bodywork sessions where we blended with the shoulder contractions, Naomi reported both a relaxing of her shoulders and a tightening around her heart. This is quite common: when one place in our body softens, another might compensate by contracting. I asked her to take several deep breaths and to make a noise with each exhale that came from the tight place in her heart. After vocalizing "Ahhhhhhhh" several times, she reported that some energy had started to pool around her heart, which now felt like it was collapsing. Naomi was visibly agitated and shaky. When I asked if any words wanted to come through, she simply said, "Help me." Then I had her say those words several times from her heart. Each time she said the words, they became more emotionally jagged until she started to cry. Energy flowed down into her arms and hands, which began trembling. She felt scared and ashamed that she asked for help.

I told Naomi to keep feeling for my presence; I wanted her to notice that she was not alone with this shame and fear. To keep the energy moving, I had her take deep breaths across the span of her chest and shoulders and down into her arms. I helped her bring more breath into her chest by tapping it and gently rocking her ribs back and forth. Naomi's arms continued to tremble, and she told me that she saw an image of herself standing in front of her locker in her predominantly white Christian middle school. Someone had written antisemitic and racist epithets on the inside of her locker door, and she remembered discovering these slurs and going into a freeze. Ashamed, she didn't want anyone else to see the graffiti, so she quickly shut her locker, and ended up just taping pictures over the words. She never told anyone about it, but the pictures she saw were a daily reminder of being threatened as an outsider in this school.

We decided to go back into that memory through bodywork so I could offer her more support and allyship. I asked Naomi what I could do or say to support her in that memory. She wanted me to stand in front of her facing out into the hallway and yell "Who did this? This isn't okay!" and "We won't allow racism or antisemitism here!" I yelled this several times as she breathed into her chest and shoulders, and she became very still. In the first round, this allyship practice had unearthed the shame of internalized antisemitism and racism intertwined with the shame of needing help.

In subsequent rounds, we decided to use our imagination to bring more supportive people into this practice. We called on Naomi's great-grandmother Esther to stand at her back, telling her that it's okay to be visible—that in fact her ancestors *wanted* her to ask for help, and that it would be healing for her ancestors to hear her ask. We brought in her partner and her best friend to stand on either side of her, to remind her that she wouldn't lose connection by showing what she needs. Her cat came in as a protector and comforter who weaved in and out through her legs. As we deepened into the practice with extra support, it started to feel like a relief to experience someone standing up for her. The possibility arose that it might not have been her fault that this antisemitic, racist incident happened or that she needed support.

Crying, Naomi slowly started to shake her head back and forth sideways as if she was saying "no." Her throat softened, and her shoulders started moving up and down in a staccato beat until that energy started to stream down her arms, which buzzed with aliveness. Many experiences and images flashed before her of times when she felt alone and too scared or ashamed to ask for help. I placed a hand on her heart and asked her to imagine the love of her partner, her best friend, and her cat coming through my hand and into her heart. We both felt an opening and softening throughout her shoulders, chest, and diaphragm. When I asked what her heart wanted to say, she replied, "It might be okay to ask for help."

After we spent several months softening her self-reliance, Naomi eventually found more suppleness in her shoulders. As her shoulders started to relax, a new story arose about being a human who needs help just like every other human. This allowed her to recognize the presence of many trustworthy people in her life, including her coworkers. In several sessions, I had her name and feel for all the supportive beings in her life, including her ancestors and the more-than-human world. We practiced being open and receptive to the love and care that was already there for her. Over time and with hard work, Naomi has started to ask for help when she needs it, delegating more, and encouraging and appreciating her coworkers' contributions. Naomi feels less anxious, and she has made more space for her coworkers to contribute more to the organization's mission.

While Naomi still has some contraction in her shoulders, some of the rigidity has started to thaw, leaving more room for her to feel her full width, her connections, and her ability to feel and be supported. There will always be times when self-reliance shows up, but now she is able to recognize when it's happening, and then to make decisions about how to relate to it. Naomi has become more congruent and trustworthy as a leader because she is cultivating other leaders and embodying more interdependence.

Re-Enlivening and Reconnecting

While our adaptations to trauma can appear as contractions in our bodies, they can also appear as emptiness, slackness, or vacancy. When parts of us have felt unseen or ignored, we can end up feeling hollow in corresponding places in our bodies. For instance, as a non-binary practitioner, I work with many trans and non-binary people. Many of us have vacated parts of our bodies that feel dysphoric to us. I also work with many clients who were ignored or neglected as children. This may translate into a hollow cavernous feeling, often in the chest or limbs, because these parts weren't seen or validated in different developmental stages. When children are forced into caretaking for the adults in their lives, this often results in slack areas of the body that represent the absence of care they experienced as children. Survivors of sexual assault may also experience a vacancy in different areas of the body including the pelvis, because it seems unsafe to feel aliveness in a place that has been violated.

When we experience a hollowness or emptiness in ourselves, we might compensate for the emptiness by bringing our attention outside of ourselves. We might track other people's expressions and gestures very carefully to determine our own states of being in relation to theirs. This attentive tracking probably kept us safe in the past because in order to identify danger, we learned to assess how the people around us were doing. At the same time, in our current lives we can end up disconnected from ourselves and reliant on other people's behavior to regulate ourselves. For some of us, this shows up as perennially adopting the role of caretaker to support others' wants and needs. When we are offered care or support, it might be hard to receive because we don't know how to allow it into the places that we have vacated. We might only feel valued for the care we offer to others, while there remains a deep yearning inside to be known for who we are and to receive care ourselves.

In addition to vacant places in our bodies, many of us experience different parts of our bodies as separate or cut off from each other. Sometimes it might feel like the right and left sides of the body are divided from each other or that our limbs are not connected to our torso. Many survivors of sexual assault, myself included, experience disconnection between our upper and lower halves. This is often a survival mechanism that allows us to contain the pain of the assault below the waist, then numb and try to cut the rest of ourselves off from it. This is a smart strategy for surviving and containing the terror of the violation, but it also cuts us off from our wholeness and leaves us feeling disconnected from the power of our pelvis and legs. Disconnection from our lower half also cuts us off from the ground, so we may feel especially ungrounded, like we're floating, instead of connected to the earth.

Bodywork can help re-enliven the places that feel empty and reconnect areas of the body that feel cut off from each other. When they came to see me, Eli—a non-binary anti-Zionist Ashkenazi Jewish writer and educator— told me they wanted to bring fragments of their soul back into their body. While they felt validated for their intellect, they often felt nothing but anxiety or blankness in their body. For many reasons, including an emphasis in Judaism on intellectual traditions of debate and commentary about written texts, there is a Jewish tradition of reliance on and validation for our intellectual acumen. It makes sense that collectively, we might avoid being in our bodies when our alleged bodily differences as Jews have been used by eugenicists to claim that Jews were and are an inferior race. However, when we are only affirmed for our minds, it can be difficult to inhabit our bodies. For many of us who have been othered as Jewish people, we see our bodies as simply vehicles to cart our minds around. However, living outside of our bodies can feel like living on the outside of our own lives.

Eli had experienced childhood sexual abuse from their father, and they had a wavering sense of self-esteem. They felt disconnected from their power, and it was very hard for them to say or know what they wanted. This made it difficult to set boundaries in the present moment and to stay in their body when they were around other people. Only much later would they realize that someone's behavior wasn't kind or respectful toward them. In relationships, they tended to go outside of themselves, so that they could figure out who or what other people wanted them to be. This left them feeling like they were never loved for who they were—partially because they weren't entirely sure who that was. Eli had a deep longing for intimacy, but it translated into accepting any form of intimacy that was on offer, even when it arrived accompanied by other harmful behavior.

As we did practices to increase Eli's somatic awareness, they noticed that they felt absent from their pelvis, and distant and disconnected from their legs. Over many bodywork sessions, when we traveled back in time to moments of abuse in their childhood home, we would have them slowly kick their legs, while imagining running away. Their legs needed to enact the impulse to flee that they were denied as a child.

When Eli was feeling more resourced in their legs from our work together, we started doing bodywork to slowly bring more presence into their pelvis. As they felt more sensation in their pelvis, more memories about their abuse arose, but then their throat would often clamp down, telling them not to reveal their family secrets. We gently worked with releasing the contractions in their throat by supporting the sides of their neck.

We then worked on reconnecting the upper and lower halves of their body by working with their psoas muscles, the only muscles in our body connecting our torso to our legs. These muscles originate on either side of the back, run through both sides of our pelvis, and through our femur—the inner thigh bone at the hip. In several sessions, we worked on opening the tightness in their psoas muscles to allow more energy to flow from their diaphragm and abdomen down through their pelvis and into their legs.

When Eli first felt more energy running through their hips, connecting their upper with their lower body, they were momentarily excited by feeling powerful. That excitement quickly morphed into terror. Feeling powerful and connected to their pelvis and legs was a new and uncomfortable sensation. Eli worried that if they felt powerful, they would cause harm to others, like their father did. This opened a new phase of work for us about how to hold power accountably. We explored how we are more likely to cause harm and enact power over others (dominating power) from a place of feeling subjectively helpless. Because Eli was also an anti-Zionist activist, we were able to discuss how we need to build our power in collaborative and collective ways to challenge domination. We will discuss more about centered accountability in the next chapter; but we experimented with feeling an accountable sense of power in their body. For Eli, it helped to imagine that they were channeling the steady power of Mount Rainier. Over time, they were able to settle into feeling more of their agency and developed a new story of themselves as a powerful person who had survived abuse and neglect—but was no longer defined by that story.

By reconnecting to their lower body, Eli was able to locate themself in relationship to the earth, to others, and to their own source of strength. Now when anxious energy builds up in their chest, they can move it down through their pelvis, thighs, calves, and feet, and into the ground. They articulate that they no longer feel valued only for their intellect, partially because they can inhabit more of their body. When taking walks, they remember that the earth is holding them, instead of feeling like they must hold themself up and away from the ground. Their legs have become a source of strength, and they trust them to run and kick and take care of them. This trust translates into a deeper knowledge of themself and a feeling that their soul has landed back in their body.

When Individual and Collective Trauma Collide

The violence and oppression we experience in our individual lives can motivate many of us to act against collective injustice, but these experiences also have the potential to pull us out of alignment with our kavanot around activism and organizing. In 2014, my individual trauma got activated by the violence in Palestine, and I had to travel back to the past to change how I could show up as an activist in the present moment.*

That summer, when the photos of Palestinian teenager Tariq Abu Khdeir's bloated face with blackened and swollen eyes first appeared on my Facebook feed, I quickly scrolled away from them.[2] I had read his story: I knew he was a fifteen-year-old Palestinian-American who was beaten and kicked unconscious by the police while protesting the murder and abduction of his cousin in East Jerusalem. Sadly, I knew his story was not unusual; it had reached the mainstream media because he was an American citizen whose attack was caught on video. When I finally turned and faced what happened to Tariq by looking at the photos and reading about this shameful attack, I was snatched out of the present and into a particularly violent incident from my childhood.

It was three AM. My sixteen-year-old sister was lying on her side on the carpeted living room floor. The dark gold carpet was divided into puffy sections separated by flat lines, which looked like little roads winding through golden fields. My dad was standing over her, kicking her. A scar marked the northeast corner of my dad's forehead, which turned a deeper red than the rest of his face when he was angry.

Driving back to our house after a late night, my sister crashed our family car—a Dodge Dart inherited from our grandfather—into a parked car. Metal collided with metal, crumpling the Dart until it was totaled. My sister was unharmed—that is, until my dad got to her. Enraged that she crashed the car while being out past her curfew, he violently attacked her.

My sister curled up into a ball to protect herself, while my dad kicked her in the head and side again and again. Blood soaked into the carpet, seeping into the golden fields. I was forced to watch her being beat up, while I sat in a dark gold-and–olive-striped chair, afraid that my dad was going to kill my sister, afraid that he might also kill me. Gnawing at my cuticles until they bled, I ripped myself out of the scene unfolding before

---

*   I originally published a version of this in *Tikkun* magazine in 2015. Wendy Elisheva Somerson, "Making Amends," *Tikkun* 30 (4): 41–43, https://doi.org /10.1215/08879982-3328877.

me. I flew through parted olive drapes, out the bay window, and into the front yard. Squinting into the dappled sun under the shade of the oak tree, I was touching the mossy hollows in the enormous tree roots where I often created dwellings for my Fisher-Price play people as a child.

Although I managed to soar away from the violence as it was occurring, this image of my dad kicking my sister tracked me down well into the future, insisting that I bear it full witness. I was jerked back to that scene of violence when I saw the image of Tariq's bloody face and read about his beating. Pulled back into this memory of family violence, I kept experiencing an intense feeling of dread connected not only to my dad's violence but also to the current violence in Palestine. As I watched the atrocities unfold in Gaza, I felt frozen in a helpless witness role, forced to watch violence that was out of my control but for which I felt responsible.

Healing from Childhood Violence

My dad has been dead for over half my life now, but his violence lives in me, impacting how I inhabit my body, navigate intimacy, and even respond to the political world around me. While we often think of healing from childhood violence as separate from social justice work, in truth the two can be deeply intertwined.

When I was in my twenties, I refused to consciously acknowledge my dad's impact, telling myself he had nothing to do with my chronic insomnia, nightmares, or chronic pain. At some point on each day of his *yahrzeit* (יאָרצײַט), the anniversary of his death, I would feel nauseated, remember what day it was, and quickly try to forget what I had just remembered.

In my thirties, as I began reclaiming my Jewish identity, I started to observe his yahrzeit with a conscious remembrance. At Shabbat dinners with friends, I would describe the positive qualities that I inherited from my father—his work ethic, his wry sense of humor, and his love of cats. I thought this might help me "forgive" him, which is what we are often told we must do in order to heal and move on. As I dove deeper into my healing through body-based therapy, I realized that healing through automatic forgiveness was simply a way to bypass my feelings and rush to resolution without doing the hard work of confronting the pain that lived in me. I needed, instead, to truly mourn this double loss—the loss of an idealized father who would have protected instead of violated me, as well as the loss of my actual father.

By encouraging us to rush to forgiveness and offering strategies to numb our feelings, our culture often reinforces our own survival mechanisms, which encourage us to dissociate from traumatic experiences. But when we turn our backs on our pain, we also turn away from feeling our aliveness. As I began acknowledging how deeply impacted I was by my father, I started using his yahrzeit to grapple with the raw and deeply uncomfortable feeling of missing someone who had caused me and my family harm. Many years ago on my dad's yahrzeit, I came to the realization that my goal was not to forgive my dad's violence, but to uphold his dignity, even though he often disrespected mine. Extending his humanity back to him is a gift I continue to offer him from the present moment.

Until I turned and faced my father's violence, I felt haunted by it, unable to shake it, but also unable to fully feel it. When I dissociated from the episodes of violence we experienced as children, it was a brilliant survival technique that kept me from drowning in horror and helplessness. However, I still carried the terror in my muscles, tissues, and bones. Although my sister survived this violence, I couldn't protect her from being harmed. Because I was neither in a position to fight back nor to help her escape, the energy from these survival reactions became trapped inside me.

Confronting Israeli State Violence

My personal healing and political work collided during Israel's devastating assault on Gaza in the summer of 2014, which killed over two thousand Palestinians. Entire extended families were destroyed, nearly five hundred children were killed, and Gaza's infrastructure was decimated. It was the deadliest attack on Gaza until 2023.

During the summer of these attacks, I oscillated between numbness and painful flashbacks as I deepened into my somatic healing work. When the Israeli attacks began, I felt horrified but numb. I couldn't connect to my feelings about the violence being done in my name as a Jew. At other times a particularly violent image from Palestine would spin me into a sense of shame at being Jewish or directly into an episode from my childhood.

And while there are clearly huge differences between the experience of violence in my Jewish family and Israeli state violence against Palestinians, these forms of violence are also interconnected. As I mentioned earlier, when I was a kid, my grandmom used to advise me repeatedly that, while friends are nice, you can only count on your family. Being told as a child that I should never trust people outside the boundary of my family contributed to my isolation and reinforced the idea that it was normal and safe to live with an unpredictably violent father.

A parallel notion of safety is passed down in Jewish families and communities when we are told that the incredibly violent nation-state of Israel will keep us safe when anti-Jewish oppression arises. The state of Israel does not keep Jews safe. Its ongoing violent occupation of Palestine endangers both Palestinians and Israelis and encourages people everywhere to conflate Jews with oppressive behavior. It makes Israelis into occupiers and the self-proclaimed "Jewish State" synonymous with ethnic cleansing. Just as I was told that the boundaries of my family would keep me safe, Jews are told that the nation-state of Israel will keep "us" safe from external threats. We don't achieve some permanent state of safety by closing ourselves off from whoever gets defined as the Other. In both cases, the threat of violence is created inside the boundaries of the system itself.

Changing the Story

To break free from feeling numb and powerless around Gaza, I needed to confront my memories of being unable to prevent the violence I witnessed as a child. My younger self needed to see that there was a way out—I was no longer stuck in that timeless place of trauma.

My somatic practitioner, Gabriel, helped me travel back to that memory. Our somatic session began with bodywork to help me feel my way into the story held in my muscles and tissues. As I lay on the table, he contacted the band across my diaphragm, which began squeezing painfully toward my center. Gabriel moved us into the scene of trauma by describing that moment when my dad was kicking my sister. He described running over to my dad, yelling, "Get off her!" and then forcibly pushing my dad away from my sister. In response, I saw myself rise from the chair, run across the room to my sister, and put my arms around her.

My sister and I were both kneeling on the gold carpet, crying, and I was crying in the present. As I comforted her in this vision, I felt my diaphragm begin to loosen. Gabriel asked me to send the powerful love I held in my heart for my sister down into my diaphragm. As I streamed energy from my heart into the constricted band, my diaphragm began humming, vibrating, and opening. It was a relief to experience my love and care for my sister without my dad in between us. While I consciously knew that my dad's violence wasn't my fault, I still held the feeling inside me that it was.

In the next session, we worked on mobilizing the stuck energy that got trapped from not being able to fight back as a kid. I held up my arms with my elbows bent, and Gabriel stood over the table, meeting my hands with his own. He gave me some of his weight, and I pushed him away by straightening my arms and saying "no." I envisioned going over to my father and pushing him off of my sister. We did this several times until my arms were trembling with exhaustion and excitement. It felt like currents were running from my heart through my shoulders, down my arms, and into my tingling fingers.

In recreating these scenarios for me to connect with my sister and fight back against my dad, we engaged my imagination and muscles to help me complete the actions that were stuck in my body. I finally viscerally understood that the violence wasn't my fault; I didn't cause it, and I couldn't stop it at that time. This is the brilliance of bodywork; it sidesteps our defenses. I had talked about this incident many times before, and I logically knew that my dad's violence wasn't my fault. Many friends and therapists had affirmed that for me, yet part of me still felt that it was. My younger parts held onto that shame as a protective mechanism until they experienced someone stepping in and stopping the violence. This allowed me to feel how powerless I was in that situation, which paradoxically freed up my energy to complete the actions of fighting back and fleeing.

The shame had a protective function; it helped me access a sense of agency in a violent situation where I actually had very little. It prevented me from feeling the full extent of my helplessness that would have overwhelmed me as a child. If some part of me held that it was my fault, there was always the chance that if I just did something different, I could stop the violence. In returning to the past through bodywork, I was able to rescue that young part of me who felt ashamed, responsible, and held hostage by that violent memory. Moving out of the frozen horror from my past allowed me to show up and speak out against Israel's current violence.

Activism and Ritual as Collective Healing

Fighting Israel's ongoing violent oppression of Palestinians is not only politically crucial, but also imperative for our healing because it breaks the cycle of collective traumatic violence we have inherited and pulls us out of a passive victim or witness stance. Connecting with our own histories of trauma and resilience, we can refuse to let violence happen in our names. We can only reassert our full humanity when we fight for the dignity of all people, including most emphatically the Palestinian people.

During the summer of 2014, I helped organize and participate in acts of civil disobedience and acts of ritual, to protest the Israeli attacks on Gaza and commemorate the Palestinian victims of these attacks. Our Seattle chapter of JVP planned a die-in at Boeing, a major supplier of weapons to the Israel Defense Forces, to draw attention to Boeing's profits from Israeli war crimes. The plan was for nine activists, locked together, to lie down and block the entrance to Boeing while fifty others would lie down on the sidewalk in front of them wearing black T-shirts that said "Shut down Israel's war machine."

At preparation meetings, I led us in a somatic centering practice to cultivate our felt sense of connection to each other and to our collective purpose. After we centered, each of us shared a personal commitment that brought us to this work. People shared moving stories about ancestors and social movement elders that helped shape their commitments. As a group, we created a collective kavanah for the direct action: to bring public attention to the companies benefiting from these attacks on Palestinians. On the morning of the protest at five AM in the park where we gathered, I led one final centering practice to help us prepare for the action.

As we gathered outside the Boeing entrance to quickly choreograph our action, many of us found it helpful to feel our individual and collective purpose for being there. It felt especially important for people who were locked down, lying on the pavement under a hot sun surrounded by police in riot gear, to feel their commitment in their bodies. When we risk getting arrested or encountering violence, we find our courage with and from each other and in our embodied convictions.

Later in the protest, my friend and I recited the Mourner's Kaddish and read the names of over one thousand Palestinians killed since the attacks on Gaza began. Western media wasn't even reporting the names of Palestinians who died, so it felt particularly important to name and honor each precious life. When I looked down at the bodies lying on the ground and heard the names being read, I started crying because I finally felt the enormity of my grief and the power embodied in this small gesture of commemoration. I don't think I could have accessed this grief if I hadn't done bodywork healing around the violence from my childhood.

As we were preparing for the action, I was mostly fueled by anger over the sickening violence taking place against Palestinians in Gaza. Anger at injustice is so important; it mobilizes us into action. However, we all know righteously angry people in social justice movements who alienate everybody around them. There's so much in our world that is enraging, but when we don't have a way to process grief and heartbreak along with the rage, we get stuck in a fight response that can make us turn against each other. We need ritual spaces both inside and outside of our actions to help us access the full range of our emotions.

That summer, through bodywork and collective action I learned that the power of healing is not linear. This allowed me to move back in time, so that I could tend to my relationship with my dad and acknowledge his humanity. It is only through finding compassion for my dad—and realizing that he must have endured some harm that contributed to his violence—that I am able to embrace the fullness of my own humanity, including the part of my father that lives inside me. I am not only a victim, but a human with the capacity to prevent, fight, and cause harm. This is as true for me as an individual as it is for my Jewish people. Although as Jews, we have been treated as less than human at various times and places, we can and must refuse to dehumanize others.

CHAPTER 8

HEALING FROM SHAME

*Shame is the lie someone told you about yourself.**

—ANAÏS NIN

Shame—that sense that something is irreparably wrong with us—is an inevitable result of the forces of oppression, internalized oppression, and sometimes privilege.† It is a stultifying feeling that we *are* inherently wrong, defective, or unworthy. Whenever there has been a violation of our dignity and an attack on our wholeness—on the individual, collective or systemic level—we experience shame.

Because shame tells us that something is wrong with us, the most common reaction to that feeling is to disconnect, withdraw, and hide from others so that they can't see our defects. We experience shame like quicksand; with every attempt to find solid footing, we sink deeper in the muck. This makes it difficult, if not impossible, for us to be present in our relationships. Mired in shame, we withdraw and hide who we really are. We believe that if people saw our true selves, nobody would ever want to be around

---

* This quote is attributed to Nin, but it is unclear whether she said these exact words.

† Internalized oppression means that we accept and internalize the negative stereotypes, beliefs, and attitudes directed toward us, often based on our identity.

us. Shame is deeply painful and confusing; we often carry the shame of previous generations and the shame of those who have harmed us. Because shame attaches itself to any dehumanizing impact, it can be difficult to untangle what is truly ours and which parts of shame rightfully belong to the people around us.

Shame is fundamentally immobilizing and isolating. When we feel shame about something we have done, we tend to freeze, withdraw, and tighten to hide the shameful parts of us. Shame lives in contractions and makes it impossible for us to show up well relationally. If we do bear some responsibility for causing harm or acting outside of our integrity, we need to transform shame into its less charged state—which is guilt—so that we can make repair. Guilt suggests that we *did* something wrong, not that we *are* wrong. From a place of guilt, we can engage with *t'shuvah* (תשובה), the process of apologizing, making amends, and taking new actions from a centered place of accountability. The next chapter will go into more detail about the process of t'shuvah, but healing shame prepares us for that process because it helps us clarify to whom we are accountable, and which pieces of the shame need to be returned to those people and systems who have harmed us.

As an embodied experience, shame plays a protective role by covering up and contracting over the deep emotions that seem too overwhelming for us to face. When we feel shame, we tend to tighten, get heavy, and collapse inward. We might contract our throat, chest, and belly, while experiencing a sense of heaviness in our pelvis or legs, like we are sinking into the ground. Our shoulders round forward, we drop our heads, and we collapse our spine.

I learned about shame in generative somatics with the helpful framing of a trampoline metaphor. The idea is that our shame-based beliefs, which include internal narratives, stereotypes, and stories, are bouncing us around on top of a trampoline. We end up stuck in repetitive beliefs that tell us we are bad, ugly, stupid, too much, too little, disgusting, etc. We may logically know that these things are not true, but part of us feels like they are absolutely true. As we are bouncing around in these beliefs, we feel increasingly unworthy of connection, and we get more tightly contracted and withdrawn.

From this place, we can tip into hopelessness, or we might take on a safety shape that tells us we just need to try harder not to be these things. If that's not possible, then we try harder to hide these things about ourselves. Shame always pulls our attention inward, so that our lives get smaller and more isolated as we bounce around on the trampoline of self-judgment.

Because we are stuck on top of the trampoline, shame keeps us from noticing what is just underneath: a roiling river of intense responses to trauma that bring us closer to the experience of death. These include helplessness, despair, terror, deep rage, irrecoverable grief, deep isolation, and fear of annihilation. These emotions and experiences overwhelm us because they feel as powerful as river rapids that threaten to pull us under. Shame protects us from the rapids by contracting us up and away from their turbulence and diverting our attention to the negative beliefs on *top* of the trampoline. However, like all protective mechanisms, shame keeps us from feeling and integrating all that is churning *underneath* the trampoline.

We may be confused to learn that there's something harder to feel than shame; shame feels bad enough. The story that something is deeply wrong with us is immensely painful and immobilizing. However, this narrative bestows upon us a sense of agency. If everything we experience results from being bad or wrong, then there's always a chance that if we just tried harder or did something better or differently, we wouldn't experience so much pain. It makes us feel hopeless to acknowledge that in some circumstances, we were powerless to stop what was happening to us. To admit this is deeply vulnerable. When we frame it as our fault, we gain a sense of control.

Blending with Shame

Given the power that shame holds over us, healing shame takes time and is broken into four phases: blending with shame, fighting for our dignity, finding centered accountability, and cultivating self-forgiveness. We need to have already engaged with some healing work, including having developed our kavanah, built a sense of trust in our ability to assess safety, and experienced opening through bodywork. Before we begin the process of healing shame, we also need to understand how shame works as a protective mechanism, and how social structures and systems of oppression can encourage shame and reinforce social hierarchies.

Learning to understand the context of our shame includes learning how we hold the shame of those who caused us harm in various contexts, ranging from personal to systemic abuse. People with power will always blame the victims, so we can end up internalizing their oppressive beliefs about ourselves. For example, David Ben-Gurion, a central proponent of Zionism and the first Israeli Prime Minister, describes feeling ashamed of his fellow Jews, just two weeks before the start of World War II. He wrote, "We are choking with shame about what is happening . . . that Jews are not daring to fight back. We do not belong to that Jewish people. . . . We do not wish to be such Jews."[1] He internalized the shame of violent antisemitism and blamed its victims for not fighting back. At that moment in time, it would have been too painful for him to acknowledge that Jews were subject to systemic violence against which they had no power.

We often have to develop our analysis and understanding about what is and isn't our fault before we work with the parts of ourselves that *feel* like something is our fault. Many of our shameful beliefs about ourselves originate in the oppressive beliefs of the culture surrounding us. We aren't trying to reason our way out of shame, but it can be helpful to understand how shame creates confusion about what is truly ours to claim. Before we can take responsibility for our actions, we need to hand back the shame that rightfully belongs to the people and systems that caused us harm.

Just as we worked to blend with safety shapes in our bodies so that they feel affirmed and to loosen their hold, we also blend with the contractions of shame. Most of us feel quite alone in our shame stories because shame has us hiding who we think we really are. Unfortunately, we can't just think ourselves out of shame, and it can actually be counterproductive for other people to try and negate it for us. From my time as a somatic practitioner, I've learned that arguing against a client's shame stories by saying things like "That's not true," or "There's nothing wrong with you" can make the client feel more isolated. They start to believe that we just can't see what is truly wrong with them, and they withdraw deeper inside. Shame will exert its grip even tighter, which leads to more contraction and isolation.

This is where the blend comes in. As a practitioner, I blend with my client's shame stories not because they are true, but because we know that contractions, including shame, only soften when we meet them on their own terms with acknowledgment and affirmation. Once we have established a client's shame story—what is bad, shameful, or unlovable about them—we reflect this story back to them. We usually position ourselves so that we are side by side and not face to face in this practice because shame doesn't like to be stared at. We will use their exact words by saying, for example, "You're bad," "You're harmful," "You are ugly," or "You are unlovable."

Through this process of affirmation and blending, the shame tends to slowly relax its hold. As we check in with clients about their emotions and sensations, we are trying to connect with the deeper emotions that lie beneath the shame contraction. Oftentimes these deeper emotions appear as impulses toward movement in the client's body, such as an urge to shake or kick. We can encourage clients to follow these impulses by shaking or stomping to start moving that energy. With a little support, this bottled-up energy can start to move through us. When we can relax some of the contractions around these enormous feelings, they start to move, release, and integrate.

Blending with Assimilation

Many of my Jewish clients who live inside Christian-dominated cultures, such as the United States, have shame about being Jewish because of antisemitism. This can show up as feeling too Jewish, too loud, too pushy, too dominating, too controlling, and too cheap, among other stereotypes. This can also show up as not feeling Jewish enough because we don't know Hebrew prayers or blessings, or information about holidays, songs, or rituals. Sometimes we flip from feeling too Jewish in Christian contexts to feeling not Jewish enough in predominantly Jewish contexts. Mizrahi and Sephardi Jews and other Jews of color might have an added layer of feeling as if they are the wrong kind of Jews because they have to navigate both antisemitism in mainstream Christian hegemonic culture and racism within Jewish communities.

For example, I worked with a client named Leo, a Jewish cis man, around his shame related to assimilation and Ashkenazi-centrism. His mother was Ashkenazi and his father was Mizrahi with roots in Iran. He grew up in a predominantly white Christian neighborhood in the South where his parents mostly wanted him and his younger sister to fit in. They told them it was okay to tell people that he was Jewish, but that maybe it shouldn't be the first thing he told them. His father spoke very little about originally being from Iran, and Leo rarely saw his father or relatives from that side of the family after his parents split up when he was ten. Leo experienced both overt and subtle antisemitism and racism growing up and didn't have anyone in his family or any Mizrahi Jewish community to help him hold this.

When he came to see me, he had recently joined a predominantly Ashkenazi Jewish congregation, but felt like his shame stories were getting in the way of connecting during services. He worried about appearing to be a "fake Jew" or "the wrong kind of Jew" because he was Mizrahi and anti-Zionist, and because he didn't know the prayers, songs, or blessings. He would often freeze during services, particularly during Hebrew prayers or songs, which made them hard to learn. Whenever a song or prayer began, Leo's breath got shallow, his vision narrowed, and his chest contracted. He would start to ruminate about his lack of Jewish knowledge in general, and whether his Mizrahi ancestors would have prayed this way, which made it hard to relax or connect with the other congregants. His anti-Zionist politics compounded his feeling of being an outsider in the congregation.

Before we began the healing shame process, we had already worked with a kavanah about reclaiming his Mizrahi Jewish identity and had done work on rebuilding his sense of trust and belonging. We decided to do a piece of work around the shame he had internalized from assimilation and racism. We began with a conversation about some of the historical forces that led to assimilation in his family. I like to frame assimilation into Christian-dominated culture as one of the quintessential Jewish experiences in the United States, because so many Jews grow up without a Jewish education or access to Jewish culture. Assimilation was a wise strategy that our ancestors used to protect their safety and dignity. Leo also faced racism within the wider culture and his Jewish community. I wanted him to hear that although he felt ashamed of the effects of assimilation, it wasn't his fault or his family's fault that they used this strategy to stay safe.

Seated next to Leo with my chair tilted slightly toward him, I began blending with Leo's shame story by saying, "You're a fraud, you have the wrong politics; you don't know your own history; you're not really Jewish—that's why you're an anti-Zionist, you hate yourself." After the first round, we noticed that he hardened even more; his face felt stiff, and he was sitting with a rigid spine and puffed-up chest. His first response had been a freeze/fight; he became still and then defended himself against the words. For the second round, we decided that I should use a gentler, more matter-of-fact tone to reflect his shame story. As I repeated the words of the shame story, Leo started to relax his face and his shoulders, which began softly shuddering, and he reported feeling a trickling sensation down the back of his throat, which he associated with the relief of someone saying out loud the words that were often spinning in his head.

When I directed Leo to drop his attention into what was even harder to feel than the shame itself, he described noticing a feeling of dread under his ribs. I asked him to take some breaths into the feeling, and he started to feel trapped and helpless. To work with the feelings underneath the trampoline, I had him lie down on the table, so that his energy could start to move down through the lower half of his body. After he took some deeper breaths, his throat started to seize up, and he reported feeling like he was being strangled. When I asked him to vocalize a "hahhh" sound on every exhale, his voice came out in a staccato crackle, and his cheeks began to flush.

As his face heated up, Leo felt like it was dangerous to make noise, and he experienced a burning sensation in his chest and throat. The rest of his body felt still and brittle. Two images arose. One was of his younger sister, cowering in the bathroom wedged between the toilet and the tub to hide from their father, who was yelling. The other was a blurry image of a dark-haired woman in a tent being forcibly restrained. Leo experienced both situations simultaneously: he was horrified that he couldn't help his sister or this woman.

To give the terror more room to move below the contraction in his neck, we worked to open and soften the space around his collarbones and upper ribs. He started to make a short staccato sound that came from the back of his throat and turned into a hoarse scream. As he continued screaming on his exhales, surges of energy shot down his legs, which began to twitch. I held up a pillow so that Leo could kick his legs into the pillow as he screamed. Sweating profusely, he screamed and kicked for several minutes, until he became exhausted, and then he slowly wept. The vibrations in his body started to subside, and he was able to take some deeper breaths.

In our debrief, Leo was surprised by how much terror he was able to feel from his experiences of powerlessness as a child and how it intersected with historical terror about ancestral trauma. Leo recognized that claiming his Mizrahi Jewish identity felt like a betrayal of his sister, who wanted nothing to do with being a Mizrahi Jew because she associated it with their abusive father. Being visibly Jewish and attending services was inherently scary for Leo, given his family history. His shame about not feeling Jewish enough was covering up this helpless terror from his childhood and continued fear about what it meant to claim a visible Jewish identity in his family. The shame story of assimilation was protecting him from feeling this hopeless terror. With this blend, the shame had at last started to shake loose.

Fighting for Our Dignity

After the shame blend, we mobilize the energy we generated from the blend into a fight for our dignity, so that we don't inadvertently slide back into more shame. Fighting for our inherent dignity in relationship with others is the opposite of feeling collapsed under shame. One way we practice fighting for our dignity is to engage martial arts and do forearm strikes with each other against Thai pads—large, rectangular pads we hold up to absorb the blows. When we do this, we can experience the physicality of fighting for ourselves and our communities. When I do this practice and hold the pads up for clients, I ask them to look me in the eyes as they hit the pads, so that they can feel seen, witnessed, and supported in their power. This act of intimacy allows us to experience our strength and connections at the same time.

After we blended with the shame of assimilation, Leo and I had a conversation about how he wanted to frame his fight. He told me he would be fighting *for* Mizrahi Jewish belonging, for his sister, for his ancestors, for a free Palestine, and for a liberated Jewishness. He was saying no or fighting *against* shame about assimilation, not feeling like the right kind of Jew, and fear of being seen in his full Jewishness. He practiced striking from his center, so that he could put his full power behind his kavanot, his boundaries, his yeses, and his nos.

As he struck the pads and yelled, he developed a good rhythm of increasing his energy and striking from his center. When he yelled "yes" or "no" on impact, I reminded him what he was fighting for by saying, for example, "yes to Jewish Mizrahi belonging" or "no to shame." Leo kept looking at the pads during his strikes. No matter what I said, he only maintained eye contact for a moment, and then averted his gaze. He told me that it felt embarrassing and vulnerable to be seen in this fight. We decided to do one round of striking in which he got to avert his gaze and notice how it felt. Leo reported feeling strong, but in a very singular focused way because he blocked out seeing or even hearing me. In the next round, he looked at me for about half the strikes, and this felt vulnerable but tolerable. We recognized that it was overwhelming for him to hear my affirmations and look at me at the same time. In the next round, I didn't say anything, and he was able to maintain eye contact for the majority of his strikes, and this allowed him to feel seen by me in his determination and strength.

Pads generate an enormous amount of energy: Leo's arms and legs were vibrating with liveliness; his face was red, animated, and shiny with sweat; and his eyes were bright and relaxed. He couldn't remember ever feeling so much energy running through his body, and it felt invigorating. I encouraged him to shake his limbs and notice that the ground was still holding him. He shook his head, shoulders, entire torso, and each arm. Then he stomped each leg to allow more of his energy to be absorbed into the earth. When I asked him what felt possible in his life from this powerful state,

Leo told me it was possible to love himself as a Mizrahi Jew and to love his people. I felt a quickening pulse of aliveness in me as I witnessed him in his full power.

Finding Centered Accountability

After fighting for our dignity, we explore how to find a centered and accountable response to our actions and histories. Because shame distorts our sense of responsibility, making it hard to determine what is and isn't our fault, we need to experience what a centered response feels like in our bodies.

It's impossible to overstate how much our carceral system of confinement, punishment, and control over people impacts how we engage with accountability. We live inside systems that shame, blame, and discipline people, instead of approaching harm with the possibility of repair and transformation. These systems encourage us to judge people as either "guilty" or "innocent," and then write the "guilty" people off as inherently unworthy. As individuals and communities, we internalize these binary systems of judgment, which make very little room to hold the breadth and complexity of people's lives.

In this process of discerning what is and is not our responsibility, shame often propels us into one of two automatic reactions: over-accountability—feeling like everything is our fault, and under-accountability—feeling like nothing is our fault or responsibility. When we tilt into over-accountability, we take responsibility for things that either were someone else's fault or have little or nothing to do with our actions. For example, when I felt responsible for not saving my sister, or when Leo felt responsible for not saving his sister, we were both taking on the shame that rightfully belonged to our parents. We became over-accountable for violence and abuse that we could not have stopped as children. Survivors and anyone targeted by oppression can lapse into over-accountability because we carry the shame of our abusers or abusive systems. Over-accountability can also show up as an immobilizing shame about privilege that makes us feel bad but doesn't spur changes in our behavior. For example, we see this in hand-wringing about privilege that isn't accompanied by any attempts to change the system of domination.

Sometimes our fear of getting stuck in the quicksand of shame moves us toward an automatic response of under-accountability, which means that we refuse to take responsibility for something we might have done by denying, minimizing, or ignoring our impact. Because shame is so painful, we will often do anything we can to avoid accountability, in order to avoid feeling shame. It's hard to take responsibility when we have internalized the carceral logic that if we caused harm, we are "guilty" and therefore unworthy. Systemic privilege also trains those of us in dominant positions of power to be under-accountable about our impact. Many of us flip between over-accountability and under-accountability, which are both automatic reactions that pull us away from a centered assessment of our impact.

Finding centered accountability as an embodied practice allows us to learn what it feels like in our bodies to respond to our impact from a centered place that is neither over- nor under-accountable. Centered accountability can be hard to define because each of us will experience our embodiment of accountability differently, but it means taking responsibility for our impact—intended or unintended—on each other, the world, and ourselves. This impact might or might not have caused harm.

We use the "grab, center, face" practice to learn how over-, under-, and centered accountability show up for each of us. In working with Leo, we wanted to find a centered response to the impact of assimilation on Leo's life. For the first round, he practiced an over-accountable reaction. I grabbed Leo's wrist and said, "You denied your Mizrahi Jewishness." After the grab, he felt all his attention and energy come through his eyes and land on me. He couldn't feel anything below his neck, and he vacated the back of his body. His first impulse was to apologize for his denial. His spine collapsed, and the narrative became, "I must hate myself."

When we practiced the under-accountable response, the front of his face froze, he contracted his chest and stared off into the distance. He couldn't really feel my presence at all, and his narrative became one of denial. He thought, "Why are they trying to force me to think about that? I will never admit to having done that," and he felt angry with me for bringing it up.

To practice centered accountability, I did the grab again, and Leo first reacted with under-accountability. After noticing the contraction, anger, and dismissiveness he felt, he consciously invited his breath to deepen. As his breath sank lower in his body, he lengthened his spine and felt the dignity of his family's survival strategies. In widening across the span of his hip bones, he remembered his kavanah around belonging. At his back, he felt more acceptance of the history of assimilation as a wise response to antisemitic violence, and in front of him, he oriented to a future of belonging in Jewish community.

Once Leo had recentered himself in his three-dimensionality and his kavanah, he turned to face me and the grab of having denied his Jewishness. From a sturdy place of neither collapse nor rigid defensiveness, he was able to experience what centered accountability felt like in his sensations and emotions. Feeling more weighted, connected to the earth, and expansive in his length and width, he noticed that he didn't need to pull away from connection or shrink his own dignity in facing his own behavior. He recognized that a centered response might be simply to acknowledge that he had sometimes hid his Jewishness, and that there were good reasons for it. The narrative became: "I have sometimes denied my Jewishness because of my family's response to antisemitism and because of racism inside Jewish communities. I'm working on reclaiming my Mizrahi Jewish identity." He also began to explore the possibility that it wasn't his fault that his sister was abused.

Finding centered accountability means that we find a way to be accountable, without giving up our dignity or refusing to acknowledge our impact if we have harmed others. When we come back to our center and our kavanot, we can find the resource to face the grab from a place of wisdom in our bodies. In Leo's case, he had internalized the lies of shame he was told about his own worthiness in both a Christian-dominated mainstream culture and an Ashkenazi-centric Jewish culture. He also internalized responsibility for his father's abuse and was causing harm to himself by taking on too much responsibility.

If he had caused harm to someone else, he would most likely need to do quite a bit more practice to find a centered and accountable response. Finding centered accountability when we cause harm to others means listening to the people we have harmed and seeking outside counsel from respected peers and mentors. As Jews healing from Zionism, we are also continuously grappling with what a centered and accountable response is to the actions being taken by the state of Israel in the name of all Jews.

Healing from shame directs us toward t'shuvah, or making amends, as we will explore in the next chapter. Making amends also requires many more actions, including gaining perspective by asking trusted people to give their feedback, and tending to the emotional and somatic experience that led us to cause harm in the first place. Fundamentally a centered and accountable response upholds our own and others' dignity as we determine what we are and are not responsible for.

Cultivating Self-Forgiveness

The last phase of healing shame is learning to embody self-forgiveness. This comes last because we have to do all the other work of healing shame, including finding centered accountability, before we arrive here. We don't want to bypass accountability for ourselves or others by starting out with forgiveness. On the other hand, we do want to develop a grounded ability to forgive ourselves and others when repair is made. Not having the ability to choose forgiveness of ourselves and others after harm has been repaired is a form of stagnation and contraction that can stifle our own aliveness.

Shame can make us feel like we are fundamentally unforgivable or encourage us to set up unrealistic conditions that we must meet to be forgivable. When I practiced with Leo, we sat side by side, and I asked him to center inside his essential dignity and worth. He took some deep breaths and softened and widened across his cheekbones, shoulders, diaphragm, and hips. I asked, "What are you forgivable for?" He responded, "I am forgivable even if I denied my Mizrahi Jewishness." I repeated back, "You are forgivable even if you denied your Mizrahi Jewishness."

We repeated this protocol with different statements, including "even if I couldn't save my sister," "even if I can't read Hebrew," and "even if I freeze during services." We kept checking in to make sure he could allow the words to land somewhere inside him, so that he could start to feel the possibility of being forgivable. Leo experienced some melting of the contractions around his throat and heart along with the sense that he might be able to forgive himself one day. Because forgiving ourselves takes time, the homework that goes with this practice is to write out these statements on slips of paper and then place them in a special container. For a set amount of time, we can take out the slips of paper once a day and read them out loud to ourselves. These declarations help strengthen the muscle of forgivability, so that we feel less caught up in our self-judgment.

Over time, as Leo has continued to reach for Jewish community and learning, he gets stuck in the muck of shame much less frequently, and he is quicker to ask for a hand from others to help pull himself out. Having sought out more Iranian-Jewish community, he is learning about this part of his ancestry. He recognized how he has inherited a safety shape of assimilation in response to antisemitism, as well as racism within the Jewish community, and he also knows how to allow that shape to soften. These shame stories haven't entirely disappeared, but they come up much less frequently and with less intensity.

The Collective Shame of Historical Wounds

Sometimes when we carry shame from causing harm, both individually and collectively, we are also carrying what is known as a *moral injury.* Susan Raffo writes about this concept, which she describes as "an injury to your values or conscience when you have witnessed, perpetrated, or failed to prevent an act that compromises your values or morals."[2] The concept of moral injury was developed to address the complexity of post-traumatic stress disorder (PTSD) in military veterans who may have participated in actions or followed orders that betrayed their own beliefs. When we experience the pain and confusion of a moral injury, we tend to justify the harm we caused—which, as Raffo describes, "only increases the pain, isolates the victim, and freezes the trauma into a repeat loop."[3] This is a version of under-accountability. The fear of feeling ashamed for having caused, enabled, or benefited from harm results in a contraction and hardening, which perpetuates more harm.

Raffo describes the founding of this country through settler colonialism and slavery as a moral injury. Generations of US citizens hold this injury from these harms, but many of us with racial and economic privilege refuse to acknowledge its impact on our collective shape. Instead, we turn to "patriotism" to justify this legacy of violence. Raffo describes how this defensive system works in our bodies as a "freeze and control" around the moral injury because "the body needs to close it off in order to move along."[4] In other words, we seal up the injury, numb ourselves so that we don't feel the pain, and never stop to confront the harm. As a result, we keep encoding the systems of domination into our cultures.

We are so deeply afraid to face the moral injuries of these original wounds because we don't want to get mired in shame. Many of us with privilege believe that to acknowledge the harm caused by our ancestors means to admit that they (and therefore we) were or are inherently bad or harmful. The elevated levels of resistance and reactivity in our culture around facing the past come from a fear that the worthiness of our existence is at stake. As I described in chapter 4, we fall into binary thinking that our ancestors were either "good" or "bad," instead of complicated people struggling to survive within cultures of domination.

Like slavery and colonialism, Zionism is a moral injury that attempted to disguise itself as a moral good. In 1901, the Jewish National Fund (JNF), created to purchase land in historic Palestine for the exclusive settlement of Jewish immigrants to the area, declared that their mission was to "redeem the land."[5] Early leaders of the JNF established the tradition, still alive today, of Jewish children from over forty countries collecting money in blue *tzedakah* (צדקה), ("charity" or "justice") boxes that went toward planting European pine trees "to make the desert bloom" in Palestine.[6]

But the land was not empty, nor was it a barren desert in need of redemption. It was already flourishing with olive trees, plants, animals, and people whose livelihoods had been intertwined with the land for centuries. Planting pine trees and uprooting indigenous olive trees was and is a key strategy of staking claim to Palestinian land and erasing its history. After razing Palestinian villages in 1948, the JNF literally covered up the remains of the villages by propagating pine trees, which were chosen for their fast growth.[7]

Pine trees also deposit acidic needles on the ground, which eradicate most smaller plants and undergrowth between the trees, making the land unusable for Palestinian shepherds. The pine trees, unlike olive trees, have been less resistant to fires, which explains why Israel has been plagued by forest fires over the years.

In *The Ethnic Cleansing of Palestine*, Ilan Pappe describes how native trees sometimes return in surprising ways in the JNF forests planted over Palestinian villages. At the site of the village of Al-Mujaydil, former residents visiting nearly sixty years later found that some of the pine trees had literally split in two, and in the middle of their broken trunks, olive trees had "popped up in defiance of the alien flora planted over them fifty-six years ago."[8] Olive trees are a symbol of Palestinian resistance and resilience.

The start of the 2023 assault on Gaza coincided with the autumn olive harvest, but the Israeli military cut off West Bank farmers' access to their trees while allowing settlers to steal the olives and destroy the trees. In Gaza farmers were cut off from their orchards, many of which were burned by missiles and tank shells. Nearly half of all cultivated land in the occupied West Bank and Gaza had more than 10 million olive trees, and around 100,000 Palestinian families relied on these trees as a source of income.[9] Yet because Israel cut off access to fuel and gas for stoves, many Palestinians were forced to cut branches off their trees to use them for firewood in order to survive. As Al Jazeera reported, people found this task demoralizing because the trees represent so much more than a livelihood for Palestinians. One woman in Gaza, Ahlam Saqr, cried when her sons cut down the trees. She explains, "I used to tell everyone that my trees have been my life companions. They've been there as I raised my children here; they've seen all the stages of our lives."[10]

The continued high level of defensiveness and reactivity in Jewish communities around Zionism arises from our attempts to avoid shame. To name the moral injury at the very foundation of the Israeli state feels akin to admitting that we are an immoral people. Even when we disagree with Zionism's conflation of the "Jewish" state with the Jewish people, it often worms its way into our psyches. It feels too threatening to our dignity as a people to acknowledge the injury, so we hold onto the moral justifications into which we have been indoctrinated. When Jews collected money in those blue boxes, we thought we were contributing to something healing for the people and land—who doesn't love trees? It is devastating to find out that we were contributing to the destruction of the land and the people who belong to it.

Facing the Nakba

In order to stop the ongoing state violence in both the US and Palestine, we must attend to the original wounds of these moral injuries. I went through a long period of denial on my own journey to face the Nakba because I had only a tenuous connection to my Jewish identity. I was afraid of stirring up a deep shame that would make it even harder to feel connected to myself and other Jews.

When I was a kid, I remember hearing my parents describe Palestinian leader Yasser Arafat, chairman of the Palestine Liberation Organization (PLO) from 1969 to 2004, as a "terrorist." Even though we had very little relationship to Judaism, let alone Zionism, I also heard that "they" were trying to push "us" into the sea as though Palestinian resistance to colonization was equivalent to hating all Jews.* I didn't really understand what the phrase meant, but this racist idea lodged itself in my brain: that some people in the Middle East wanted "us" to die. This idea got reinforced when I started dating my first boyfriend, a Turkish immigrant. My parents made snide comments about how I was dating an "Arab," and that neither of us understood our histories.

Many years later, when I was a graduate student in transnational feminist studies, I read Edward Said's The Question of Palestine. I remember feeling activated every time Said characterized Israeli Jews as oppressors. Because I wasn't rooted inside my Jewishness, it felt destabilizing to hear about Jews misusing power. As a graduate student, I loved Said's other

---

* This statement might originate from a 1967 Israeli media campaign. See Moshe Shemesh, "Did Shuqayri Call for 'Throwing the Jews into the Sea?'" Israel Studies 8 (3), (Fall 2003): 70.

book, *Orientalism*, and I had a cognitive framework for understanding set-tler colonialism, but I literally couldn't make sense of his argument about Palestine. I just kept thinking, "He's saying that Jews are oppressors, but I only heard stories in my family of Jews being oppressed." Instead of trying to learn more, I shut the book and moved on to other things. Mind you, I was literally studying race, racism, and US identity in the era of trans-nationalism, but I somehow managed to avoid Palestine. I experienced an automatic reaction of under-accountability, and I chose to avert my gaze.

Finally, in my thirties after feeling more rooted in Jewish community, I dove into learning about the history of Zionism with a group of queer Jews. With a supportive community to hold the emotions that arose, I finally faced the horrifying history of the Nakba, which contradicted everything I was told growing up. While I had been taught that Palestinians volun-tarily abandoned their homes in 1948 and only wanted to come back to dis-place Jews, I later learned that Jewish forces inflicted widespread terror that forced Palestinians out of their homes. In March 1948, David Ben-Gurion implemented the strategy of Plan Dalet, which declared the intention to eth-nically cleanse as much of Palestine as possible to control as much land as possible with the least number of Palestinians left on the land.[11]

To accomplish this task, Jewish military forces, essentially terrorist orga-nizations, were told to carry out this campaign in the following manner: "Either by destroying villages (by setting fire to them, by blowing them up, and by planting mines in their debris)" or by "encirclement of the villages, conducting a search inside them. In case of resistance, the armed forces must be wiped out and the population expelled outside the borders of the state."[12] As this violent colonial strategy was implemented, these militias committed many massacres, including in the village of Deir Yassin on April 9, 1948, where more than one hundred Palestinian village residents, most of them unarmed, were murdered. Atrocities like this terrorized the Pales-tinian population and encouraged flight from the surrounding villages.[13] When I first read about these massacres, I felt nauseous. I couldn't under-stand why this history was told to me as if we were the victims.

Once I learned about Israel's violent origin story, I started to wonder about what other lies I had been told. In another stunning reversal, I found out that the notion that "they" wanted to "push us into the sea" was literally what Jewish terrorist organizations did to Palestinians. When I read Ilan Pappe's *The Ethnic Cleansing of Palestine*, I learned that many Palestinians were pushed into the sea during the ethnic cleansing of Haifa. The largest Jewish militia, the Haganah, terrorized Palestinian neighborhoods with gunfire until inhabitants rushed to the harbor to escape. "Men stepped on their friends and women on their own children," Pappe writes.[14] He also describes how "the boats in the port were soon filled with living cargo. The overcrowding in them was horrible. Many turned over and sank with all their passengers."[15]

This tactic of oppressing and dispossessing a population and then treating them as a threat to justify their continued oppression is a state tactic used against communities in both the US and Palestine. In the aftermath of the police killings of Michael Brown, Eric Garner, and countless other Black people, officials and the media portrayed these men as "thugs" and "criminals" to justify their murders. As Nadia Barhoum, a researcher at UC Berkeley, argues in "Rhetoric of Racism, from Ferguson to Palestine," the media promotes the fear and bias built into the nation-building project of dispossession.[16] Whipping up fear is meant to drown out any empathy and encourage people to condone state violence as protection from the imagined threat of the "racialized other."[17] While Black people are equated with "thugs," Palestinians are often equated with Hamas or "terrorists," "the Palestinian equivalent of 'thug,' bearing its own set of racist stereotypes."[18]

Once I turned and faced the Nakba, the catastrophe of ethnic cleansing that began in 1948, I started to realize how Zionism and the supposed threat of the Palestinian "other" permeated my consciousness as a kid even though I felt disconnected from my Jewishness. My family gave me the impression that Israel was a benevolent Jewish relative—a precarious refugee from antisemitism who needed help defending herself against the terrorists who surrounded her. Any criticism of her was portrayed as an attack on all Jewish people, like the many attacks throughout our history as a people.

The ongoing Nakba continues to wreak havoc, killing and displacing Palestinians. When Israel annexed the West Bank and Gaza Strip in 1967,

Israel displaced close to 300,000 more Palestinians.[19] Between 1967 and 1994, Israel revoked the citizenship of close to 250,000 Palestinians by refusing to allow Palestinians from the West Bank and Gaza Strip to leave for extended periods of time.[20] Since 2005, according to Badil Resource Center for Palestinian Residency and Refugee Rights, almost 12,000 Palestinians in the West Bank and East Jerusalem have watched the Israeli government demolish their homes.[21] And, as I write this, over 40,000 Palestinians in Gaza have been killed and 62 percent of all homes destroyed in the Gaza Strip.[22]

I couldn't confront my shame over the Nakba on my own. Most anti-Zionists choose to grapple with the Nakba at some point in their politicization. I'm more than a little embarrassed that it took me so long. For those of us who inherited Zionism through our families, we often get politicized during one of Israel's military operations, which kills and injures hundreds or even thousands of Palestinians. Countless Jews are being politicized right now around the genocide in Gaza that began in the fall of 2023. The incontestable and wildly disproportionate violence is shaking some of us out of the complacency instilled by Zionist propaganda. When we recenter ourselves in the current reality of Israel's murderous attacks, we can turn and face the roots of this violence—Israel's founding as a settler colonial state.

The Temptation to Look Away

For those of us in the long-haul struggle to end the ongoing Nakba, we make a choice to continue turning and facing the relentless violence with each and every attack on Palestine—most of which don't get reported in mainstream Western news outlets. It's easy to be grabbed by the repetitive nature of Israeli state violence, and then go into a numb or frozen state. Although I have chosen to face the Nakba, this isn't a one-and-done action. It's a choice I must keep making over and over. And the only way to find the strength to face this violence is to do so in connection with others.

In the fall of 2014, I had a chance to gather with thirty-six artists in Connecticut for a weekend of remembrance and collaboration at the first-ever convening of the national Jewish Voice for Peace Artists and Cultural Workers Council. One day during the retreat, the facilitators printed out pictures and descriptions of Palestinians who died in the most recent attacks on Gaza and laid them out on the floor of the synagogue space. One of the facilitators cried upon introducing the display, and we were invited to learn about the lives of the people who died.

Our group wandered around looking at the pictures, feeling the poignancy of honoring and mourning Palestinian lives in a Jewish religious space—where, at best, congregations tend to ignore Palestinian deaths and, at worst, justify them. Looking at the face of a young Palestinian girl who had loved to sing and longed to swim in the ocean, I was shocked by how hard it was for me to stay present. I felt a deep restlessness in my legs and an urge to leave the space, to walk in the nearby forest, to turn my attention elsewhere.

It was hard to feel the weight of responsibility for these lives taken by a state that claims to speak for me and is funded by a government that claims to represent me. Honestly, if other people weren't around, I might have left. But I took some deep breaths, and I looked around at my comrades. Some were tightening their jaws and holding back tears; some had tears streaming down their face, and some looked a bit lost, rapidly moving from picture to picture. Feeling for my kin reminded me of my own obligation to try to stay present for the sake of helping create a container in which we could grieve. I finally slowed down and let myself cry with the other mourners. How could we do this work and forget the importance of grieving? How could we refuse to mourn these precious lives, each an integral thread in a web of connection?

Finding Accountability around the Nakba

Since that time, I've done a lot of work studying, discussing, and helping others face the Nakba, but I'm not immune to feeling blasts of shame. Most recently, I was watching the brilliant and devastating film *Farha*, about a young Palestinian girl who lived through the assault on her village in Palestine in 1948. Watching Jewish soldiers torment and kill an entire Palestinian family created an upswell of shame in me that I am still processing. While I was watching *Farha* (foolishly, by myself!), I literally held my phone up between my face and the TV screen, so I could scroll through some pictures to mitigate the growing horror I felt. I can't imagine that anyone could watch these scenes of torture without feeling appalled, but I felt something more akin to shame.

It wasn't until the next day that I realized how much shame got kicked up. During my singing lesson I was having a hard time connecting to the words of "Shalom Aleichem," about the angels of peace who descend on Shabbat. I love this song, but the words were coming out stilted and affectless. When my singing teacher asked me to make the song my own, I couldn't summon any emotion until I started crying and had to stop singing it altogether. Scenes of soldiers speaking Hebrew from *Farha* were still floating through my head, and it felt hypocritical to sing a song about peace in Hebrew after watching such brutality. What was wrong with my people? How could we commit such atrocities? Why weren't we all doing everything we could to stop the ongoing Nakba? At that moment it felt like nothing else mattered.

In anti-Zionist Jewish circles, we often see this kind of shame spiral into over-accountability whereby we feel so devastated about the Nakba that we accept the conflation of Judaism with Zionism. We might then categorize anything Jewish as regressive and distance ourselves from other Jews and Jewishness. Some Jewish people don't claim their Jewish identity because they don't want to align themselves with an identity that feels inherently oppressive. This is often because they were raised in a Jewish community with oppressive dynamics around Zionism and racism. This brand of over-accountability frames Jewishness itself as inherently oppressive and disappears the roles of Christian Zionism and US imperialism in upholding and maintaining Israeli apartheid.

This over-accountability is an understandable reaction to the many established Jewish organizations and communities who continue to be completely unaccountable for the harm caused by their unwavering support for the state of Israel. However, this collapse into over-accountability and distancing doesn't serve our movements because we end up ceding Jewishness to the relatively recent force of Zionism and abdicating our responsibility to move our fellow Jews toward true justice.

As Jews (and US citizens or any citizens whose governments give military aid to Israel) we all must grapple with finding a centered response to the violence being done in our names. In the following days and weeks after watching *Farha*, I was able to process my shame through connecting with other anti-Zionist Jews and rededicating myself to the collective work of ending the ongoing Nakba. None of us can hold the enormity of our shame and grief about the Nakba by ourselves, but we can face it together in community. We can examine where we have numbed against feeling, how we attempted to seal off the injury, and where we continue to defend domination. What is possible when we are neither defensive nor collapsed in facing the Nakba? How do we stay in our dignity, while clearly acknowledging the collective harm we have caused? What kind of repair is being called for? These questions clear the space to begin the process of t'shuvah.

CHAPTER 9

MAKING AMENDS: T'SHUVAH AND TOCHECHA

The longer the Nakba continues, the deeper this Jewish moral exile becomes. By facing it squarely and beginning a process of repair, both Jews and Palestinians, in different ways, can start to come home.[1]

—PETER BEINART, "TESHUVAH: A JEWISH CASE FOR
PALESTINIAN REFUGEE RETURN"

Healing shame prepares us to engage in t'shuvah, a powerful process that teaches us how to take both individual and collective responsibility, which are essential skills for engaging with transformative justice (TJ), one of the foundations of healing justice that I discussed in chapter 3. As a political framework, TJ provides an approach for responding to harm without creating more harm through the dehumanizing and punitive systems that promote state violence—including mass incarceration, which traumatizes vulnerable communities. By addressing the root causes of harm, transformative justice aims to transmute systems of power and oppression.

Because TJ insists that we build alternatives to state violence and punishment, it necessitates that our communities develop the skills to hold ourselves and each other accountable when we cause harm. As a Jewish healing modality, the framework of t'shuvah provides a pragmatic path for developing individual and collective accountability. Or, as I like to say, TJ is built into Judaism.

While the Hebrew word *t'shuvah* often gets translated as "repentance," it means "to turn, return, or transform." T'shuvah provides a path for returning home to ourselves—our kavanah, our purpose, and our center—after we have strayed from our integrity. The forty-day period from the new moon of the month of Elul (אלול), through the holiest day of the year, Yom Kippur (יום כיפור), is devoted to t'shuvah, a process of healing repair for causing ethical injury, taking unjust action, or causing moral harm. This season offers us an opportunity to reflect on our past year and the ways that we might have missed the mark, and make amends before we enter the New Year. During this time, we are supposed to atone for our transgressions against G-d by confessing, apologizing, and promising not to repeat the action. When we hurt others, we must go through a lengthier process of t'shuvah to make amends by taking specific reparative actions.

T'shuvah moves us away from denial and toward accountability because we are being asked to face our actions and be honest with ourselves and others about where we have missed the mark in our lives. Taking responsibility is a holy task that moves us toward right relationship with ourselves, each other, and G-d or spirit. According to the rabbis, t'shuvah existed "before the mountains were brought forth," or the world was created.[2] This means t'shuvah is woven into the very tapestry of our existence; it acknowledges the inevitability of humans causing harm to ourselves, each other, and the natural world, as well as the ever-present potential for repair and transformation.

In the ancient days of the first and second temples, on Yom Kippur the High Priest sacrificed a goat to clear out the sins of all the people. After the second temple was destroyed, the High Priest no longer had a central location to do this purification. Individuals had to start taking their own responsibility for addressing the harm they had caused during the year leading up to Yom Kippur. The *Mishnah,* the first major work of rabbinic literature and law compiled around 200 CE, mentions this process for making repair with each other and with G-d.[3]

The laws of t'shuvah are explained in the Talmud, a commentary on the *Mishnah* and textual record of rabbinic debate about law, philosophy, and biblical interpretation, compiled between the third and eighth centuries.* Moses Maimonides, a twelfth-century Sephardic Jewish philosopher and scholar, created a comprehensive study of t'shuvah called *The Laws of Repentance,* which is part of a larger work called the *Mishnah Torah.* Maimonides wrote the *Mishnah Torah* to help Jews follow Jewish law without having to study the Talmud—which can be difficult to interpret, partially because it includes detailed debates about the meaning of the Torah (the first five books of the Hebrew Bible) and the *Mishnah.* This robust template for accountability from Maimonides is just as relevant to our lives today as it was in the twelfth century.

It is important to note that unlike Christianity, Judaism doesn't emphasize the need for forgiveness. Our Christian-dominated culture in the US promotes the notion that experiencing harm should immediately lead us to "forgive" those who have harmed us and "forget" about the harm they caused. This "forgive and forget" orientation toward harm—which is promoted as spiritual fortitude—translates into denial, minimization, and a lack of accountability from people who have caused harm.

T'shuvah focuses on *how* we make repair and amends after we cause harm with very little focus on whether or not we are forgiven. In fact, those who have been harmed should *not* forgive the person who caused them harm until that person engages in the challenging work of t'shuvah. We should offer the person the opportunity to find right relationship with us, but we are not required to forgive them if they have not engaged with the demanding work of repair. As Danya Ruttenberg writes in her book

---

* The most significant discussions on the topic can be found in Tractate Yoma of the Babylonian Talmud. In addition to Yoma, t'shuvah is also discussed in other tractates and chapters throughout the Talmud, such as Tractate Rosh Hashanah, Tractate Ta'anit, and Tractate Berakhot, among others.

about t'shuvah, *On Repentance and Repair*, "In Judaism, a person can do real, profound, comprehensive repentance work and even get right with G-d—experience atonement—even if their victim never forgives them. Repentance and forgiveness are separate processes."[4]

Beginning the Process of T'shuvah

I'm going to outline the process of making amends for individual harm before widening out to consider how we make repair for collective harm. Two prerequisites must be met before the process of t'shuvah even begins. First, the harm or violence must stop. Second, we must engage in self-reflection about our behavior that caused harm. This reflection, referred to as *cheshbon hanefesh* (חשבון הנפש), means an "accounting of our soul." In order to begin the process of t'shuvah, we must have already engaged in a sober reflection about our past actions. The shame-healing practices described in the last chapter, including fighting for our dignity, finding centered accountability, and cultivating self-forgiveness, are integral to this work of soul accounting. In particular, practicing centered accountability with "grab, center, and face" helps us learn what a centered response feels like in our bodies.

Until we do this work of healing shame, it can be difficult, if not impossible, to engage in this spiritual accounting because shame hijacks our inner world. When we are spinning in a self-contained vortex of shame, we are unable to look outside ourselves to examine the impact we may have had on others. As discussed in the last chapter, we tend to respond to shame by flipping between an under-accountable and over-accountable response. As part of our practice of finding a centered and accountable response when we cause harm, we should consult with trustworthy people who can give us honest feedback about our actions. We must be willing to take a hard look at ourselves, including the parts that don't match our self-image of who we think we are or who we wish we were.

In the past, two of my friends, Alicia and Jory, with whom I spent the majority of my organizing and social time, started dating. Prior to this, the

three of us did many things together, including group vacations and celebrating holidays. We all organized with JVP, but after they started dating, I
withdrew from our individual and collective friendships, which impacted
our whole chapter. I had a disproportionate reaction to their dating because
it tapped into my wounds around belonging in my family of origin.
Although the three of us discussed how I was feeling, it was hard to explain
the intensity of my reaction because I didn't understand it very well myself.
Because I was so agitated, I started to withdraw from intimacy with these
friends, and I got more rigid and less inclusive during our chapter meetings.

When I was activated around our shifting relationship during meetings,
I felt a hard shell come over my face, chest, and belly. It felt harder to track
what was happening, and I became very invested in my own opinions. I felt
like I needed to be right to be valued in the group. When I talked to other
people about these two friends, I developed a story about all the things they
had not communicated well with me, which made me harden even more.
This overly rigid shape and repetitive thought pattern was not a centered
response, and it was also under-accountable to our many years of friendship as well as my investment in our chapter's sustainability.

Although I knew that I hadn't behaved well, I was so scared of spiraling
into shame about my own worth that I became hardened and defensive
about my actions. Over much time and reflection with others, I recognized
that I had disinvested from my friendships without acknowledging it and
was not showing up well to support our chapter. I think of myself as a reli-
able friend and organizer who shows up decently in conflict, so it was hard
to face this truth. I had always assumed that I could prioritize my political
commitment over any personal challenges with people in the chapter. After
close to a year, I was finally able to recenter and recognize how my actions
had been hurtful to my friends and to our collective. Before I could do anything differently, I had to acknowledge that I didn't show up well to this
challenge. This was the accounting I needed to do before I even began the
process of t'shuvah.

Maimonides tells us that once the active harm has ceased, and we have
engaged with cheshbon hanefesh, the first official step in making t'shuvah

is to admit we had a negative impact and speak out loud the specifics of the wrong (publicly if it was a harm caused to another person). In other words, we need to own the harm that we have caused. Why does Maimonides emphasize a public confession? He wants to make sure we acknowledge our impact to anyone who was present. For example, if someone says something hurtful to someone in a group, they should acknowledge the harm to everybody who heard that comment, not just the person to whom the comment was directed. If an institution harms an entire community through its actions, then that institution needs to make a public apology.

After we confess to what we have done, the second step is to resolve in our hearts never to repeat that action. Maimonides tells us that "a person who confesses with words but does not resolve in his heart to abandon the sin—behold, he is like one who immerses in a ritual cleansing bath while holding a lizard in his hand. The immersion will have no effect."[5] We can't be cleansed by the water of the ritual bath when we are clasping a dead lizard, which is inherently not Kosher!* In other words, a rote apology or performative confession is not true t'shuvah. Just as important as the confession itself is our commitment to doing the hard work of transformation. We have to understand what led us to cause harm and engage in healing practices, so that we don't take the same harmful action all over again.

The Perspective of Exile

How do we find this resolve in our hearts to transform our behavior? Interestingly, Maimonides suggests that we need to become a new person, or, in other words, a person who won't cause that same kind of harm again. He tells us that a person committed to the process of t'shuvah "will change his name, as if to say, I am another person, I am not the person who behaved that way."[6] This is no small thing! We are being called upon to become someone else. Although most of us today won't change our name after causing

---

*   A *mikveh* can only work its magic if a person fully immerses themselves in the water.

harm—which might lead to confusion and even less accountability—we can extrapolate that the process of t'shuvah demands that we undergo a significant and radical transformation.

According to Maimonides, not only might a person change their/her/his name, but he should "exile himself from his home because exile atones for sin, since it causes him to be lowly, humble, and of contrite spirit."[7] Again, most of us today won't literally leave home after causing harm, but we can explore what he means by exile or *galut* (גלות). The root of exile *(gimel, lamed, hey)* means "to expose, uncover, or reveal." In a sermon given during the beginning of the Covid pandemic, Rabbi Ari Lev Fornari describes how being in exile means being exposed: "It is a vulnerable place to be, dispersed from our center of protection. But it is also a powerful spiritual state. Because in the state of exile, everything is revealed."[8] Although Rabbi Fornari is referring to the exile of being kept from our gathering places during the lockdown at the beginning of the pandemic, he is linking this to the shift in perspective we can choose in order to find humility as part of the process of t'shuvah.

How might we choose the humbleness of exile, of being away from home, lost, and in need of assistance? One way is to leave behind our familiar and comfortable surroundings. We have to admit what we don't know (for example, about ourselves, about other's experiences), and how our ignorance might have led us to cause harm. This might mean putting ourselves in uncomfortable and disorienting situations and conversations in order to gain different perspectives. To do the deep work of transforming ourselves and resolving to take a different path, we must be vulnerable and reveal to others and ourselves where we went wrong and the places where we lack this understanding. Then we can ask for guidance and feedback, which may arise from unexpected and surprising places on the path to becoming this new person.

Maimonides suggests many methods for dedicating ourselves to this metamorphosis in our hearts, including prayer, helping others, making financial sacrifices, avoiding temptation, changing our name, and going into exile. Today we might rely on some of the same methods, including prayer and financial sacrifice, but we also need modern methods that can support a similar transformation in our identities. These can include but are not limited to many forms of healing, including body-based healing, therapy, culturally specific healing, group healing, ritual, creative practice, and engaging with mentors and people willing to support our change.

After I acknowledged that I caused harm in my friendship with Alicia and Jory as well as our chapter when I withdrew from intimacy, I had to deeply reflect on what I didn't yet understand, which was the intensity of my reaction. Through somatic healing work and reflection, I learned to notice what happened in my body right before I felt the urge to withdraw. I noticed a squeezing sensation in my chest, which felt like terror and dread, and then a dissociative urge to move up into my head and away from the terror. When we worked on diving into this feeling through bodywork, I remembered overhearing my father telling my older sister who was away at college about something "bad" I had done.

My parents pitted my siblings and me against each other throughout our childhood. It often felt like a competition for positive attention, which was in short supply. The spotlight on who was deemed "good" and who was deemed "bad" shifted frequently. And when we were deemed bad, we faced violence and shunning. The dynamic of feeling excluded inside of this friendship triggered my fear of being excluded from our organizing collective. Group dynamics in organizing collectives, where we develop intimate relationships, can activate our wounds from our families of origin. We don't often acknowledge this or have tools for how to work with these dynamics when they do arise.

When I was activated by my friends' choice to date each other, it felt like my ability to survive was under threat just as it had been in my family of origin. I felt excluded and terrified, like something bad was about to happen at every meeting. I had to work with my young parts who felt stuck in a model of scarcity and competition to show them the difference between the past and the present, so that I could make different choices in the future.

After we have confessed to the harm that we caused and begun the often-lengthy process of becoming the kind of person who won't cause that type of harm again, only then do we take the third step of making restitution or rectifying the harm we have caused. This order is important because we must first understand ourselves and make a resolution to be different, so that we show up with sturdiness and sincerity to ask the person or people we harmed what actions would feel reparative to them. In some cases, the actions we take to rectify the harm might appear straightforward: We should return what we have stolen or fix what we have broken.

Often the context is more complicated, but reparative action might include financial restitution, donating time or money to an organization chosen by those harmed, and taking any steps that might lessen the consequence of our previous harmful actions. In the case of my broken friendship, I communicated about my behavior with friends we had in common and some people in my organizing collective to start repairing the community fractures.

The Life-Changing Work of Transformation

Finally, after making restitution, we apologize to the person or people we harmed. Because we don't want to cause more harm to our victims with an unskillful or uncentered apology, we only engage with them when we have already done our own work and taken reparative steps. In reality, sometimes we have already made an initial apology, but it may not hold much weight if we haven't yet done the work of understanding our impact.

For example, I know that at times when I have hurt someone's feelings with a thoughtless comment, I might apologize the moment I recognize the hurt. Only later am I capable of a deeper apology after I try to understand what led me to make that comment. If the people we harmed are willing to be in conversation with us, then we can also ask them what else they might like to hear in an apology that would feel truly reparative. When I withdrew from Alicia and Jory, it took me three years of time, space, and healing around the situation before I could offer a sincere and thorough apology to them without blaming them or needing anything in return. I first asked for their consent, and then I offered a simple apology for withdrawing from our friendships. I heard from them about what might feel good in shared community spaces, and I try to honor their wishes.

According to Maimonides, the highest level of t'shuvah occurs when we are in the same situation in which the original harm occurred, but we take different actions. We might wonder if the circumstances will repeat themselves, but in reality, they always do. As Rabbi Alan Lew writes in *This Is Real and You Are Completely Unprepared: The Days of Awe as a Journey of Transformation,* "The unresolved elements of our lives—the unconscious patterns, the conflicts and problems that seem to arise no matter where we go or with whom we find ourselves—continue to pull us into the same moral and spiritual circumstances over and over again until we figure out how to resolve them."[9] If we have experienced the transformative work of t'shuvah, when we encounter the same pattern, we will make different choices, perhaps clumsily, that are more in alignment with our kavanot.

In my case, I didn't return to the exact same situation, but I experienced similar feelings of exclusion when an old friend of mine and a newer friend started dating. Although I was initially very activated, I was able to understand why I felt so upset more quickly, communicate about what was coming up for me, take some space, and eventually reengage with those friendships in months, not years! I also try to engage more thoughtfully around interpersonal conflict in organizing spaces, knowing how much we all want and need belonging with each other. When we can make repair inside of our organizing spaces, we also strengthen our movements.

Maimonides tells us that when we have reached this level of t'shuvah where we make different choices in similar situations, we become very holy and beloved to G-d. In fact, we become closer to G-d than those who have never caused harm to begin with because we have engaged with the life-changing work of transformation. The Torah tells us that after our ancestors turned away from their covenant with G-d, G-d says to them, "Return to Me and I will return to you."[10] When we return to the path, to our kavanah, to our purpose, we return to holiness. When we have completed this round of t'shuvah, we become "among those who have a share in the World to Come, for nothing can stand against t'shuvah."[11]

The orientation of t'shuvah as a healing force is an antidote to shame. T'shuvah reminds us that we aren't inherently bad, selfish, flawed, or broken if we did something that caused harm or ruptured a relationship. We are simply human. Perhaps t'shuvah predates our world because it is actually the whole point of being in this world. Isaac Luria, a sixteenth-century Jewish mystic and one of the most influential figures in the development of Kabbalah, a mystical tradition within Judaism, proposed that the purpose of human existence is to make repair.

Luria taught that before the creation of the universe, G-d existed in a state known as both the *ain sof* (אֵין סוֹף), "the endlessness," and the *ain* (אֵין), "the emptiness." This powerfully charged state wouldn't allow anything to exist in its presence, so in order to create the universe, G-d had to contract G-dself in an act known as *tzim-tzum* (צמצום), which removed G-d's presence from a tiny speck at the center of the emptiness. This speck was the creation of the universe. The divine light of the ain sof was so powerful that it had to be contained in vessels in order for this little universe to survive, but the vessels weren't strong enough to contain the light. A cosmic catastrophe known as *shevirat hakelim* (שבירת הכלים), "the shattering of the vessels," occurred, and the divine light was scattered throughout creation, becoming embedded within the material world. This scattering created a broken, imbalanced, and chaotic world.

According to Luria, the central task for humans is tikkun olam, repairing the world, through gathering and elevating the holy sparks. When we engage in acts of justice, compassion, loving-kindness, and t'shuvah, we bring the sparks together. In our broken, beautiful, and imperfect world, we cause harm and make mistakes, but that is how we learn to make this repair. We actually can't unite the sparks by being perfect; we can only repair the world by repairing our relationships with each other. Our sparks join together to form a beacon of light when we heal, transform, and make amends.

Tochecha, or Calling In Our People

What are some of the obstacles on the path toward t'shuvah? While there are many roadblocks, Maimonides calls our attention to two in particular: the first is avoiding speaking out against someone else who is causing harm, and the second is getting defensive or refusing to take feedback when we are being called to account. In other words, we have inherited a directive to give feedback if we witness someone else causing harm and to listen and receive feedback when someone tells us that we are causing harm.

Maimonides uses the concept of *tochecha* (תוכחה), a "loving rebuke," to discuss how we call each other into accountability. He tells us, "Call out from your throat, do not hold back," to let others know when they have missed the mark.[12] If we don't call out, we bear responsibility for the harm they have caused because we didn't try to stop it. This is true on both a personal and collective level. The Talmud tells us that not only are we responsible for calling in members of our immediate circle, but also if anyone "is in a position to protest the sinful conduct of the people of his town, and he fails to do so, he is apprehended for the sins of the people of his town. If he is in a position to protest the sinful conduct of the whole world, and he fails to do so, he is apprehended for the sins of the whole world."[13] We are responsible for each other inside of our intimate relationships, but also inside of our communal ones. We are implicated in harm that we fail to speak out against. If we rebuke the people or systems causing harm, we might be able to prevent more harm by inviting those who are causing harm to make t'shuvah.

Although the word *rebuke* sounds harsh, we are told to rebuke someone with love, humility, and honor for their experience. As it is written in Leviticus, the third book of the Hebrew bible, we are not supposed to shame them "until their face changes color" because that causes further harm, and ultimately does not make them receptive to taking responsibility for their actions.[14] So how do we rebuke people and communities with love, care, and respect? The Rabbis from the third century CE describe the extreme difficulty of this task: Rabbi Tarfon said: "In this generation there is no one capable of rebuking." Rabbi Elazar ben Azariah added: "In this generation there is no one capable of receiving rebuke."[15] Rabbi Akiva responded: "In this generation there is no one who knows how rebuke ought to be worded."[16] In other words, it is hard to name someone's impact in a way that respects their dignity. It is also very difficult to hear that we have caused harm without getting defensive and spiraling into shame. However, just because the task is hard doesn't mean we shouldn't attempt it. Rabbi Yosi ben Chanina tells us, "A love that is not willing to reproof, is not really love," and "peace unaccompanied by rebuke is not peace."[17]

As anti-Zionist Jews, we are constantly navigating this conundrum of how to love our people enough to call them into account in a way that at least some of them can hear! As people grappling with the harm of the ongoing Nakba, we are not striving for the false peace of complicit silence in our Jewish communities about the Nakba. We are striving for a peace that can only be achieved by ending Israeli apartheid and colonization. As we call in our Jewish people to join us in ending the violence, we need to employ different strategies for engaging with tochecha on an institutional, versus an individual, level.

To fight the governments and institutions—including Jewish institutions—that uphold Zionism, we need to use all the power at our disposal. As the brilliant abolitionist and former enslaved person Frederick Douglass said in 1857, "If there is no struggle there is no progress. Those who profess to favor freedom and yet deprecate agitation are men who want crops without plowing up the ground; they want rain without thunder and lightning. They want the ocean without the awful roar of its many waters."[18] He goes on to remind us that "power concedes nothing without a demand. It never did and it never will."[19] Being part of the struggle to end the Nakba means using all our strength to demand that these institutions stop their harmful actions. Indeed, in that same passage from Leviticus about not embarrassing those we rebuke, we are told that if we have tried to give people feedback several times and they still don't cease causing harm, then we may need to make our rebukes public.

On the other hand, I think we can heed the principles of tochecha to call in individual people with love, respect, and care. This is not an easy task. Toggling between these two modes of engagement is quite difficult, and I often fail at it because I get angry, upset, and truly hurt by other people's investment in and refusal to stop the violence of the ongoing Nakba. At that same protest at Boeing I mentioned earlier—when our JVP chapter temporarily shut down the factory—my rage about the attacks on Gaza got in the way of making a human connection. When we were on the sidewalk in front of the factory, one of the Boeing workers came by to find out what we were doing. After he approached me about why we were there, I angrily told him how many Palestinians had died in the attacks on Gaza. He replied, "That many?" in a stricken voice. While this was an opportunity to connect and possibly organize someone who seemed to care about Palestinians, I felt myself freeze because I couldn't get out of an antagonistic way of communicating. I felt tight and angry. This makes sense to me; I was enraged at Boeing and our government for profiting off the deaths of Palestinian people, but I also missed that opportunity to recenter myself.

As I mentioned previously, our righteous anger is powerful, useful, and it fuels action. We need our anger, just like we need the roar of the waters, but we must find other ways to invite individual people into the struggle against racial injustice, including our struggle to end the Nakba. I always return to the concept of calling people in with *humility*. When I think about how long it took me personally to face the Nakba, it is easier to be empathetic to other people's journeys. I didn't just wake up one day as an anti-Zionist Jew because I read Edward Said, saw the latest news out of Palestine, or witnessed a protest. I needed connection with other Jews who were willing to be in conversation and learning alongside me. I am grateful to the hard work of other queer Jews in Seattle who prioritized relationship-building and education as part of their organizing. Providing these kinds of opportunities is integral to our work of bringing other Jews into the movement.

Humility in giving and receiving feedback is essential to the process of transformation. I am still practicing giving feedback in a way that respects the other person's agency and humanity. If I had recentered myself in that moment with the Boeing worker, I might have invited him into a conversation about the attacks on Gaza. I could have asked, "How does it make you feel to hear that number?" or "How does it make you feel to see this protest?" These questions could have led to a conversation about how he could put pressure on Boeing from within the company.

T'shuvah or tochecha cannot be practiced without humility. It is an act of humility to give and receive feedback, admit that we caused harm, and make restitution. How can we cultivate humility when we hear about the impact of our actions? We can practice identifying humility in our bodily sensations. Over time, I have noticed that when I am open to receiving and giving feedback in a centered way, my face softens and widens. I feel tingling and a sense of permeability on the surface of my arms and a softness at the front of my chest. My feet feel sturdy and connected to the ground, and I experience movement and aliveness at the back of my body.

When I receive feedback, I can cultivate this openness and initiate a set of practices that help me stay centered. Because I don't want to collapse under the weight of assessment, I focus on maintaining my dignity. I breathe down into my center and lengthen up through the crown of my head, while rooting my legs and feet into the ground. Instead of tightening against feedback, I try to soften my edges with a particular focus from my collarbones out to my shoulders. Finding my width helps me remember the importance of my relationships and why listening and receiving feedback matter to me. I also wake up the energy in my back body to help me meet the feedback with a sense of discernment that arises from the wisdom of my past experiences.

Collective T'shuvah through Ritual

With this emphasis on humility, accountability, and transformation, t'shuvah offers us a model for undoing dominance in our individual and collective shapes. Collective rituals can help Jews experience the first step of t'shuvah around the Nakba by coming together in community to name and take responsibility for the harms of the Israeli government that are being done in our names. Although the active harm of the Nakba hasn't ceased, we can still name the ongoing and devastating impact of Zionism on Palestinians, the land, and indeed, all people.

In 2006, our chapter of JVP organically created rituals to meet the local political moment and help us find the ground we needed to move into action together. As I mentioned in chapter 2, when Israel attacked Lebanon and Gaza with air strikes that summer, our nascent chapter of JVP joined a protest against Israeli military aggression at a Stand with Israel rally. We held signs that said, "As a Jew, I cannot support bombing civilians," and "Judaism taught me to question the justification of war for peace." When we tried to join the rally, we were stopped by the police. They told us we couldn't enter the rally with our signs, although many people attending the rally had signs—just ones with different messages.

The police didn't know how to deal with us as Jewish protesters. They were told to keep protesters out, but many of us had been invited to the rally by our own congregations. Did we belong inside or outside? Finally, we just strode into the rally and positioned ourselves under a tree with our signs. The police let us stay, but various people at the rally were infuriated by our presence: some insisted that we leave; some tried to argue with us; many yelled at us, calling us "traitors" and "self-hating Jews."

As we stood under the tree, we were all shaken; some of us were angry, and some of us were crying. Bewildered and disoriented, I felt as if I were floating a few inches above the ground. It was destabilizing to be so new to claiming my Jewish activist identity and experiencing so much vitriol from Jews supporting nationalist violence. I didn't know how to take up space at the rally; my shoulders hunched together protectively, and I collapsed my length and my dignity.

When the rally came to an end, we stood on a hill near the exit where we spontaneously began singing peace songs in Hebrew. Our mood began to lift as we felt the strength of our voices. As people left the rally, they heard us singing familiar Jewish songs. Many of them began unconsciously singing or humming along to *"Lo Yisa Goy"* ("A Nation Shall Not Raise Swords"), and *"Od Yavo Shalom Aleinu"* ("Peace Will Come upon Us"), only to stop themselves when they glanced up and realized we were the ones leading the songs. I remember feeling my feet root into the dirt of the hill; hearing my comrades' voices helped me relax my shoulders and extend upward through my spine. With our singing, we had managed to carve out a small ritual space for us to reclaim the best of our Jewish tradition in the midst of rejection and unthinking support for violence. This was my first taste of the embodied power of ritual.

Five days later an armed man entered the Jewish Federation in Seattle and shot six women, injuring five and killing one. Although we were shattered by the shootings, my friends and I were scared to mourn this act of violence in the ritual spaces created by establishment Jewish organizations. That autumn, we created our own space to grieve both the local and global violence. Our chapter of JVP led our first Tashlich L'tzedek, casting-off ceremony, during the Days of Awe. Since the late medieval period, Jews have been holding tashlich rituals, typically on the first day of Rosh Hashanah, the Jewish New Year. The ceremony helps us reflect on what we need to release from the past year in order to be in more alignment with our kavanot in the new year. We symbolically cast away our transgressions by throwing breadcrumbs or pebbles into a body of water. The gesture is based on several passages, including this one in the Book of Micah (7:9): "You will tread our sins underfoot and hurl all our iniquities into the depths of the sea."[20] Although this is a symbolic act, the physical motion of casting off invites us to experience a sense of release in our bodies.

On a sunny day in fall 2006, by the shores of Lake Washington in Madrona Park, about one hundred of us came together to cast off the transgressions of the Nakba and the transgressions of antisemitism. As part of our ritual, we acknowledged that we do not "throw away" or suddenly rid ourselves of these sins, but we set our intention to transform them as a community in the year to come. We framed our practice as a way to shed the calcified husks of protection we have built up over the year. We ask the water to soak off the husks and revive our seeds, which contain the holiest sparks of ourselves.

In casting off the sins of the ongoing Nakba, we named the violence against Palestinians being committed in our names, the continuous theft of Palestinian land, and the destruction of Palestinian homes and olive groves. We also cast off the sins of failing to speak up against antisemitism when we see or hear it happening, and refusing to see the connection between antisemitism and white supremacy. As we tossed each rock into the lake, we named the transgression, and then we said, "We take responsibility" in unison. We also called in our commitment to end the Nakba, challenge white supremacy, and build coalitions strong enough to face these enormous tasks ahead.

As our rocks hit the surface of the lake, a series of ripples expanded out in concentric circles overlapping each other. The snowy peak of Mount Rainier loomed over us, bearing witness to our ceremony. Hearing the cacophony of voices declaring our responsibility, I felt a sense of grounded hopefulness along with expansive width in my chest, tingling in my cheeks, and a stirring sense of purpose in my belly and pelvis. Instead of feeling shut down and contracted in the grief and fear I had been holding since the summer, I felt connected to my community through our collective act of t'shuvah.

This space of collective ritual enabled many of us to expand our energy wide enough to hold the contradictions we were experiencing as Jews in that moment. In the midst of mourning and protesting Israeli aggression, we lived through a violent act of antisemitism in our community. We were trying to hold this truth in a context where false accusations of antisemitism are routinely weaponized to silence criticism of Zionism and the Israeli state. As Jews, we felt simultaneously targeted and implicated in the violent actions of Zionism. The weight of contradictions that summer caused many of us to freeze, shrink, or focus on only one aspect of the violence—either antisemitism or state-sanctioned violence. The ritual helped widen the scope of what we could feel so that we could hold the complexity of our position and maintain the steadiness of our political purpose.

T'shuvah and the Nakba

The Nakba rolls on, harming the people and the land every single day. As I write this, the genocide continues in Gaza. As Jewish communities, we have not met the prerequisites for making t'shuvah around the Nakba because the violence has not ceased, nor have most Jews acknowledged the harms of a state that claims to speak for us. Some of us are heeding the call of tochecha by challenging Jewish institutions and inviting individual

Jews to learn more about the Nakba. We are creating rituals, writing articles, protesting, taking direct action, building campaigns, and building our base, so that more Jews come to understand our responsibility in this ongoing atrocity.

We also know that individual Jews are not solely responsible for the state of Israel's actions. Zionism was a response to the brutal history of European antisemitism, and there would be no Nakba if the US government didn't continue to fund the Israeli military. Christian Zionists make up the largest movement outside the Israeli state that supports the fascist policies of the Israeli government. They are motivated primarily by their belief in the prophecy that Jews must control the biblical land of Israel in order to make way for the second coming of Jesus and the end of the world. According to this prophecy, when Jesus arrives, Christians will reach salvation and non-Christians—including Muslims and Jews—will be annihilated. Christian Zionists are estimated to number at least in the tens of millions, far greater than the global population of Jews.[21] Jewish Zionists in Europe seeking to form a Jewish state made alliances with Christian Zionists that continue to this day—in spite of the deep antisemitism and Islamophobia embedded in Christian Zionist doctrine.

While we certainly need to hold Christian Zionists, the US government, and all the funders of the ongoing Nakba accountable, I feel compelled to work first and foremost with my Jewish people because I understand the cultural context in which Zionism formed as a reaction to trauma. As a collective safety shape, Zionism was a reaction to the persecution and oppression faced by European Jews. Early Zionists were trying to create a space for Jews that could keep them safe from violence. However, when we respond to violence by emulating the people who oppress us, we end up replicating that oppression.

When we contracted ourselves into this collective safety shape, we lost some of our humanity, including our ability to empathize. In an interview with NPR, Stanford psychology professor Jamil Zaki described how "empathy and power have an inverse relationship." According to Zaki, "The more powerful people are, the less likely they are to have empathy because they're less likely to need other people."[22] In gaining and leveraging the power of colonialism and nationalism, we collectively became less empathetic to the plight of Palestinians. This is how systems of domination work; in exchange for the illusion of safety and control, we give up a piece of our humanity by agreeing to exploit others. We committed a moral injury that continues to cause great harm to Palestinians and ourselves.

How do we end the continuing violence of the Nakba and regain the humanity we lost in this bargain? Our Jewish tradition offers a clear path forward through t'shuvah. The first step for Jewish communities is to engage with cheshbon hanefesh, so that we can start acknowledging—instead of denying—the ongoing Nakba. In "Teshuvah: A Jewish Case for Palestinian Refugee Return," professor and journalist Peter Beinart points out the deep hypocrisy in Jews demanding that Palestinians "repudiate the very principles of intergenerational memory and historical restitution that Jews hold sacred."[23] Our tradition demands that we remember and mourn events that happened over a thousand years ago: the destruction of the first and second temples and our many exiles. In fact, Beinart points out that the Zionist movement relied on Jewish collective memory to create a nation-state in a land most Jews had never even seen.

At the same time, as Beinart reminds us, "Jewish leaders keep insisting that, to achieve peace, Palestinians must forget the Nakba, the catastrophe they endured in 1948."[24] Indeed, the state of Israel has attempted to outlaw memory for Palestinians. In 2011, Israel formally enacted a so-called Nakba law, to reduce state funding to any institution that rejects Israel as a Jewish state or commemorates Israel's so-called Independence Day as a day of mourning or Nakba commemoration.[25] Israel has used this law to criminalize protests, forbid the display of Palestinian flags, and censor any mention of the Nakba in textbooks. But true peace will never come through dispossession followed by denial. As Beinart suggests, "It is more accurate to say that peace will come when Jews remember."[26]

Beinart walks us through what it might mean if we, as Jews, could end the violence, acknowledge our wrongdoing by taking public responsibility, and engage in the third step of t'shuvah—restitution—by ensuring that Palestinians regain citizenship and the right to return home. In Beinart's words, "The better we remember why Palestinians left, the better we will understand why they deserve the chance to return."[27] While Zionists claim that it's impossible for Palestinians to return given the size of the state, Beinart points out that Israel has already shown it knows how to quickly resettle vast numbers of people into a small space as it did after the Nazi Holocaust. Zionists also argue that it's impossible to compensate Palestinians for their stolen land; however, many Jewish institutions have certainly found ways to demand compensation for Jewish survivors and their descendants whose property was stolen during the Nazi Holocaust.

Palestinians and some Israelis have begun creatively envisioning different options for Palestinians to return home. For example, some Palestinians have put forth a vision of rebuilding houses where former Palestinian villages once stood. Since many Palestinians might not want or be able to return to the agricultural areas where their former villages were located, they could be compensated to live wherever they choose. In addition, the government could build housing for Palestinians in urban areas with accompanying access to jobs. Two organizations, Badil Resource Center, which promotes Palestinian refugee rights, and Zochrot, an Israeli organization that raises awareness about the Nakba, have partnered to come up with a proposal for compensating Palestinians when Jewish Israelis occupy former Palestinian homes or when institutions operate on the land of these former homes.

Return is possible if we do the deep work to resolve in our hearts that we are committed to liberation instead of colonization. We must ensure the right of return for Palestinians, make reparations, and ask what else we can do to support Palestinian-led healing from the trauma of colonization and dispossession. We must, finally, deeply apologize on behalf of the state of Israel and all the institutions and people who have inadvertently or blatantly upheld this system of violence and domination.

Beinart reminds us that t'shuvah is never a transformation only for the sake of those harmed; it offers transformation for us all. He tells us, "In Jewish tradition, return need not be physical; it can also be ethical and spiritual. Which means that the return of Palestinian refugees—far from necessitating Jewish exile—could be a kind of return for us as well, a return to traditions of memory and justice that the *Nakba* has evicted from organized

Jewish life."[28] Through making t'shuvah, we regain some of the humanity we lost as Jews. This isn't the primary goal of ending the Nakba—which is to end the violence against Palestinians. However, the healing waters of t'shuvah ripple outward to include everybody.

An Ocean of Healing

As a young kid growing up in landlocked Ohio, when I first heard the phrase, "They want to drive us into the sea," it didn't make sense to me. I wondered, "What is so bad about the sea?" I had a strong desire to dive into this thing called the ocean. The Passover story reminds us that if we are willing to risk moving toward the sea, the water will part and reveal the path toward liberation. Perhaps this childhood vantage point can offer us a shift in perspective, which is exactly what the process of t'shuvah demands. What might happen if we divert our gaze away from the land and out toward the sea?

What if we took the vast oceanic perspective that comes from our journeys as a people who crossed many oceans in the diaspora to escape the violence directed against us? What might be revealed? This shift in perspective, this exile from homeland, might help us turn to face the watery depths of history that contain the horrors of humanity—from the Middle Passage to pogroms to the Nakba. When we can acknowledge this ocean of suffering that we are a part of—both as people who have been harmed and as people who have caused harm—we can start a process of healing.

As a system of domination, Zionism tells us we could only escape suffering through exploiting others and stealing their land. We prioritized ownership of the land over our shared humanity. We attempted to find safety by mimicking the colonialism, nationalism, and militarism of the people who oppressed us. This left us continuously grasping for more land and power while policing our boundaries with ever-increasing force and violence.

But other choices and journeys have always been and are always possible. The perspective of the sea might help us acknowledge the precarious and temporary nature of human lives in the face of natural forces. Land is impermanent; it shifts around in geologic time: land becomes water, and water becomes land. Try as we might to dominate the land and each other, we won't have the power to do that for much longer. Defending these temporary lines on a map doesn't help us recover our lost humanity, and it certainly doesn't move us toward liberation. In the deep waters of the ocean, humanity's stories of suffering and resilience bump into each other, merge, and reemerge differently. These porous underwater currents might help us find a new shape for being Jewish that emphasizes our ability to find safety by reaching for connection, rather than enforcing these violent separations.

CHAPTER 10

JEWISH EMBODIED RESILIENCE, RITUAL, AND GRIEF

If ocean-full our mouth were with music

Our tongues singing

like the ceaseless surf

Our lips praising You to the skies

Our eyes blazing like sun and moon

Our arms spread like soaring eagles

Our legs sprinting like those of deers

We could not thank You enough[1]

—*NISHMAT KOL CHAI* (נשמת כל חי), TRANSLATED BY
RABBI ZALMAN SCHACHTER-SHALOMI

The waterways of Seattle drew me west from landlocked Ohio over two decades ago. I landed in central Seattle where I developed a practice of walking down to Lake Washington several times a week. I love witnessing the life of the lake: the cormorant perched on a buoy stretching out its glossy wings, the heron stalking the edges of the shore, and ospreys torpedoing down into the water to catch fish. About a year ago, I moved to West Seattle, which is on a peninsula that extends into the Salish Sea. At my new neighborhood beach, I discovered the magic of low tides when the moon and the sun beckon the water toward them, revealing sea life that is usually submerged. Along with many others, I rush down to exclaim over the creatures exposed at low tide, including the shockingly bright red blood stars clinging to rocks, the nudibranchs waving the frosty white tips of their cerata, and the iridescent seaweed glimmering in the sunlight. When I am near large bodies of water—a source of resiliency for me—a corresponding sense of spaciousness opens up inside my body. My chest cavity expands, and my limbs feel fluid and free.

A couple months ago, I was sitting on a park bench with a friend, staring out into the Salish Sea, when we spotted three enormous dorsal fins of a mama orca whale and her two babies headed north. One of the baby whales kept enthusiastically breaching, tossing her shiny black-and-white body up toward the sky. A small crowd of people gathered behind our bench, and we shrieked in unison each time the calf leaped out of the water. We experienced a collective sense of awe and resilience watching the orca whales. For the rest of that day, I was enlivened by the orcas' energetic presence; the surface of my arms and face were buzzing; my face hurt from smiling so much, and I couldn't speak of anything else.

Just as all of us develop safety shapes because we are born with survival reactions, we are also born with an inherent capacity for resilience and connection. Resilience refers to our ability to feel buoyed, enlivened, and awed by the beauty of life. Our resilient impulses include moving toward connection with humans and animals and the natural world, and creative art or play. As social animals, we are also drawn toward experiences of collective resiliency, including participating in rituals, singing, dancing, and celebrating together.

Resiliency helps us return to ourselves and our kavanot during and after experiencing hardship. It allows us to shift from a state of traumatic reactivity (our safety shapes) to a relaxed and reconnected state. Whereas safety shapes tend to restrict our range of sensations, resilience helps us feel more of our aliveness. When we access resilience, we often experience a sense of movement in our bodies, including tingling, buzzing, or streaming, particularly in our limbs. Our chest and throat might feel open, and our shoulders and jaw relax down. We might notice a sense of comforting warmth, particularly in our chest, diaphragm, and belly.

While resilience is inherent to our humanity, the concept sometimes gets misused in social justice movements and the wider culture. We should never suggest that individuals or communities need to be "more resilient" without holding that we need to shift the structural and institutional systems that create oppressive conditions. We should neither blame anyone for their supposed lack of resiliency, nor justify oppression by suggesting certain communities can "handle the stress" because they're resilient. Instead, our work is to build resilient and effective social justice movements that challenge systems of domination, so that more people can access their resiliency more of the time.

Whereas our safety shapes encourage disconnection from each other, the land, and spirit, resiliency helps us perceive our place in the ecosystem. Instead of feeling separate from other humans, plants, and animals we often experience a sense of kinship. Inside of these connections, we become more hopeful, even in the face of daunting oppression. This is not a shallow sense of optimism, but a rooted sense of possibility. As the poet Jericho Brown articulates so beautifully, "Hope is the opposite of desperation . . . it is always accompanied by the imagination, the will to see what our physical environment seems to deem impossible. Only the creative mind can make use of hope. Only a creative people can wield it."[2] Hope fuels our ability to imagine and build toward a future beyond our current systems of oppression, including white supremacy, the carceral state, and Zionism.

Practicing Resilience

By consciously practicing resilience, we develop our ability to recognize and generate the feelings and sensations of joyful aliveness. When I work with clients around resilience, I have them choose and describe an activity, relationship, place, or practice that brings them joy—including what they can see, hear, smell, touch, and taste when they are in that resilient practice. For example, I worked with a trans masculine Ashkenazi Jewish teacher, Ethan, who felt enlivened and joyful when he went swimming in Lake Washington. He described a specific moment when he was standing on the dock about to dive into the lake. The sun warmed his cheeks, neck, and shoulders. The sounds of the boats and people splashing nearby surrounded him with ambient noise. He saw rippling patterns of light on the blue water, turtles on a log reaching their necks up to the sun, and the branches of a nearby willow tree that dipped gracefully into the lake. Smelling algae and sunscreen, he anticipated the joy of diving in.

I had him close his eyes and imagine standing on the dock. I helped set the scene by describing back to him what he experienced from the warmth of the sun to the light on the water. When I asked about his sensations and emotions, he reported a warm energy flowing from his heart down through his arms. The tips of his fingers were tingling, and his chest felt bubbly and warm. His thigh muscles were trembling with readiness to launch him off the deck. His cheeks felt wide and flushed, and his mood was excited anticipation. I prompted him to increase the intensity of his sensations by envisioning a dial that he could turn to the right, bringing more flowing energy to his arms and legs, faster bubbling and increased warmth in his chest, and more heat to his cheeks. For Ethan, turning up the sensations made his entire body shake, and he felt an uncomfortable pressure in his chest, like he was about to explode. We returned to a more comfortable level of sensation.

When Ethan turned the dial down to the left to decrease the intensity of sensation and emotion, he felt subdued. He could only feel some light trembling in his legs and a thin stream of energy in his arms. He described feeling like something upsetting had pulled his attention away from his experience. We returned to the sweet spot where we began, where he felt excited without feeling overwhelmed.

In our debrief, Ethan described his delight at discovering that he could control the volume of his sensations. He felt both powerful and awed by the amount of sensation he was able to generate in this practice. We talked about how he can cultivate this resilience in several ways. Whenever he goes swimming in the lake, he can consciously linger in the moment by noticing his sensations and emotions. As Ethan builds up this awareness of how he experiences resilience in his body, it will be easier for him to notice smaller joyful moments throughout his days by tuning into his body. When he needs more resourcing, he can also generate resilience by closing his eyes and returning to the felt sense of being on the dock by the lake.

Like many somatic practices, the resilience practice is a simple one, which is also deeply stirring. It's one of my favorite practices because witnessing my clients in their joy and exuberance increases my own sense of excitement. Resilience is contagious. When we sing, dance, play, and enact rituals together, we are exponentially increasing our individual and collective resiliency.

I often bring aspects of resiliency into more intense practices with clients because delving into healing from trauma requires us to feel resourced. Before the end of each session, I track whether a client is feeling more or less alive. If I sense that they are feeling numb, brittle, or frozen, I will often remind them of some aspect of their resilience. For instance, one time when Ethan and I were doing bodywork around transphobia in his family, I noticed him slipping into a state of despair. In that moment he was feeling small and ashamed and couldn't envision ever feeling different. I asked him to close his eyes and revisit the experience of standing on the dock, ready to jump into the water. By recalling the warmth of the sun on his skin, the smell of the algae, and the feeling of anticipation, Ethan was able to reconnect to a sense of greater possibility.

Jewish Resilience through Sanctifying Time

Resilience is built into Judaism in numerous ways. The life cycle of the year includes time to grieve, commemorate, and celebrate through the seasonal holidays. In the month of Adar (אדר) between winter and spring, we are told to increase our joy. If we can't access joy, we are told to *perform* joy until we can *feel* joy, an ancient version of "fake it until you make it." Adar includes the celebration of Purim (פורים), which commemorates how a Jewish woman, Esther, saved the Jewish people from Haman, who was planning to annihilate all the Jews of ancient Persia. Purim celebrations include feasting, redistributing wealth, giving out treats, performing drag, challenging binaries, and retelling the story of Esther.

While many annual Jewish holidays help us access our resilience, we also have a beautiful resiliency practice built into every single week of our calendar. The Jewish holiday of Shabbat begins every Friday evening at sunset and ends on Saturday evening when three stars are visible in the night sky. A sacred time for rest and reflection, Shabbat connects us to the Jewish story of creation. The Book of Genesis, the first book of the Hebrew bible, tells us that after six days of creating the earth and heaven, on the seventh day, G-d ceased and took a breath. This breath completed the universe. G-d's act of creation required not only action, but breath, rest, and renewal. The first time the word *kadosh* (קדוש), or "holiness," appears in the Torah, it refers to Shabbat; rest is the first concept to be sanctified as holy.

We usher in the sacredness of Shabbat on Friday night by slowing down, taking a breath, and lighting candles. Many of us have an embodied tradition of scooping the light toward our eyes three times with our hands in a circular motion to welcome the light of Shabbat into our souls, before we close our eyes and say the candle blessing. This ritual invites us into our bodies; we breathe in the light and draw our attention inward. For six days of the week, our attention is focused out toward the world, and on the seventh day, we turn inward to attend to our soul. On Shabbat, we even receive a bonus soul! During the rest of the week, we have a soul that enlivens our body, our nefesh, but on Shabbat we also gain an extra soul—our *neshama yeteirah* (נשמה יתרה)—which offers an enhanced spiritual state. These two souls intermingle on Shabbat to help us connect to the vastness of spirit through our bodies.

On Friday night, we separate ourselves from the world of work and enter into a time of resilient practices and spiritual reflection. Shabbat historically included everybody involved in Jewish community. In the days of agricultural work, even at plowing and harvesting time, there was a historical requirement that workers and strangers were allowed to rest, just like the farm owners. Once we leave the world of work, we are invited into the pleasurable activities of wandering, napping, eating, singing, praying, playing, reading, cuddling, gathering, lingering, and simply losing track of time.

Shabbat beckons us into an experience of time that isn't controlled by the clock of capitalism, but by the act of creation. As Rabbi Abraham Joshua Heschel describes in his seminal work, *The Sabbath,* we learn to "celebrate time rather than space. Six days a week we live under the tyranny of things of space: on Shabbat we try to become attuned to holiness in time."[3] We "turn from the results of creation to the mystery of creation, from the world of creation to the creation of the world."[4] We enter a cathedral in time where our focus shifts from the material world of acquiring things, including economic and political power, to a holy world of assisting G-d in the creative acts of repairing and healing.

Rabbi Zalman describes this entry into the cathedral of Shabbat as a transition from "commodity time" to "organic time."[5] In commodity time, we focus on efficiency for the sake of productivity and acquisition: everything we do, from exercising to eating, is dictated by the time frame of capitalism. Inside organic time, we encounter time as nature holds it, not as capitalism does. With this slowing down, we undergo a shift in perspective. As minister and writer Ana Levy-Lyons explains, "The goal of Shabbat is not to patch us up and send us back out to the violent secular world . . . it is to reconstruct the rest of time from the viewpoint of Shabbat as unjust and untenable."[6] We not only gain an extra soul on Shabbat, but we gain a wider perspective on our world.

Released from the constraints of clock time, we are free to expand beyond the limits that capitalism imposes on our imagination. As Rabbi Watts Belser writes in *Loving Our Own Bones,* "Shabbat is a way of unwinding the lies that make work the measure of our worth, the cultural patterns that tie our basic value as people to our ability to labor, produce, accomplish and earn."[7] Shabbat, she poses, is the antidote to ableism, which helps drive capitalism. We are reminded that our dignity and belonging are not dependent on what we produce.

While much is made of the limits on Shabbat (anything related to work), these limits also expose the ableist capitalist myth of limitlessness, or the idea that we're only living our fullest life when there are no limits on where we can go and what we can do. The very idea of "no limits" on human activity or the resources of the earth grows out of a colonialist Western expansion myth; "no limits" for some depends on violent restrictions for others, and making the earth uninhabitable for all of life. As Watts Belser reminds us, the limits of Shabbat actually help us expand into a different kind of time, a practice that helps us recognize "rest and renewal not simply as a spiritual good but as a spiritual obligation."[8]

Shabbat offers us a glimpse of the world to come—a world that exists outside of labor, a world of rest and surrender, a world in which we are not striving to accomplish anything in the material world of commerce. Heschel tells us that Shabbat encompasses both this world and the world to come because it is "joy, holiness, and rest; joy is part of this world; holiness and rest are something of the world to come."[9] We experience the beauty of this world through our resilient practices, yet we rest as though all our tasks are complete, as they will be in the world to come.

On Saturday night, we complete Shabbat with a Havdalah (הבדלה) ritual that separates the holiness of Shabbat from the rest of our week. We bless an overflowing glass of wine, which reflects the abundant gifts of Shabbat that will flow into the other six days. To fortify our remaining soul as our additional soul departs, we smell b'samim (בשמים), fragrant spices that remind us of the beauty of this earth. We light a braided candle with many wicks, representing the entanglement of the spiritual and material worlds. Gazing at the half-moons on our fingernails and the light in each other's eyes reflected from the candle, we acknowledge that we are all both earthly and spiritual beings. Finally, we douse the candle in the wine to complete the ritual. As we demarcate the boundary of Shabbat, we engage our senses to remind ourselves of our kavanah to allow Shabbat to transform the rest of our week.

Releasing Capitalism with Shmita

I am going to zoom out from the Jewish holiday that occurs every seven days to a holiday that occurs every seven years in the Jewish agricultural calendar called the *Shmita* (שמיטה) year, or Sabbatical year. *Shmita* means "release." According to rabbinic law, this is the year we cease cultivation of the land, free enslaved people, and forgive debts—an opportunity to start over by releasing what we once held onto so tightly. During this year, agricultural activities such as planting, pruning, and harvesting are prohibited, so that the land can rest and be restored to its natural fertility. The produce that grows naturally during this time is considered communal property, free and accessible to all including "your hired servant and the traveler who sojourns with you; and your cattle and the wild beasts that are in your land."[10] In this same text in Leviticus, we are told to physically open our hands to release the debt owed to us, to free our people who were enslaved, and to help all those in need. We should not send our formerly enslaved people away empty-handed. Keeping our hands open, we should offer them livestock, grain, and wine.

As a collective Shabbat, Shmita offers rest to the entire ecosystem as we acknowledge that the land, money, people, and animals were never truly "ours" as possessions but remain "ours" as responsibilities in the web of connection. In *Shabbat Ha'Aretz*, published in 1909, Rabbi Kook describes the Shmita year as "a year of peace and quiet without oppressor and tyrant . . . there is no private property and no punctilious privilege."[11] Holiness is no longer profaned by attempting to profit off the fruits of the land and acquiring wealth via commerce and trade. According to Kook, this year corrects "this situation of inequality and societal rifts, by removing a major source of power of the elite: debts owed to them."[12]

Shmita feels even more politically directive than Shabbat because it urges us not just to pause, slow down, and breathe, but to stop engaging with profit for a whole year. Seven years of Shabbats were not enough. Now we are commanded to stop feeding the busy machine of capitalism and reconsider how we want to be in relationship with each other and the natural world. Shmita makes it abundantly clear that slowing down and resting are acts with radical consequences. We are reminded not only that our dignity does not depend on our productivity, but that our productivity has been coopted as an instrument of capitalism to desecrate our holy world.

Shmita, like Shabbat, offers us a framework for social change that comes from pausing, breathing, and resting. As activists and people dismayed by the dire situation of our current world, we tend to be driven into action by a sense of urgency. We might wonder how we could possibly stop to take a breath in the face of myriad climate catastrophes, the violence of the racist state, the colonization of Palestine, and the colonization of the land we are on. Yet hurtling into action in response to domination while ignoring our breath and our bodies encourages numbness, disconnection, and dehumanization—the tools capitalism uses to separate us from each other, spirit, and the land. We become tangled in a fight against domination that inevitably replicates domination.

To take deliberate action grounded in an understanding of our interdependence, we have to be able to feel ourselves, each other, and the rhythmic breath of life inside us and around us. Breath is not stillness; breath is movement that reveals our entanglement with the natural world. We inhale; our diaphragm contracts, allowing the rib cage and lungs to expand and gather oxygen that is offered to us by the trees, plants, and algae. We pause. We exhale; our diaphragm relaxes, causing the rib cage and lungs to contract and expel carbon dioxide that is transformed by the flora into energy and oxygen through photosynthesis. We pause. And then another inhale occurs. Every seven years, we are invited to be conscious of this cycle of contracting and expanding and pausing. We discover what might happen when we attune to the rhythmic breath of life, which connects us to the world of trees, plants, and even algae in the ocean, not the imposed rhythms of late capitalism. Even when we stop cultivating the fields, the cycle of life continues at its own pace. Seeds scatter, sprout, mature, bloom, fruit, and reseed on their own schedule. The world whirls, the seasons shift, the moon waxes and wanes, the tides ebb and flow.

Shmita and Shabbat do more than help us cultivate our resilience for the sake of joy; they help us remember the gifts of being attuned to natural cycles of life, instead of trying to command, manipulate, or devour nature. On a recent trip to the Washington Coast, I hiked down to my favorite wild and rugged beach, Cape Alava, at low tide. As I walked through the maze of rocks separated by tide pools, I saw some expected friends: piles of seals lounging on rocky outcrops in the ocean, otters gliding through the water on their backs, and plovers probing the sand for mollusks. I also encountered some unexpected visitors: a deer scrounging for kelp and a black mama bear with her cubs digging for clams on the beach. As I sat under a madrone tree watching the bears forage, my breath and pulse slowed down. Along with the briny air, I breathed in the slow and steady rhythm of coastal time.

Witnessing the abundance of food that low tide provided for this array of creatures brought into stark relief the scarcity, exploitation, and extraction created by capitalism. Nature has provided human and animal alike with plenty to eat, but we are so attached to exploitation and profit that we hoard resources and let people and animals starve. When we slow down to pay attention, the cycles of nature can remind us of what is possible. Human domination and exploitation require great expenditures of energy. For example, the system of Israeli apartheid demands tremendous resources of money, technology, and military labor. The border wall, checkpoints, and surveillance systems are partially funded by $3.8 billion in annual US military aid.[13] In this country, we spend hundreds of billions of dollars funding the criminal injustice system that cages and kills our siblings.[14] What if we stopped working so hard to maintain white supremacy, racialized capitalism, and Israeli apartheid? What changes could we see in our world if we paused, took a breath, and listened for a different rhythm?

Maybe this is the collective equivalent to what Maimonides suggests about going into exile, so that we can transform our perspective. Entering the holy palace of time can help illuminate a different path through this world. As Aurora Levins Morales often says, those in power insist that the way things are is the way things have always been and the way they will always be. We need to be reminded that there is nothing natural or inevitable about racialized capitalism. Humans created this system, and we can certainly stop our efforts to maintain it and come back into a reciprocal relationship with the natural world. Resilience helps us encounter, imagine, and foster a world that emerges between the cracks of capitalism.

Resilience and Grief

Slowing down, noticing our breath, and purposefully celebrating Jewish holidays and rituals help us strengthen our resilience, so that we can find the fortitude to face and grieve the ongoing domination of people and destruction of our environment that characterizes our current era. It's no coincidence that I became politicized around Palestine through political conversations that began by welcoming in Shabbat. Participating in ritual with other Jews helped me break out of the denial, isolation, and freeze that I experienced in the face of Israeli state violence. Rituals have the power to make the invisible visible. In other words, they provide a collective container where we can express the intense or overwhelming feelings that have been repressed or suppressed because they feel too big for us to hold by ourselves.

Inside the intentional and sacred space of ritual, we agree to let go of decorum and stop tamping down our feelings and emotions. In this portal between the material and spiritual worlds, we are able to perceive and experience ourselves differently than in our everyday lives. As Rabbis Jessica Rosenberg and Ariana Katz write,

> Our Jewish traditions include millennia of wisdom that speak to commemorating and moving through grief and loss; transforming hurt and harm; cultivating gratitude, joy, and connection; marking liminal moments and transitions; being present in the current moment; connecting the seasons, the earth, and our ancestors; asking for help; and more.[15]

We invite forces larger than ourselves—spirit, nature, ancestors—to help us hold and transform the feelings that threaten to subsume us on our own. We increase our collective resilience through rituals because they allow us to witness each other's raw, untamed emotions so they can be unleashed and released or integrated into our collective body.

In reviewing the many political rituals I've helped create and participate in over the years for this book, I was reminded that most of them centered around mourning. Mourning is always present in Palestinian solidarity work because the Israeli government continues to murder Palestinians as part of its strategy of ethnic cleansing. When we publicly mourn the Palestinian lives lost to the apartheid regime of Israel, we are acknowledging our deep grief about the violence done in our names, committing to ending the ongoing Nakba, and challenging the erasure of Palestinian lives and deaths in most Western media. It was just recently in 2021 that the *New York Times* first published the names and faces of Palestinian children killed by Israeli forces.[16] Many of us bitterly noted the importance of this shift that promoted empathy toward Palestinian children, even as it reinforced the tragedy of their deaths.

How do mourning rituals help us access resiliency, which is frequently associated with joy? Resiliency does increase our capacity for joy, but it also increases our ability to experience the depth of all our feelings, including the life-altering experience of grief. In his book on grieving, *The Wild Edge of Sorrow*, psychotherapist Francis Weller reminds us that "while it is difficult to embrace grief and be moved by its muscular demands, without it we would not know the heartening quality of compassion, could not experience the full breadth of love, the surprise of joy, we could not celebrate the sheer beauty of the world."[17],* Grief demands that we stretch our hearts to hold more, feel more, and confront the mystery of our connections with each other in this world and the world beyond this world.

We don't engage with Jewish ritual as a spiritual bypass to escape the difficult and heartbreaking experiences in both our personal and political worlds. We engage with Jewish ritual to increase our capacity to feel more, including joy, grief, sorrow, and awe. In his book *Inciting Joy*, poet Ross Gay asks, "What if joy is not only entangled with pain, or suffering, or sorrow, but is also what emerges from how we care for each other through those things?"[18] Gay contends that our sorrows cause us to fall apart and come

---

*   It is important to note that Weller trained with the West African healer Malidoma Patrice Somé for two years in the US, and then accompanied Somé back to his home country of Burkina Faso for further study.

undone. If we draw close to each other through these losses, we fall into each other's arms.

Loss is an integral part of life, but many Western cultures do not provide space for us to fully experience these losses. We are often urged to quickly "move on," dissociate, and constrict around our losses. This constriction leaves us feeling rigid, flat, and dull because this constriction freezes our sorrow. Grief is more than an emotion; it is a doorway into a process of change; when we refuse to enter the portal, its demands don't ease. Instead, the loss wraps itself around us like a heavy chain, pulling us away from our own aliveness. We might be able to drag ourselves through the motions of life, but we can't access our full vitality.

When we turn toward our grief instead of suppressing or ignoring it, we discover it is suffused with raw life force. As Weller reminds us, "There is some strange intimacy between grief and aliveness, some sacred exchange between what seems unbearable and what is most exquisitely alive."[19] At the heart of grief is a lesson about allowing ourselves to be changed through loss. Grief honors the depth of our love. Whether we are grieving the loss of a relationship with a person, community, animal, landscape, or ecosystem, we honor the sacredness of that connection and how our lives are beautifully tangled up together.

While we live inside a larger mainstream culture that often denies death and tries to sidestep the demands of grief, Judaism offers us ritual, structure, and physical movements that help us move through the stages of mourning the loss of a loved one. The first stage, which begins when a loved one dies and lasts until the burial, is called *Aninut* (אנינות) and a mourner is called an *onen* (אונן), someone who straddles the world of the living and the world of the dead. Stunned by the pain of death, we may engage with the ancient tradition of *kriah* (קריעה), the tearing of our garments when we hear about our loved one's death or in a ritual prior to the burial. With this rending of our clothes, our hands express the way we are being torn apart by grief. This tearing creates an opening or a portal into the life-changing process of grieving before we enter the next stage, *Shiva* (שבעה).

After the funeral, Shiva lasts for seven days. For these seven days, we separate ourselves from our everyday lives. We remain at home, receiving visits and food from our community, praying and reflecting on our loss. Staying close to the ground in which we just buried our loved ones, we sit on low stools or pillows or on the floor itself. We refrain from activities that draw our attention outward: personal grooming, adornment, sex, entertainment, and celebrations. To keep our focus away from our appearance rather than our internal journey, we also cover our mirrors with black cloth.

During this period, we begin reciting the Mourner's Kaddish (קדיש), the prayer for the dead, every day. We need a quorum of ten people to say the Kaddish prayer; we are not meant to grieve alone. During Shiva, we hover between the worlds of the living and the dead, but our communal recital of the Mourner's Kaddish provides an anchor to ensure that we don't drift too far from the earthly realm. In fact, the Kaddish doesn't once mention death, but instead uses mourning as an occasion to praise the beauty of life.

Kaddish helps the living remember the wonder of life and connects us to the dead; praising life is meant to help elevate the souls of the deceased on their journey. Kaddish also connects us to G-d. Because each person on this earth is made in the image of G-d, each death diminishes G-d's presence in this world. When we say *yitgadal* (יתגדל), the first word of Kaddish, which means "may you be increased," we are trying to comfort G-d about G-d's loss. We console G-d that more life will follow the diminishing of G-d's presence. When we say *yitkadash* (יתקדש), the second phrase, "may you be made holy," we are acknowledging that one unique expression of G-d has been lost to this world, but we reassure G-d that holiness is still present. We still honor spirit. We soothe G-d, and in turn, we ask for soothing.

At the close of the seven days, loved ones might join us for a brief walk outside to represent our reentry into the world. After Shiva ends, we enter into Sheloshim (שלושים), a period of mourning that lasts for thirty days after the burial. We leave our homes, returning to some of the duties of life, but we still avoid celebrations. We continue to recite the Mourner's Kaddish daily for up to eleven months for close family members. On the anniversary of our loved one's death, their yahrzeit, we light a candle to remember them. On the final day of services for many Jewish holidays, we may join in special *yizkor* (יזכור), memorial prayers at synagogues.

These three stages of mourning provide a sturdy vessel in which we can fully encounter grief without fear of drowning in its ocean. In Aninut, we physicalize the depth of grief ripping apart our heart. During Shiva, our community supports us to stay close to our beloved dead through remembrance, while the Mourner's Kaddish provides a tether to the world of the living. Sheloshim transitions us back into more of our daily lives, while still tending to our relationships with those on the other side. Instead of shutting down or shutting out the grief, we are invited to fully feel the grief as we are ushered through the stages of deepening, softening, opening, and being transformed by grieving. This time-bound structure allows grief to have its way with us—to undo us without sinking us, so that we can reemerge from this process with a deeper sense of gratitude and reverence for the interdependence of our lives.

Rituals and Resilience

The Jewish cycle of grieving is meant to help us mourn the loss of individual people in our lives, but Jewish rituals can also help us mourn in the face of collective violence. During the height of the pandemic in the spring of 2021, Israel launched a deadly attack on Gaza, killing at least 260 Palestinians, including 66 children, and injuring over 1900 Palestinians. In Israel, thirteen people were killed.[20] I remember the familiar shock and numbness when I read about the deaths, which felt especially difficult to absorb in the midst of pandemic isolation. Our chapter of JVP wanted to help our community come together to acknowledge, grieve, and fight back against these deadly attacks.

We participated in a nationally coordinated action by JVP to hold "Shabbat in the Streets" to demonstrate solidarity with Palestinian resistance to Israeli apartheid and colonization.* In Seattle, we held our Shabbat in front

---

* Jessica Rosenberg and Alana Krivo-Kaufman helped create the ritual for JVP that we adapted for our local context.

of Temple de Hirsch Sinai, a centrally located Reform synagogue that frequently sponsors Zionist events, whose leader has consistently undermined local movements for racial justice.[21] Earlier that week, we sent a letter to Temple de Hirsch and other local synagogues and Jewish institutions to invite them into a conversation with us about the attacks on Gaza. Motivated by our deep care for our Jewish people and our longing for them to join us in supporting the Palestinian struggle for freedom, we asked them to support the Palestinian call for BDS. Although it seemed unlikely that we would get a response (indeed, we did not), we attempted to call in our community members with this act of tochecha, loving rebuke.

With the support and coordination of our chapter, three of us led a service outside the synagogue to welcome in the light of Shabbat, to honor the lives lost, and to recommit ourselves to creating a different world. We were making space for ourselves to be changed by these losses and reclaiming our traditions, in the face of the Israeli government deploying Jewishness to oppress Palestinians. To our side was an altar laden with flowers, candles, and the names and pictures of those killed in the attacks. Gathered around us in the street in front of the synagogue was a multiracial group of over one hundred mourners, including Jews, Muslims, and Christians crying and holding onto each other.

We included traditional prayers, songs, and moments in the service for all of us to look around and notice the tremendous community sorrow about Gaza, as well as the support for a Jewishness beyond Zionism that honors all life. As leaders, we saw and felt the ways our gathering created a collective space for all of us to break through the numbness to feel grief. Celebrating the steadfastness of Palestinian resistance and resilience, we read the words of Palestinian activists and artists, including Mahmoud Darwish's poem "I Belong There," about his homeland.[22]

During our service, we noted that our ritual was taking place the same week as Shavuot (שבועות), a Jewish holiday that celebrates receiving the wisdom of the Torah at Mount Sinai. We explained how we were heeding the Torah's commandment to love the stranger as we love ourselves. The Torah reminds us how to treat the stranger thirty-six times, its most repeated injunction. In Leviticus, we are told that "The stranger who resides with you shall be to you as one of your citizens; you shall love him as yourself, for you were strangers in the land of Egypt."[23] Not only were we once strangers, but we are also likely to become strangers again. In fact, as Maimonides suggests, we might even choose exile in our attempts to make t'shuvah around the Nakba. When we oppress the stranger, we end up cutting off parts of ourselves, estranging ourselves from the holiness that comes from our empathetic connections to each other.

We lifted up this lesson from the Torah about the need for solidarity with those who have been exiled from their land or from power. I chose to tell a story from our collective history to create a new possibility for the future. In his article, "When Genya and Henryk Kowalski Challenged History—Jaffa, 1949," Professor Alon Confino describes how two survivors of the Nazi Holocaust returned the keys they were given to a house in Jaffa. In Genya's broken Hebrew, she describes:

> The house was beautiful, but we didn't even enter the house because in the yard there was a round table set with plates, and as soon as we saw this . . . we were frightened. And besides the fear, we could not look, it hurt us, how could people, it reminded us how we had to leave the house and everything behind when the Germans arrived and threw us into the ghetto.[24]

When the majority of Jews in Israel were stealing Palestinian land, livestock, and the homes from which Palestinians were expelled, the Kowalskis made a different choice.

When I first read these fragments, "It hurt us, how could people, it reminded us . . ." I felt a shiver of recognition run down my spine. These words express the bewildering shock of emotions I experience whenever I hear about Israel's vicious treatment of Palestinians. Seeing their community displace Palestinians was hurtful, abhorrent, and confusing to them because it mimicked their own recent dispossession. They wondered how Jews could escape the devastation of Europe only to reenact this violence in Palestine. The Kowalskis created an empathetic bridge from their own very fresh traumatic experiences to the owners of this house who were forced to flee mid-meal. They instinctively clung to their humanity, instead of dehumanizing others.

I honored our ancestors, the Kowalskis, for this simple act that went against the grain of history. In the words of Professor Confino, "Their act declares, by whispering not by shouting, the moral obligation of the victim toward other victims, particularly toward the victims created by one's own actions."[25] In reclaiming the holiness of the Kowalskis' act, we refused to cede our Jewishness to the institutions—like the synagogue behind us—that show disdain for the holiness of life. We were forwarding an alternative vision of Jewishness that values Palestinian lives. That was the wisdom we celebrated receiving at Sinai.

It was devastating to lead this ritual in a time of escalating violence, but it also felt crucial to grieve together in community. After it was over, I was sitting in my friend's car, trying to convey how confusing it felt that this tragedy brought us all together for the first time since the beginning of Covid. I had barely begun articulating this thought when my voice began cracking, my throat constricted, and my chin started trembling. A minute later, I was full-body sobbing. Because I was helping facilitate the ritual space for others, I had a delayed reaction. It was hard to fully experience my feelings as the ritual was happening, but the potency of the ritual reverberated through me afterward. Our ritual allowed me to start grieving the heart-wrenching attacks on Gaza that I couldn't grieve sitting at home alone reading the news on my laptop between client sessions. I could only grieve when I knew that my tears could flow into the collective river of grief within a community committed to stopping the violence.

Rituals in the face of atrocities help us remember and memorialize what the dominant powers would rather have us forget. As Weller describes, "Some losses should never be allowed to settle, like silt, to the bottom of our memory."[26] We are not trying to move on from these losses, but to combat their erasure and denial by memorializing them and holding them close to our hearts. Rituals like these are not enough in and of themselves; they are meant to change us and fuel our actions. But our campaigns, protests, and actions can become brittle and lifeless if we don't find ways to resource ourselves, experience our feelings, and take action from a place of empathetic connection.

Toward a Collective Diasporic Jewish Identity

We have inherited the technology of ritual from our ancestors, many of whose lives were deeply intertwined with the world of nature and spirit. To keep facing and transforming the violent systems of domination that seem bent on destroying life on this earth, we also have to revel in the beauty of the earth. Ritual is one way to access both our pain and deep awe for this miraculous world. In the words of Jewish poet, singer, and songwriter Leonard Cohen, "You look around and you see a world that is impenetrable, that cannot be made sense of. You either raise your fist or you say hallelujah. I try to do both."[27] Susan Raffo writes that our challenge as healers and change makers is "to sit with both hands, one filled with horror and loss, the other filled with love and intimate connection, and feel them both at the same time."[28] As people determined to breathe a new world into being, we hold the tension of the anguish next to the reverence, which creates space for the possibility of transformation.

One of the tensions we are holding as Jews right now is how to breathe new life into our traditions of healing and justice, while simultaneously acknowledging how our Jewish lives are fundamentally intertwined with the rest of the human and more-than-human world. As somatic healer Abigail Rose Clarke reminds us in her book *Returning Home to Our Bodies*, our bodies can offer a model for this kind of interdependence. Our skin is a boundary that holds us intact, while remaining porous and receptive. The trillions of cells within our bodies each have a membrane that holds their integrity as it facilitates an exchange of salt, water, and nutrients with the cells around it. In Clarke's words, "The cell membrane teaches that integrity, individuality, and interdependence can be held through adaptive and permeable boundaries."[29]

What kind of collective Jewish shape maintains integrity while facilitating connection and exchange with the world around us? At the end of her groundbreaking book on Jewish racial politics, *The Colors of Jews: Racial Politics and Radical Diasporism*, Melanie Kaye/Kantrowitz proposes a collective Jewish identity that is contained not by the rigid boundaries of a nation-state but by the porous, flexible, and shifting boundaries of the diaspora. She names this concept "Diasporism," which "begins but does not end with Jewish diversity and boundary crossing."[30] "Where Zionism says go home," writes Kaye/Kantrowitz, "diasporism says we make home where we are."[31]

Diasporism centers an aspect of Jewish identity—our dispersal—which has been denigrated by Zionists, but upheld by our anti-Zionist ancestors, particularly the Bundists. By embracing our own identities as strangers and exiles, we widen out to welcome in the strangers among us as we reach beyond the narrow nationalist conception of Judaism. As settlers on many lands, how do many of us make our homes in the diaspora, even as we acknowledge, honor, and make reparations to the original and forever stewards of the land we are on? In her beautiful poem "Land Days," Aurora Levins Morales puts forth a vision for Jews to nourish the land wherever we have landed. She encourages us to "be like the common/plantain, low to the/ground, rooting only/where there is room/between the conversations/of moss and stars." She asks us to "join, not destroy, the ecosystems/join, not erase, the whole story," so that we can "belong to the land," but never "own" it.[32]

If we imagine a collective shape of joining—joining within and across identities, joining the land, and joining the plants and the animals, what opens up for Jews? If we experience how we are intertwined with all of life, we can no longer accept the constraints of a Zionist identity that insists that we guard our boundaries with fear and aggression. When I read Levins Morales's poem, my whole body relaxes and widens because I sense what can unfurl from our current world if we make different choices.

If we choose to nurture the land and all its beings, we can expand beyond the limits of Zionism or any artificial national borders. If we choose to heal our trauma through our bodies, we can reach for each other beyond the boundaries of our identities. If we choose to honor the whole story of history, we can make amends and heal from history's ruptures.

Honoring the whole story means that we emphasize our interdependence, rather than our isolation, when we tell our Jewish stories. As I write this conclusion during Passover, I've been thinking about how we might retell the iconic story of the Exodus—our journey to liberation. In the traditional story, Moses leads the Israelites to escape from *Mitzrayim*, "the narrow place," where they have been enslaved under the dictatorship of Pharoah. In the climax of the story, they arrive at the shores of the Red Sea, only to find themselves trapped between Pharoah's army, hot on their heels in pursuit, and the depths of the sea. Moses calls out to G-d, who parts the sea into two towering walls of water with a dry path in between, so the Israelites can cross over to solid land. Once they reach safety on the opposite shore, the waters close back in, drowning their pursuers.

However, the sea did not part for the Israelites alone. The Torah actually refers to *erev rav* (ערב רב), "the mixed multitude," who crossed with them. Although we rarely hear about the *erev rav*, our people did not journey into the wilderness of freedom by themselves. Who were the mixed multitude? Commentators who mention them throughout the years have categorized them variously as non-Israelite people enslaved under Pharoah, people of other nations who married Israelites, people who found kinship with the Israelites, and even magicians and witches drawn to the seemingly magical powers of Moses.[33]

Some commentators categorize the *erev rav* dismissively as "riffraff" and "rabble" whom they also blame for later building the idolatrous golden calf, which brought down G-d's fury on the Israelites.[34] Not surprisingly, in modern-day Israel, the term *erev rav* is sometimes used to delegitimize Jews with varying political viewpoints, including the Jewish left.

What if we instead honored and celebrated the magical mixed multitude as righteous rabble-rousers who were integral to our ancestors' journey to freedom? I imagine Shifrah and Puah, the defiant midwives who refused to slaughter Hebrew sons, linking arms with Miriam to cross the Red Sea. What if the lesson from this journey to liberation is that we simply cannot get free alone? As our bodies remind us from the microcellular level to the organ of our skin, we cannot survive or thrive without permeable boundaries that invite connection and exchange.

When the Red Sea parted, its spiritual power caused every single body of water on earth to part as well. One people's journey into liberation reverberated around the world, carving out new pathways to freedom everywhere. This time Palestinians are the ones struggling to escape the oppression of the Israeli state. Our role right now as Jews is to join the mixed multitude of troublemakers, risk-takers, and agitators to do everything in our power to support Palestinians on their journey to liberation. Perhaps these acts of solidarity are what it will take to unite our disparate sparks of light and create a force powerful enough to repair this broken world. And this time, when the sea parts, when Palestine becomes free, so will we.

NOTES

Chapter 1

1 Jacqueline Rose, *The Question of Zion* (Princeton, NJ: Princeton University Press, 2007), 145.

2 Rose, *The Question of Zion,* 160.

3 Elissa Nadworny, Samantha Balaban, Sawsan Khalife, Anas Baba, and Claire Harbage, "As Israel Forces Workers from Gaza Back, Thousands More Remain Stuck in the West Bank," NPR, November 3, 2023, www .npr.org/2023/11/03/1210441078/israel-palestinian-gaza-workers -stuck-west-bank.

4 Al Jazeera, "Israel Revises Down Toll from October 7 Attack to 'Around 1,200,'" Al Jazeera, November 10, 2023, www.aljazeera.com /news/2023/11/10/israel-revises-death-toll-from-october-7-hamas -attack-to-1200-people.

5 Alyssa Fowers, Leslie Shapiro, Cate Brown, and Hajar Harb, "Friends, Family, Acquaintances: What Would Have Happened to Them If Gaza Was Home?" *Washington Post,* accessed May 13, 2024, www.washington post.com/world/interactive/2024/gaza-numbers-killed-displaced-scale.

6 "Daily Death Rate in Gaza Higher than Any Other Major 21st Century Conflict—Oxfam," Oxfam International, January 16, 2024, www.oxfam .org/en/press-releases/daily-death-rate-gaza-higher-any-other-major -21st-century-conflict-oxfam.

7 "We had Dreams" video, Visualizing Palestine, accessed May 13, 2024, https://visualizingpalestine.org/visual/we-had-dreams-palestinians -living-and-dying-under-siege-in-gaza.

8 Mishnah Sanhedrin 4:9; Babylonian Talmud, Tractate Sanhedrin 37a.

9   Ruwaida Amer, "Remembering a Vibrant Artist and Mother Killed in Gaza, Baraa Abu Mohsen," Al Jazeera, accessed April 4, 2024. www .aljazeera.com/features/2024/1/21/remembering-a-vibrant-artist -and-mother-killed-in-gaza-baraa-abu-mohsen.

10 Abubaker Abed, "My Friend Al-Hassan, a Liverpool Fan Who Dreamed Big, Killed in Gaza," Al Jazeera, accessed April 4, 2024, www.aljazeera .com/features/2023/12/19/my-friend-al-hassan-a-liverpool-fan -who-dreamed-big-killed-in-gaza.

11 Ethar Shalaby, "A Doctor, Tailor, and Bride-To-Be: Stories of Those Killed in Gaza," BBC, November 3, 2023, www.bbc.com/news/world -middle-east-67278549.

12 "Israel-Hamas War Live Updates: Biden 'Outraged' at Israel over Gaza Aid Convoy Deaths," NBC News, April 3, 2024, www.nbcnews.com /news/world/live-blog/israel-hamas-war-live-updates-rcna146148.

13 "We Had Dreams" video, Visualizing Palestine.

14 Julian Borger, "The Plight of Gaza's 'WCNSFs'—Wounded Child, No Surviving Family," The Guardian, December 22, 2023, www.theguardian .com/world/2023/dec/22/the-plight-of-gazas-wcnsfs-wounded-child -no-surviving-family.

15 Masha Gessen, "In the Shadow of the Holocaust," The New Yorker, December 9, 2023, www.newyorker.com/news/the-weekend-essay/in -the-shadow-of-the-holocaust.

16 "Israel's Apartheid against Palestinians," Amnesty International, June 23, 2023, www.amnesty.org/en/latest/campaigns/2022/02/israels -system-of-apartheid.

17 Gadi Zaig, Zvika Klein, and Tovah Lazaroff, "Erdan Blasts Hamas Final Solution Wearing Yellow Star at UNSC," The Jerusalem Post, October 31, 2023, www.jpost.com/international/article-770921.

18 Associated Press, "Israeli Finance Minister Calls for Reestablishing Israeli Settlements in Gaza," PBS, January 8, 2024, www.pbs.org/news hour/world/israeli-finance-minister-calls-for-reestablishing-israeli -settlements-in-gaza.

19 Adam Fulton, Cash Boyle, Charlie Moloney, Gloria Oladipo, Maya Yang, Rebecca Ratcliffe, Peter Beaumont, et al., "Netanyahu Speaks in

Tel Aviv, Pledges to 'Abolish This Evil' – as It Happened," *The Guardian*, October 29, 2023, www.theguardian.com/world/live/2023/oct/28/israel-hamas-war-live-gaza-phone-and-internet-cut-off-as-israel-intensifies-bombardment.

20   "Netanyahu's References to Violent Biblical Passages Raise Alarm among Critics," NPR, November 7, 2023, www.npr.org/2023/11/07/1211133201/netanyahus-references-to-violent-biblical-passages-raise-alarm-among-critics.

21   Linda Kinstler, "'Never Again' after October 7th," *Jewish Currents*, November 29, 2023, https://jewishcurrents.org/never-again-after-october-7th.

22   Steven Wineman, *Power-Under: Trauma and Nonviolent Social Change* (Wineman, 2003), 23.

23   Wineman, *Power-Under*, 21.

24   Naomi, Klein, *Doppelganger: A Trip into the Mirror World* (New York: Farrar, Straus and Giroux, 2023), 57.

25   Klein, *Doppelganger*, 12.

26   Klein, 299.

27   Klein, 301.

28   "2014 Gaza Conflict," UNRWA, accessed March 15, 2024, www.unrwa.org/2014-gaza-conflict.

29   "2014 Gaza Conflict," UNRWA.

30   Law for Palestine, January 4, 2024, Database of Israeli Incitement to Genocide, https://law4palestine.org/law-for-palestine-releases-database-with-500-instances-of-israeli-incitement-to-genocide-continuously-updated.

31   Emanuel Fabian, "Defense Minister Announces 'Complete Siege' of Gaza: No Power, Food or Fuel," *The Times of Israel*, October 9, 2023, www.timesofisrael.com/liveblog_entry/defense-minister-announces-complete-siege-of-gaza-no-power-food-or-fuel.

32   Noah Lanard, "The Dangerous History behind Netanyahu's Amalek Rhetoric," *Mother Jones*, November 3, 2023, www.motherjones.com/politics/2023/11/benjamin-netanyahu-amalek-israel-palestine-gaza-saul-samuel-old-testament.

33 Jaclyn Diaz, "9 U.S. Citizens Have Died in the Israel-Gaza Conflict, U.S. Officials Say," NPR, October 9, 2023, www.npr.org/2023/10/09/1204 639253/israel-gaza-hamas-us-citizens-killed.

34 Fatima Al-Kassab, "A Top U.N. Court Says Gaza Genocide Is 'Plausible' but Does Not Order Cease-Fire," NPR, January 26, 2024, www.npr.org /2024/01/26/1227078791/icj-israel-genocide-gaza-palestinians-south -africa.

35 "What Qualifies as Genocide? Breaking Down the ICJ Case against Israel," *Washington Post*, January 11, 2024, www.washingtonpost.com /world/2024/01/11/what-is-genocide-definition-courts.

36 Patrick Kingsley, "Accused of Genocide, Israelis See Reversal of Reality. Palestinians See Justice," *New York Times*, January 12, 2024, www .nytimes.com/2024/01/12/world/middleeast/israel-palestinians -icj-genocide.html.

37 Kingsley, "Accused of Genocide."

38 Klein, *Doppelganger*, 93.

39 Toni Morrison, *Beloved* (London, UK: Vintage International, 1987), 35.

40 "'This Is Your Money': Palestinian Father Pleads with Americans to Stop Funding Israeli Aggression," *Democracy Now*, accessed April 6, 2024, www.democracynow.org/2023/11/2/gaza_media.

41 USAFacts, "How Much Military Aid Does the US Give to Israel?" USA-Facts, May 20, 2021, https://usafacts.org/articles/how-much-military -aid-does-the-us-give-to-israel.

Chapter 2

1 Mike Comins, *Making Prayer Real: Leading Jewish Spiritual Voices on Why Prayer Is Difficult and What to Do about It* (Woodstock, VT: Jewish Lights Publishing, 2010), 48.

2 Mohammed Haddad, "Nakba Day: What Happened in Palestine in 1948?" Al Jazeera, May 15, 2022, www.aljazeera.com/news/2022/5/15 /nakba-mapping-palestinian-villages-destroyed-by-israel-in-1948.

3 Alissa Wise, "Rabbi Alissa Wise's Love Letter to Anti-Zionist Jews, as She Leaves Ten Years' Work with JVP," Medium, March 24, 2021, https://

jewish-voice-for-peace.medium.com/rabbi-alissa-wises-love-letter-to
-anti-zionist-jews-as-she-leaves-ten-years-work-with-jvp-d04776df54ff.

4 Arielle Angel, "Shedding Thick Skin," *Jewish Currents,* accessed April 6,
2024, https://jewishcurrents.org/shedding-thick-skin.

5 Angel, "Shedding Thick Skin."

6 Zalman Schachter-Shalomi, *First Steps to a New Jewish Spirit: Reb Zalman's Guide to Recapturing the Intimacy & Ecstasy in Your Relationship
with God* (Nashville, TN: Turner Publishing Company, 2013), 39.

7 Daniel Boyarin, *Carnal Israel: Reading Sex in Talmudic Culture* (Berkeley,
CA: University of California Press, 1993), 5.

8 Julia Watts Belser, *Loving Our Own Bones: Disability Wisdom and the Spiritual
Subversiveness of Knowing Ourselves Whole* (Boston: Beacon Press, 2023), 22.

9 Irit Reinheimer, *Push the Water* (Philadelphia: Thread Makes Blanket
Press, 2023), 85.

10 Audre Lorde, "The Uses of the Erotic" in *Sister Outsider: Essays and
Speeches* (Freedom, CA: Crossing Press, 1984), 58.

11 Lorde, "Uses of the Erotic."

12 André Aciman, *Call Me by Your Name* (New York: Picador, 2007), 224.

13 Zisl, *CrossCurrents: God, the God of Unmet Desire* (Chapel Hill, NC: Association for Public Religion and Intellectual Life, 2022), 16.

14 Zisl, *God of Unmet Desire,* 36.

15 Zisl, 81.

16 Zalman Shachter-Shalomi and Joel Segel, *Davening: A Guide to Meaningful Jewish Prayer* (Woodstock, VT: Jewish Lights Publishing, 2012), 12.

17 Watts Belser, *Loving Our Own Bones,* 210.

18 Shachter-Shalomi, *Davening,* 25.

Chapter 3

1 Aurora Levins Morales, *Medicine Stories: Essays for Radicals* (Durham,
NC: Duke University Press, 2019), 101.

2 "Why Birthright Israel Is More than a 10-Day Trip," Birthright Israel
Foundation, January 10, 2021, https://birthrightisrael.foundation/blog
/why-birthright-israel-is-more-than-a-10-day-trip.

3 "Understanding Antisemitism: An Offering to Our Movement," Jews for Racial and Economic Justice, accessed March 15, 2024, www.jfrej.org /assets/uploads/JFREJ-Understanding-Antisemitism-November-2017 -v1-3-2.pdf, 13–14.

4 Arthur Gobineau and Mark Tyson, *An Essay on the Inequality of the Human Races: The Hidden Causes of Revolutions, Bloody Wars, and Lawlessness* (CreateSpace Independent Publishing Platform, 2016).

5 "The Door Slams Shut—Jewish Immigration to America—YIVO Online Exhibitions," YIVO, accessed March 27, 2024, https://immigrationusa .yivo.org/exhibits/show/immigrationstories/1870s1920s/doorslams.

6 Emma Green, "Antisemitism at the Deadly Charlottesville Protests," *The Atlantic,* August 15, 2017, www.theatlantic.com/politics/archive /2017/08/nazis-racism-charlottesville/536928.

7 Nicole Chavez, "Pittsburgh Synagogue Gunman Said He Wanted All Jews to Die, Criminal Complaint Says," CNN, October 28, 2018, www .cnn.com/2018/10/28/us/pittsburgh-synagogue-shooting/index.html.

8 Staci Haines, *The Politics of Trauma: Somatics, Healing, and Social Justice* (Berkeley, California: North Atlantic Books, 2018), 74.

9 Cara Page and Erica Woodland, *Healing Justice Lineages: Dreaming at the Crossroads of Liberation, Collective Care, and Safety* (Berkeley, CA: North Atlantic Books, 2023), 122.

10 Page and Woodland, *Healing Justice,* 144.

11 Susan Raffo, *Liberated to the Bone: Histories. Bodies. Futures* (Chico, CA: AK Press, 2022), 22.

12 Eric L. Goldstein, *The Price of Whiteness: Jews, Race, and American Identity* (Princeton, NJ: Princeton University Press, 2008), 145.

13 Uri Schreter, "'The Most Awful Scenes': The Tulsa Massacre and Racist Violence in the Yiddish Press," *In Geveb,* accessed March 29, 2024, https:// ingeveb.org/blog/the-most-awful-scenes.

14 Michael Paul Rogin, *Blackface, White Noise: Jewish Immigrants in the Hollywood Melting Pot* (Berkeley, CA: University of California Press, 1998).

15 Goldstein, *Price of Whiteness,* 154.

16 *The Jazz Singer,* film directed by Alan Crosland (Warner Brothers, 1927).

17 *The Jazz Singer.*

18 Karen Brodkin Sacks, *How Jews Became White Folks and What That Says about Race in America* (New Brunswick, NJ: Rutgers University Press, 2010).

19 Levins Morales, *Medicine Stories*, 101.

20 Levins Morales.

Chapter 4

1 Paul Chiariello, "A Note in Each Pocket: A Parable on Humility, Pride, & Comparative Religion," *Applied Sentience*, September 3, 2013, https://appliedsentience.com/2013/09/03/a-note-in-each-pocket-a-parable-on-humility-pride-comparative-religion.

2 Richard C. Schwartz and Martha Sweezy, *Internal Family Systems Therapy* (New York: The Guilford Press, 1997).

3 Steven Wineman, *Power-Under: Trauma and Nonviolent Social Change* (Wineman, 2003).

4 Aurora Levins Morales, "Red Sea," accessed March 28, 2024, www.auroralevinsmorales.com/red-sea.html.

5 Paul Kivel, "Challenging Christian Hegemony | Practical Tools for Recognizing and Resisting Christian Dominance," accessed March 27, 2024, https://christianhegemony.org.

6 "Pilpul," Jewishencyclopedia.com, accessed April 4, 2024, https://jewishencyclopedia.com/articles/12153-pilpul.

Chapter 5

1 David Biale, *Power and Powerlessness in Jewish History* (New York: Schocken, 1989), 164.

2 Rotem Shtarkman and Lior Dattel, "What Really Happens on Israeli Students' Holocaust Trips to Poland?" *Haaretz*, May 6, 2016, www.haaretz.com/israel-news/2016-05-06/ty-article/what-really-happens-on-students-holocaust-trips-to-poland.

3 "It's Clear to Everyone Gazans Must Be Destroyed, Israeli Lawmaker Says," *Haaretz*, January 3, 2024, www.haaretz.com/israel-news/2024-01-03/ty-article/its-clear-to-everyone-gazans-must-be-destroyed-israeli-lawmaker-says.

4 Chaim Weizmann and Barnet Litvinoff, "The Cultural Question in Zionism," speech to the fourth Zionist Congress, August 16, 1900, in *The Letters and Papers of Chaim Weizmann*, Series B (New Brunswick, NJ: Transaction Books, 1983), 3.

5 Joseph Massad, "Zionism, Antisemitism and Colonialism," Al Jazeera, www.aljazeera.com/opinions/2012/12/24/zionism-antisemitism-and-colonialism.

6 "Zionism's History Is Also a History of Jewish Anti-Zionism," Jacobin.com, January 28, 2024, https://jacobin.com/2024/01/shaul-magid-interview-zionism-anti-zionism-judaism-history.

7 Martin Buber, "Zionism and Nationalism" in *The Martin Buber Reader: Essential Writings* (New York: Palgrave Macmillan, 2002), 278.

8 Molly Crabapple, "My Great-Grandfather the Bundist," *The New York Review of Books*, October 6, 2018, www.nybooks.com/online/2018/10/06/my-great-grandfather-the-bundist.

9 Klein, *Doppelganger*, 301.

10 Buber, "Zionism and 'Zionism,'" in *The Martin Buber Reader*, 290.

11 Martin Buber, "Politics and Morality," in Martin Buber and Paul R. Mendes-Flohr, *A Land of Two Peoples: Martin Buber on Jews and Arabs* (Chicago: University of Chicago Press, 2005), 172.

12 Crabapple, "My Great-Grandfather the Bundist."

13 Haddad, "Nakba Day: What Happened in Palestine in 1948?"

14 "After 74 Years Palestinians Pass down Keys and Dreams of Return," The Palestinian Information Center, May 20, 2022, https://english.palinfo.com/opinion_articles/After-74-years-Palestinians-pass-down-keys-and-dreams-of-return.

15 Mari Cohen, "The Numbers Game," *Jewish Currents*, accessed April 6, 2024, https://jewishcurrents.org/the-numbers-game.

16 Anti-Defamation League, "Audit of Antisemitic Incidents 2022," ADL, March 23, 2023, www.adl.org/resources/report/audit-antisemitic-incidents-2022.

17 Daniel Boyarin, *Unheroic Conduct: The Rise of Heterosexuality and the Invention of the Jewish Man* (Berkeley, CA: University of California Press, 1997).

18 Boyarin, *Unheroic Conduct*, 254.

19 "The Body Issue," Association for Jewish Studies, accessed April 3, 2024, www.associationforjewishstudies.org/publications-research/ajs -perspectives/the-body-issue/muscular-judaism.

20 "Hillel's Actions," Palestine Legal, accessed April 6, 2024, https:// palestinelegal.org/hillels-actions.

21 "Remarks by Jonathan Greenblatt to the ADL Virtual National Leadership Summit," ADL, accessed March 15, 2024, www.adl.org/remarks -jonathan-greenblatt-adl-virtual-national-leadership-summit.

22 "Remarks by Jonathan Greenblatt."

23 "Remarks by Jonathan Greenblatt."

24 "Jewish Federation of Greater Seattle," Change.org, accessed April 3, 2024, www.change.org/p/concerned-seattle-jews-protect-the-sanctity -of-tikkun-olam/responses/39191.

25 Alex S. Vitale, *The End of Policing* (London: Verso, 2017), 34.

26 Libby Denkmann, Alec Cowan, and Amy Radil, "After 11 Years, Seattle's Federal Consent Decree Reaches the 'End of the Beginning,'" KUOW, September 13, 2023, www.kuow.org/stories/after-11-years -seattle-s-federal-consent-decree-reaches-the-end-of-the-beginning.

27 Law Enforcement and Society: Lessons of the Holocaust, training course, Washington State Criminal Justice Training Commission, accessed April 3, 2024, www.cjtc.wa.gov/training-education/law-enforcement-training -and-community-safety-act-(letcsa)-mandated-courses/law-enforcement -and-society-lessons-of-the-holocaust.

28 James Q. Whitman, *Hitler's American Model: The United States and the Making of Nazi Race Law* (Princeton, NJ: Princeton University Press, 2017).

29 "American Law Enforcement Learns Anti-Terror Tactics from Israeli Experts," *The Jerusalem Post*, September 9, 2015, www.jpost.com/Israel -News/American-law-enforcement-delegation-learn-anti-terror-tactics -from-Israeli-experts-415757.

30 "Jewish Federation of Greater Seattle," Change.org, www.change. org/p/concerned-seattle-jews-protect-the-sanctity-of-tikkun-olam /responses/39191.

31 "Holocaust Education: Examining and Addressing the History of Antisemitism," Seattle ADL, accessed April 3, 2024, https://seattle.adl .org/holocaust-edu-history-of-antisemitism.

32 Levins Morales, *Medicine Stories*, 70.

33 Tallie Ben Daniel, "Antisemitism, Palestine and the Mizrahi Question" in *On Antisemitism: Solidarity and the Struggle for Justice,* Jewish Voice for Peace (Chicago: Haymarket Books, 2017).

34 April Rosenblum, *The Past Didn't Go Anywhere: Making Resistance to Antisemitism Part of All Our Movements*, accessed May 2, 2024, www .aprilrosenblum.com/thepast.

35 Jewish Voice for Peace, *On Antisemitism: Solidarity and the Struggle for Justice* (Chicago: Haymarket Books, 2017), 77.

Chapter 6

1 Mariame Kaba and Andrea J. Ritchie, "Reclaiming Safety," Inquest, August 30, 2022, https://inquest.org/reclaiming-safety.

2 "Remarks by President Biden at a Hanukkah Holiday Reception," The White House, December 12, 2023, www.whitehouse.gov/briefing -room/speeches-remarks/2023/12/11/remarks-by-president-biden -at-a-hanukkah-holiday-reception.

3 Michelle Goldberg, "Opinion | At a Hearing on Israel, University Presidents Walked into a Trap," *New York Times,* December 7, 2023, www.ny times.com/2023/12/07/opinion/university-presidents-antisemitism.html.

4 Yousef Munayyer, "What Does 'From the River to the Sea' Really Mean?" *Jewish Currents,* accessed May 9, 2024, https://jewishcurrents.org /what-does-from-the-river-to-the-sea-really-mean.

5 Lex Dobkin, "Rashida Tlaib's 'From the River to the Sea' Post Sparks Outrage," *Newsweek,* November 4, 2023, www.newsweek.com/rashida -tlaibs-river-sea-post-sparks-outrage-1840959.

6 Maha Nassar, "Opinion | 'From the River to the Sea' Doesn't Mean What You Think It Means," *The Forward,* December 3, 2018, https:// forward.com/opinion/415250/from-the-river-to-the-sea-doesnt-mean -what-you-think-it-means.

7 Geoff Bennett and Shoshana Dubnow, "College Leaders Face Congressional Hearing over Antisemitism and Islamophobia on Campus," PBS NewsHour, December 5, 2023, www.pbs.org/newshour/show/college-leaders-face-congressional-hearing-over-antisemitism-and-islamophobia-on-campus.

8 Johanna Alonso, "Columbia Suspends 2 Pro-Palestine Groups," Inside Higher Ed, November 10, 2023, www.insidehighered.com/news/students/free-speech/2023/11/10/columbia-suspends-two-pro-palestinian-groups.

9 Ayana Archie, "New York Police Arrest 300 People as They Clear Hamilton Hall at Columbia University," NPR, May 1, 2024, www.npr.org/2024/05/01/1248401802/columbia-university-protests-new-york.

10 Robin D.G. Kelley, "Letter to Columbia President Minouche Shafik," *Boston Review*, April 29, 2024, www.bostonreview.net/articles/letter-to-columbia-university-president-minouche-shafik.

11 "The Palestine Exception," Palestine Legal, accessed March 29, 2024, https://palestinelegal.org/the-palestine-exception-appendix.

12 "The Palestine Exception."

13 "The Palestine Exception."

14 Jessica Rosenberg, "Reunderstanding Jewish Historical Trauma: Moving from the River to the Watershed," Evolve, December 27, 2021, https://evolve.reconstructingjudaism.org/reunderstanding-jewish-historical-trauma-moving-from-the-river-to-the-watershed.

15 James Baldwin, "As Much Truth as One Can Bear," *New York Times*, January 14, 1962, www.nytimes.com/1962/01/14/archives/as-much-truth-as-one-can-bear-to-speak-out-about-the-world-as-it-is.html.

Chapter 7

1 Raffo, *Liberated to the Bone*, 32.

2 Michael Schaeffer Omer-Man, "American Teen Beaten by Israeli Police Is Cleared of Wrongdoing," *+972 Magazine*, January 28, 2015, www.972mag.com/american-teen-beaten-by-israeli-police-is-cleared-of-wrongdoing.

Chapter 8

1 David Ben-Gurion's memoirs, cited in Rose, *The Question of Zion*, 123.

2 Raffo, *Liberated to the Bone*, 189.

3 Raffo, 192.

4 Raffo.

5 Dan Leon, "The Jewish National Fund: How the Land Was 'Redeemed,'" *Palestine-Israel Journal of Politics, Economics and Culture*, accessed May 4, 2024, https://pij.org/articles/410/the-jewish-national-fund-how-the-land-was-redeemed.

6 Jessica Buxbaum, "Making the Desert Bloom? How Israel Is Greenwashing Its Land Theft in the Negev," The New Arab, February 1, 2022, www.newarab.com/analysis/making-desert-bloom-israels-greenwashing-negev.

7 Liat Berdugo, "A Situation: A Tree in Palestine," Places Journal 2020 (January), https://doi.org/10.22269/200107.

8 Ilan Pappe, *The Ethnic Cleansing of Palestine* (London: Oneworld, 2006), 337.

9 Marta Vidal, "Palestinian Olive Farmers Hold Tight to Their Roots amid Surge in Settler Attacks," Mongabay Environmental News, November 30, 2023, https://news.mongabay.com/2023/11/palestinian-olive-farmers-hold-tight-to-their-roots-amid-surge-in-settler-attacks.

10 Ruwaida Amer, "The Olive Tree, Symbol of Palestine and Mute Victim of Israel's War on Gaza," Al Jazeera, January 22, 2024, www.aljazeera.com/features/2024/1/22/the-olive-tree-symbol-of-palestine-and-mute-victim-of-israels-war-on-gaza.

11 "Ethnic Cleansing in Palestine," Al Jazeera, accessed May 13, 2024, www.aljazeera.com/gallery/2023/5/15/ethnic-cleansing-by-zionists-in-palestine.

12 Pappe, *Ethnic Cleansing of Palestine*, 79.

13 "The Deir Yassin Massacre: Why It Still Matters 75 Years Later," Al Jazeera, April 9, 2023, www.aljazeera.com/news/2023/4/9/the-deir-yassin-massacre-why-it-still-matters-75-years-later.

14 Pappe, *Ethnic Cleansing of Palestine*, 158.

15 Pappe, *Ethnic Cleansing of Palestine.*

16 Nadia Barhoum, "Rhetoric of Racism, from Ferguson to Palestine," Al Jazeera, September 4, 2014, www.aljazeera.com/opinions/2014/9/4/rhetoric-of-racism-from-ferguson-to-palestine.

17 Barhoum, "Rhetoric of Racism."

18 Barhoum.

19 "Seventy+ Years of Suffocation," Amnesty International, accessed May 11, 2024, https://nakba.amnesty.org/en/about.

20 Akiva Eldar, "Israel Admits It Revoked Residency Rights of a Quarter Million Palestinians - Haaretz Com," *Haaretz,* June 11, 2012, www.haaretz.com/2012-06-12/ty-article/israel-admits-it-revoked-palestinians-residency-since-1967/0000017f-f95b-d044-adff-fbfb0f8e0000.

21 "House Demolitions and Israel's Policy of Hafrada,"Al-Majdal, Badil Resource Center for Palestinian Residency and Refugee Rights, accessed April 4, 2024, www.badil.org/publications/al-majdal/issues/items/1421.html.

22 "Gaza Infrastructure Damages Estimated at $18.5bn in UN-World Bank Report," Al Jazeera, accessed April 4, 2024, www.aljazeera.com/news/2024/4/2/gaza-infrastructure-damages-estimated-at-18-5-bln-in-un-world-bank-report.

Chapter 9

1 Peter Beinart, "Teshuvah: A Jewish Case for Palestinian Refugee Return," *Jewish Currents,* accessed May 2, 2024, https://jewishcurrents.org/teshuvah-a-jewish-case-for-palestinian-refugee-return.

2 Psalms 90:2–3, Sefaria, accessed May 15 2024, www.sefaria.org/Psalms.90.3.

3 "Mishnah Torah Repentance 2:2," Sefaria, accessed April 7, 2024, www.sefaria.org/Mishneh_Torah%2C_Repentance.2.2.

4 Danya Ruttenberg, *On Repentance and Repair* (New York: Beacon Press, 2022), 25.

5 Henry Abramson and Moses Maimonides, *Maimonides on Teshuvah: The Ways of Repentance* (Lulu.com, 2020), 38.

6 Abramson and Maimonides, *Maimonides*, 40.

7 Abramson and Maimonides.

8 Rabbi Ari Lev Fornari, "We Don't Know What Comes Next: Teshuvah, Exile, and Impermanence," Kol Tzedek, accessed May 5, 2024, www .kol-tzedek.org/we-dont-know-what-comes-next-teshuvah-exile-and -impermanence.html.

9 Alan Lew, *This Is Real and You Are Completely Unprepared: The Days of Awe as a Journey of Transformation* (New York: Little, Brown, 2003), 42.

10 "Malachi 3:7," Sefaria, accessed May 2, 2024, www.sefaria.org /Malachi.3.7.

11 Abramson and Maimonides, 94.

12 Abramson and Maimonides, 103.

13 "Shabbat 54b:20," Sefaria, accessed May 2, 2024, www.sefaria.org /Shabbat.54b.

14 Hannah Pollak, "The Mitzvah of Tochacha," Sefaria, accessed May 2, 2024. www.sefaria.org/sheets/446789.

15 Getzel Davis, Sifra 89a-89b, in "Rebuke: Hard but Sometimes Necessary?" Sefaria, accessed April 20, 2024, www.sefaria.org/sheets/53174.8.

16 Davis, "Rebuke."

17 "Bereshit Rabba 54:3," in "Rebuke & the Limits of Live & Let Live," Sefaria, accessed May 2, 2024, www.sefaria.org/sheets/84905.

18 "Frederick Douglass Project Writings: West India Emancipation | RBSCP," Rochester.edu, 2018, https://rbscp.lib.rochester.edu/4398.

19 "Frederick Douglass Project Writings."

20 Holy Bible: New International Version online, Book of Micah 7:9, https://web.mit.edu/jywang/www/cef/Bible/NIV/NIV_Bible /MICAH+7.html.

21 Jonathan Brenneman and Aidan Orly, "Progressives Can't Ignore Role of Christian Zionism in Colonization of Palestine," Truthout, May 20, 2021, https://truthout.org/articles/progressives-cant-ignore-role -of-christian-zionism-in-colonization-of-palestine.

22 Shankar Vedantam, Parth Shah, Tara Boyle, and Jennifer Schmidt, "You 2.0: The Empathy Gym," NPR, accessed May 13, 2024, www.npr .org/2019/07/22/744195502/you-2-0-the-empathy-gym.

23 Beinart, "Teshuvah."

24 Beinart.

25 "'Nakba Law'—Amendment No. 40 to the Budgets Foundations Law," Adalah, accessed April 2, 2024, www.adalah.org/en/law/view/496.

26 Beinart, "Teshuvah."

27 Beinart.

28 Beinart.

Chapter 10

1 Aharon N. Varady (transcription), Zalman Schachter-Shalomi, "נִשְׁמַת כָּל חַי | Nishmat Kol Ḥai, Interpretive Translation by Rabbi Zalman Schachter-Shalomi, The Open Siddur Project, January 19, 2020, https:// opensiddur.org/prayers/lunisolar/pilgrimage/passover/leil-pesah /hallel-leil-pesah/nishmat-kol-hai-interpretive-translation-by-zalman -schachter-shalomi.

2 Krista Tippett, "Jericho Brown—Small Truths and Other Surprises," The On Being Project, accessed May 13, 2024, https://onbeing.org /programs/jericho-brown-small-truths-and-other-surprises.

3 Abraham Joshua Heschel, *The Sabbath: Its Meaning for Modern Man* (Boulder, CO: Shambhala Publications, 2003), xvii.

4 Heschel, *The Sabbath*, xviii.

5 Zalman Schachter-Shalomi and Joel Segel, *Jewish with Feeling: A Guide to Meaningful Jewish Practice* (Woodstock, VT: Jewish Lights Publishing, 2013), 36–37.

6 Ana Levy-Lyons, "Sabbath Practice as Political Resistance: Building the Religious Counterculture," *Tikkun*, October 2, 2012, www.tikkun.org /sabbath-practice-as-political-resistance-building-the-religious -counterculture.

7 Watts Belser, *Loving Our Own Bones*, 199.

8 Watts Belser, 209.

9 Heschel, *The Sabbath*, 9.

10 Zann Jacobrown, "Leviticus 25:1-7," "Shmita" Sefaria, accessed May 2, 2024, www.sefaria.org/sheets/344224.

11 Abraham Isaac HaCohen Kook, *Shabbat Ha'Aretz*, Sefaria, accessed April 5, 2024, www.sefaria.org/Shabbat_HaAretz.

12 "Re'eih: The Word of Shemitah," Rav Kook Torah, accessed April 5, 2024, www.ravkooktorah.org/REEH60.htm.

13 Yousef Munayyer, "Ending Military Aid to Israel: The Death of a Taboo?" Arab Center Washington DC, August 21, 2023, https://arab centerdc.org/resource/ending-military-aid-to-israel-the-death-of -a-taboo.

14 "Budget Justice," Vera Institute of Justice, 2020, www.vera.org/spotlights /election-2020/budget-justice.

15 Ariana Katz and Jessica Rosenberg, *For Times Such as These: A Radical's Guide to the Jewish Year* (Detroit, MI: Wayne State University Press, 2024), 49.

16 Mona El-Naggar, Adam Rasgon, and Mona Boshnaq, "They Were Only Children," *New York Times*, May 26, 2021, www.nytimes.com/interactive /2021/05/26/world/middleeast/gaza-israel-children.html.

17 Francis Weller, *The Wild Edge of Sorrow: Rituals of Renewal and the Sacred Work of Grief* (Berkeley, CA: North Atlantic Books, 2015), 9.

18 Ross Gay, *Inciting Joy* (Chapel Hill, NC: Algonquin Books, 2022), 3.

19 Weller, *Wild Edge*, 1.

20 "2021 Israeli–Palestine Crisis," "Casualties and Damage," accessed August 21, 2024, https://en.wikipedia.org/wiki/2021_Israel%E2%80 %93Palestine_crisis#Casualties_and_damage.

21 Wendy Elisheva Somerson, "OPINION: The Movement for Black Lives Honors the Radical Legacy of John Lewis," South Seattle Emerald, August 12, 2020, https://southseattleemerald.com/2020/08/12/opinion -the-movement-for-black-lives-honors-the-radical-legacy-of-john-lewis.

22 Mahmoud Darwish, "I Belong There," Poets.org, https://poets.org /poem/i-belong-there.

23 "Leviticus 20:18," Sefaria, accessed May 2, 2024, www.sefaria.org /Leviticus.20.18.

24 Alon Confino, "When Genya and Henryk Kowalski Challenged History—Jaffa, 1949" in *The Holocaust and the Nakba: A New Grammar of*

Trauma and History, edited by Bashir Bashir and Amos Goldberg (New York: Columbia University Press, 2018), 172.

25 Confino, "When Genya and Henryk Kowalski Challenged History."

26 Weller, *Wild Edge,* 18.

27 *Hallelujah: Leonard Cohen, A Journey, A Song,* film directed by Daniel Geller and Dayna Goldfine (Roadside Attractions, 2019).

28 Raffo, *Liberated to the Bone,* 63.

29 Abigail Rose Clarke, *Returning Home to Our Bodies: Reimagining the Relationship Between Our Bodies and the World—Practices for Connecting Somatics, Nature, and Social Change* (Berkeley, CA: North Atlantic Books, 2024), 95.

30 Melanie Kaye/Kantrowitz, *The Colors of Jews: Racial Politics and Radical Diasporism* (Bloomington: Indiana University Press, 2007), 199.

31 Kaye/Kantrowitz, *Colors of Jews,* 221.

32 Aurora Levins Morales, "Land Days," RIMONIM, accessed April 5, 2024, www.rimonim-liturgy.org/land-days.html.

33 Rabbi David J. Zucker, "Erev Rav: A Mixed Multitude of Meanings," TheTorah.com, accessed April 14, 2024, www.thetorah.com/article /erev-rav-a-mixed-multitude-of-meanings.

34 Zucker, "Erev Rav."

INDEX

K

ACKNOWLEDGMENTS

A deep bow of gratitude to the land, sea, and creatures of the Coast Salish land that held me as I wrote this book, and to the original and forever stewards of the land, the Duwamish and Coast Salish peoples. I am also deeply grateful to the Quileute tribe who have welcomed me countless times to their land where the ocean meets the mouth of the river.

I honor all of my ancestors, particularly Maurice and Peggye Oren, David and Gertrude Somerson, Cecilia Orenbach, Surah and Mendel Shameson, Norman Somerson, Stephen Lane, and Doris Lane. Your memories bless me.

I also offer appreciation to the lineages of Jewish anti-Zionist and anti-nationalist thinkers, including Hannah Arendt, Melanie Kaye/Kantrowitz, Leslie Feinberg, Naeim Giladi, and Marek Edelman, among many others.

I will be forever grateful that my friend Penny Rosenwasser introduced me to the concept of Jewish healing and inspired me with her work.

I offer undying gratitude and love to my dearest teacher, mentor, and friend, Jennifer Ianniello, who made it possible for me to heal and become a healer.

I trained in the lineage of generative somatics out of the Bay Area that came through Richard Strozzi-Heckler and Staci Haines. Generative somatics emerges out of learnings from Aikido from Japan, yoga and meditation from Tibet, and speech theory from Chile; as well as Western body-based healing methodologies. Sometimes oral traditions have been ignored or erased, so I hold this lineage somewhat loosely, assuming and honoring that there are more influences than I am conscious of, and I am grateful to all my teachers and all the beings who contributed to this path.

Thank you to the healers for your vision and clarity, Susan Raffo, Aurora Levins Morales, Stacy Torres, Dori Midnight, Jo Kent Katz, Simon Wolf,

Danica Bornstein, Socket Klatzker, Stacey Prince, Sage Hayes, and Jeremy Hulley.

Thank you to the many felines, past and present, who have shown me how to give and receive love unconditionally. Extra love to Shmuli, the anti-Zionist tuxedo cat we've all been waiting for.

Thank you to some of my first readers and dear friends, Jennie Goode, Stefanie Fox, and Eli Briskin for your brilliance and encouragement.

To the editors who make all things happen! Gratitude to Shayna Keyles, for holding the big picture with wisdom, enthusiasm, and kindness; Wendy Call, for being an early reader who helped make my manuscript feel like a book; Trisha Peck for guiding me through production; and Sandra Korn, for encouraging me and generously helping me understand the book publishing process.

Much gratitude to the readers of the first chapter that I wrote in my devastation after October 7: Jennie Goode, Stefanie Fox, Emily Warn, and Jessica Rosenberg.

I am forever grateful to Ronni Klompus and Jo Kent Katz for organizing queer Jews in Seattle; and to all the Jews of those early days with whom I broke bread, had hard conversations, and made good trouble. Thank you for creating ritual with me over the years, Susie Levy, Shelby Handler, Zoh Lev Cunningham, Hillary Blecker, and countless others.

Thank you for years of engaging conversation, ritual, and action around anti-Zionism, Stefanie Fox, Socket Klatzker, Danica Bornstein, Jo Kent Katz, Zoe Bermet, Jennifer Greenstein, Janet Nechama Miller, Stacey Prince, Diana Falchuck, Eitan Isaacson, Deborah Massachi, Jessica Rosenberg, Emily Warn, Matt Weiner, Jen Kagan, Eva Dale, Keshet Ronen, Eliana Horn, Shelby Handler, Evelyn Shapiro O'Connor, and many more!

Thank you for helping me find my voice through song, Rebekka Goldsmith.

I am beyond grateful to the folks I have organized with and continue to organize with in the Seattle chapter of Jewish Voice for Peace. Shout out to the ritual and art spokes! Respect to the national organization, the JVP Artist Council, and the wider community of chapters. Thank you for being my political home.

Acknowledgments

Thank you to all the Ruach participants who continue to bring this material to life in surprising and moving ways. Thank you to Zoh Lev Cunningham, Ariel Marks, and Rivka Yeker for assisting with various iterations of Ruach.

So much gratitude to Dona Hirschfield White for joining me in the Ruach endeavor. Thank you for getting weird with me and for being such a loving, fun, and brilliant collaborator.

I am grateful for my colleagues in somatics, including Elizabeth Payne, Danica Bornstein, and devon de Leña, for accompanying me in the depths.

Thank you to all my clients for allowing me to accompany you in your depths.

Thank you for many years of collaboration and friendship, Selma Al Aswad, Stacy Torres, Acca Warren, Deborah Massachi, Cricket Keating, Jennie Goode, Kristin Pula, Alia Fink, Kim Ulmer, and Gillian Harkins.

Thank you to Stefanie, Nason, and Jonah Fox for being my family. Thank you to my mama, my five siblings, and the next generation of awesome niblings, their kids, and the generations to come! May you all experience Jewishness beyond Zionism, a free Palestine, and a liberated world.

ABOUT THE AUTHOR

Wendy Elisheva Somerson (Wes) is a queer non-binary, disabled, cat-loving Ashkenazi Jewish somatic healer, writer, activist, and visual artist residing on Duwamish and Coast Salish land. One of the founders of the Seattle chapter of Jewish Voice for Peace, they have been active in Palestinian solidarity work for more than two decades. In their art and organizing they create ritual, images, and stories that help envision Jewish life beyond Zionism. As a politicized healer, Wes works at the intersection of personal and collective healing with individuals, groups, and organizations. They are the creator and facilitator of Ruach, an ongoing anti-Zionist, body-based Jewish healing group. At low tide, you can find them investigating tide pools. During high tide, they are likely covered in linoleum shavings and ink from their latest linocut creation.

ABOUT NORTH ATLANTIC BOOKS

North Atlantic Books (NAB) is an independent, nonprofit publisher committed to a bold exploration of the relationships between mind, body, spirit, and nature. Founded in 1974, NAB aims to nurture a holistic view of the arts, sciences, humanities, and healing. To make a donation or to learn more about our books, authors, events, and newsletter, please visit www.northatlanticbooks.com.Index